NEO-NAXAL CHALLENGE

Issues & Options

NEO-NAXAL CHALLENGE

Issues & Options

Giridhari Nayak

PENTAGON SECURITY
INTERNATIONAL
AN IMPRINT OF PENTAGON PRESS

Neo-Naxal Challenge: Issues & Options / Giridhari Nayak

ISBN 978-81-8274-519-3

First Published in 2011
Revised: 2012

Publishedlby
PENTAGONOOECUOITYOINTEONATIONAL
AnlImprintlof
PEhT AGOh PRESS
206, Phhcock Lhnh, Shhhpur Jht
hhw Dhlhi-110049
Phonhs: 011-64706243, 26491568
Thlhfhx: 011-26490600
hmhil: rhjhn@phnthgonprhss.in
whbsith: www.phnthgonprhss.in

Prited at Aegean Offset Printers, Greater Noida, U.P.

Dedicated to
all the brave souls
who went for heavenly abode
while performing their duty

डॉ. रमन सिंह
मुख्यमंत्री

Dr. RAMAN SINGH
CHIEF MINISTER

मंत्रालय
रायपुर, छत्तीसगढ़

MANTRALAYA
RAIPUR, CHHATTISGARH
Ph.- (O) 0771-2221000-01
Fax - 0771-2221306
Ph.- (R) 0771-2331000-01

FOREWORD

Ideas are important than weapons in fighting Naxalism. Documented ideas & good practices prevent institutional amnesia. At the outset I congratulate Shri Nayak for making efforts to prepare a book on the burning topic of Naxalism. Utilising his first hand knowledge of Naxal problem the writer Shri Nayak empirically analysed ground situtaion, mixed it with historical and analytical facts and presented correct perspective about naxlism and counter measures. He has created conceptual framework to analyse and to deal with this problem. I am sure, the principles & concepts enshrined in the book would serve as guideposts for security force in combat.

I wish the book & author grand success.

(Dr. Raman Singh)
Chief Minister

Preface

Left-wing extremists in India have a blue print which follows the M-L-M theory and accordingly they continue their offensive, political, military and information operations, accordingly. The security forces take time to understand the game plan and develop counter-strategies. As a result, countermeasures are constrained by a late start and limits of understanding. Further, many of the counter-measures also involve adequate up gradation of men and material, which in turn may be adversely affected by budgetary constraints. I recall an incident, in 2004, when some senior colleagues directed the planting of thorny trees around police stations to prevent attacks on them. Combat, Left-wing extremism and allied subjects are vast and dynamic; and nobody can claim absolute mastery over them. However, each person dealing with the problem needs deep insight.

Many of my colleagues dislike conceptual discussions, alleging that theory is not needed on the ground, and paper work is of no use in combat. However, they forget that a correct plan can only be made after concrete analysis and precise evaluation of possibilities. A theoretical concept is the summation of practical experiences. Before constructing a building even an engineer needs a blueprint on paper. More importantly, unless the problem is explained to the public nobody can achieve its support. With this plain and simple idea in mind I started studying the phenomena of Naxalism and allied concepts on the ground and also from books and journals. I also discussed issues with people and started writing articles on the subject since 1998. It was only in 2009 that I made serious efforts to write a book on the problem highlighting historical, analytical, and conceptual thematic issues pertaining to various facets of the Naxal problem. This publication is a result of that effort.

People say that all genuine knowledge originates from direct experience. Knowledge begins with practice; and theoretical knowledge which is gleaned through practice must return to practice. An analytical frame-work of pragmatic general principles and theoretical postulations deduced from messy and confused ground situations can further be applied to strategic, tactical, and operational situations of combat. The primary purpose of this book, therefore, is to frame concepts, and clarify ideas that have become confused and entangled. Practice gropes in darkness if its path is not illumined by theory.

The capacity to act comes from thought which can crystallize into theory. Problem appraisal and solution identification is important. Perseverance in the face of pessimism is required. Rethinking roles, restructuring organisations, processes and reorienting the players within the system can help in achieving a mission. If we can manage to be ready in time, we shall withstand the Naxalite offensive. However much we may study it, perfect operations will always remain just beyond the intellectual capabilities of even the best of us. Yet the very best will get so close that perfection seems tantalizingly almost within their grasp.

The experiences and analysis offered here should contribute to clearer and effective approaches to conflict resolution. It contains a fusion of empirical conceptual formulas that respond to the messiness of the current realities. I fervently hope that the suggestions/recommendations put forward will cause a rethinking on various issues. Problem diagnosis at macro and micro level has been done. Concept papers make clear the need for various efforts, institutions and ideas. Perspective and theory can guide policy choices. Wisdom is better than weapons. Use the ideas, seize the day to cease the decay is the order of the day.

I am indebted to my parents, my wife, daughter, son, my brother and his wife for inspiring me in completing the work. I thank profusely doyen of Indian Police Service Shri K.P.S. Gill Padma Shree for his guidance during his stay in Chhattisgarh as Adviser to Chhattisgarh Government, my mentors Shri P.V. Rajgopal Ex-Director N.P.A., Shri Vishwa Ranjan D.G.P. Chhattisgarh Shri S.K. Rout D.G.P. M.P., and Shri K. Vijaya Kumar D.G.P., C.R.P.F. for their valuable guidance. I am grateful to my friends Shri D.M. Mitra, Smt. Reena Mitra, Shri A.K. Maliwal, Shri B.B. Mishra, Shri Harshbardhan Raju, Shri S.P. Singh, Shri S.K. Bhardwaj, Shri Rishi Shukla, Shri A.K. Pattanaik, Shri Ranjit Pachhananda, Shri S.K. Sharma, Shri Shirish Jain, Shri Mahinder Reddy, Shri D.P. Tarenia, Shri Surendar Sinh, Shri B.Basu, Shri S.N. Pradhan, Shri Rajeev Kumar, Shri B.M. Kumar, Shri R.N. Das, Shri B.K. Patshahani, Shri Raghunath Mahapatra, Mrs Tejdeep Kaur Menon, Mr L.D. Pangari, Mr Ramesh Parida, Master A. Nayak, Miss S. Nayak and Prof. Debal Singh Roy for their support & assistance. I also thank Shri P.V. Ramnna and Shri Nihar Ranjan Nayak of IDSA, Special thanks are owed to my steno, Chudamani, for his sincere assistance in this project. Finally, I thank my publisher Shri Rajan Arya of Pentagon Press for giving concrete shape to the project. Last, but not least, I thank all my well wishers and the readers of my articles for their efforts and encouragement to me to undertake this project.

Giridhari Nayak
girinaya@yahoo.co.in

Contents

ANNEXURES

Abbreviations

ACM - Area Committee Member
ACS - Area Committee Secretary
AFSPA - Armed Forces Special Powers Act
AGL - Automatic Grenade Launcher
AICCCR - All India Coordination Committee of Communist Revolutionaries
AILRC - All India League For Revolutionary Culture
AIMCC - All Indian Mahila Coordination Committee
AIMO - All India Mass Organisation
AIPRF - All India Peoples Resistance Forum
AIPRF - All India peoples Revolutionary Front
AIRSF - All India Revolutionary Student Federation
AISC - All India Special Conference
AOB - Andhra Orissa Border
APRCP - Andhra Pradesh Revolutionary Communist Party
BJSAC - Bihar Jharkhand Special Area Committee
BSNL - Bharat Sanchar Nigam Limited
CAF - Chhattisgarh Armed Force

CATAS	-	Committee for the Assistance of Tribals Affected by Salwa Juddum
CAVOW	-	Committee Against Violence On Women
CBB	-	Comprador Bourgeois Bureaucrat
CC	-	Central Committee
CCOMPOSA	-	Coordination center of Maoist Parties and organisations of South Asia
CGS	-	Central Guerrilla Squad
CKS	-	Communist Kranthikari Sanghatan
CMC	-	Central Military Commission
CNM	-	*Chetana natya mandali*
CPB	-	Central Publishing Bureau
CPI	-	Communist Party of India
CPI-ML (SNS)	-	Satya Narayan Singh
CPI-ML	-	Communist Party of India (Marxist-Leninist)
CPMF	-	Central Paramilitary Force
CPML-JS/KR	-	CPML-Jana Shakti/Kurra Rajanna
CPUSI/BCP	-	Communist Party of United State of India/ Bahujan Communist Party
CRB	-	Central Regional Bureau
CRC	-	Central Regional Command
CRPP	-	Committee for Release of Political Prisoners
CTC	-	Central Technical Committee
DCM	-	Divisional Committee Members
DCS	-	Divisional Committee Secretary
DIR	-	Defence India Rule
DK	-	Dandakaranya
DAKMS	-	Dandkaranya Adiwasi Kisan Mazdoor Sangh

DKSZC	-	Dandakaranya Special Zonal Committee
DRP	-	District Reserve Police
DVC	-	Divisional Committee
EOD	-	Explosive Ordnance Disposal
ERB	-	Eastern Regional Bureau
ERC	-	Eastern Regional Command
ERC	-	Education Rectification Campaign
GF Rifle	-	Grenade-firing Rifle
GRC	-	Gram Rajya Committee
GRP	-	Government Railway Police
HQ	-	Headquarter
IAPL	-	India Association of Peoples Lawyers
IAS	-	Indian Administrative Service
ICDS	-	Integrated Child Development Services
IG	-	Inspector General
INSAS	-	Indian Small Arms System
IO	-	Information Operation
IPS	-	Indian Police Service
ITI	-	Industrial Training Institute
JLT	-	Jharkhand Liberation Tigers
JPC	-	Jharkhand Prastuti Committee Revolutionary Communist Centre
JSJMM	-	Jharkhand Sangharsh Jana Mukti Morcha
KABS	-	Krantikari Adivasi Balak Sangh
KAMS	-	Krantikari Adivasi Mahila Sangh
KKC	-	Krantikari Kisan Committee
LGS	-	Local Guerrilla Squad
LMG	-	Light Machine Gun
LOS	-	Local Organising Squad

LWE	-	Left-Wing Extremism
MB	-	Mobile Bunker
MCC	-	Maoist Communist Centre
MI	-	Military Intelligence
MISA	-	Maintenance of Internal Security Act
MIT	-	Military Instructor Team
M-L-M	-	Marxist-Leninist-Maoist
MNC	-	Multi-National Corporation
MNREGA	-	Mahatma Gandhi National Rural Employment Guarantee Act
MOPAS	-	Mobile Political Academy & Schools
MOU	-	Memorandum of Understanding
NMS	-	Nari Mukti Sangh
NRHM	-	National Rural Health Mission
NSCN	-	Nationalist Socialist Council of Nagaland
NTSZC	-	North Telangana Special Zonal Committee
OSINT	-	Open Source Intelligence
PB	-	Polit Bureau
PDFI	-	People's Democratic Front of India
PDS	-	Public Distribution System
PGA	-	People's Guerrilla Army
PHQ	-	Police Headquarters
PLA	-	People's Liberation Army
PLFI	-	People's Liberation Front of India
PLGA	-	People's Liberation Guerrilla Army
PMGSY	-	Prime Minister Gramin Sadak Yojana
POL	-	Petrol oil and Lubricants
POR	-	Political Organisation Review
POSCO	-	Pohang Steel Company

POTA	-	Prevention of Terrorist Activities
PPC	-	Platoon Political Committee
PPW	-	Protracted People's War
PS	-	Police Station
PSCC	-	Progressive Students Coordination Committee
PSS	-	People's Security Service
PW	-	People's War
PWG	-	People's War Group
R&D	-	Research & Development
RB	-	Regional Bureau
RC	-	Regional Committee
RDF	-	Revolutionary Democratic Front
RIM	-	Revolutionary International Movement
ROP	-	Road Opening Party
RPC	-	Revolutionary Peoples Committee
RUF	-	Revolutionary United Front
SAC	-	Special Area Committee
SCOMA	-	Sub-Committee on Military Affairs
SCOPE	-	Sub Committee on Political Education
SDPO	-	Sub-divisional Police Officer
SEZ	-	Special Economic Zone
SHO	-	Station House Officer
SLR	-	Self-Loading Rifle
SMC	-	State Military Command
SP	-	Superintendent of Police
SPO	-	Special Police Officer
SSA	-	Sarva Siksha Abhiyan
SSB	-	Sashastra Seema Bal

SST	-	Sainik Sanchalan Team
SUCOMO	-	Subcommittee on Mass Organisation
SUF	-	Strategic United Front
TADA	-	Terrorism and Disruptive Activities
TATA	-	There Are Thousand Alternatives
TCOC	-	Tactical Counter Offensive Campaign
TD	-	Technical Department
TDC	-	Technical Department Committee
TINA	-	There Is No Alternative
TOR	-	Technical & Organisation Review
TSC	-	Technical Sub Committee
TSPC	-	*Tritiya Sammellan Prastuti Committee*
TUF	-	Tactical United Front
UAPA	-	Unlawful Activities Prevention Act
UCCRI-ML	-	Unity Centre of Communist Revolutionaries of India-Marxist-Leninist
UG	-	Under Ground
ULFA	-	United Liberation of Asom
USC	-	Urban Sub-Committee
VIP	-	Very Important Person
VVJVA	-	Visthapan Virodhi Jan Vikas Andolan
ZC	-	Zonal Committees

List of Figures, Maps and Charts

Annexures

1

Nature, Dimensions and Dynamics of LWE

Naxalism is back in India with vengeance. After being subdued by the Government offensive of "Operation Steeple Chase" in 1972, the surviving active die-hard cadres of Naxalites retreated to the areas of Bhojpur of Bihar and Telengana forest areas of Andhra Pradesh; and clandestinely conspired to reconstruct the movement. Kondapalli Seetaramiah, Kanai Chatterjee and others like Narayan Sanyal, Sushital Roy, Kishanda—the *prima linea* and a second generation of leaders Ganapati, Kishanji, Ganganna (who are presently politbureau members) and others made efforts to revive Naxalism. It remained in a moribund stage and hibernated for a decade. People thought that Naxalism was dead. It was scotched, not killed. They underestimated the tenacity of the problem. Left wing extremism (LWE) has a tendency to grow from ashes. It re-grows when it gets a congenial environment and good breeding centres. In 1972, there was no final full stop, only dots which suggested that the act was not over, the curtain again rose.

In the 1970s the Naxalites remained low in the wilderness of the jungle and rural areas of Andhra Pradesh and Bihar. In the 80s they resurfaced after regrouping and reorganizing themselves in the forested rural areas of Telengana of Andhra

Pradesh, Bastar of Madhya Pradesh and Purnea, Mungher of Bihar. In the 90s they sneaked into few more states, conducted sporadic incidents, gaining strength and spatial spread. In spite of many setbacks in the millennium decade the bigger streams of Naxalites merged, further militarised, made rapid strides and posed a serious challenge to Indian democracy.

Complex Naxalite Phenomena

Naxalite's activity is a jigsaw of terrible complexities. Naxal problem is protracted in time, enduringly diffuse on focus, potentially still very much unresolved and formidably occluded. The most visible manifestations of the Naxal situation is banditry, extremism and episodes of extremely violent destructive rebellions and the most insidious activities of subtle revolutionary politics. The Naxalites are able to confuse people with their underdog image. Their organisation, like other extremists organisations, is Janus-faced with one side appearing as a saviour of people and the other side is their killer appearance—killer of people and democracy. For many years it was able to cover its killer face by camouflaging and concealing its objectives, face of the organisations and its members. Their dim visibility shrouded mystery over the phenomena. Obscurity and invisibility added to its power.

Naxalites claim their organisation as political party; some gullible people may believe it, but in no stretch of imagination it can be termed as political party. It is basically extremist unlawful organisation which has political objectives; but no faith in the political system, democracy and constitution of India. Naxalism thrives in the dark and withers when stripped of its invisibility. As people are unable to see things in the correct perspective, they start interpreting it in a manner which suits the Naxalites perfectly. This is not a traditional law and order problem; though it has some component of law enforcement and maintenance of order. It will be grossly wrong to diagnose or categorise it as a simple law and order problem. The problem should be seen from different perspective. At the group level it is widespread, and a form of socio-political banditry. It is a violent politico-administrative threat to Indian democracy. At the individual level it is psycho-social. Charu Mazumdar, after being defeated in the 1963 Assembly bye election, became more radical. Similarly, a number of top and middle level Naxalites, when they did not get scope to fulfil their ambition, became totally radical. It is pertinent to quote the words of Nobel Laureate Albert Camus:

> *"In every act of rebellion, the man concerned experiences not only a feeling of revulsion at the infringement of his rights but also a complete and spontaneous to certain aspect of himself. He is torn between the idea of romanticism and desire to kill. With him the rebellion of reason ends in madness."*[1]

It is obvious that the effects of spreading of Naxalism are very pernicious. Solving a problem is easier than detecting and recognizing a problem. Some people project it as socio-economic problem; some describe it as law and order problem. Mostly people suffer from an elephantine syndrome while dealing with this problem. A deeper analysis of many issues reveals that most of the problems e.g. gambling, dowry, usury, bonded-labour, prostitution etc. can be categorised as socio-economic problem. In fact any problem can be branded as such. Socio-economic under-development is the justification for their violence. Socio-economic causes are not the motivation for violence. Rather than being the result of a spontaneous popular upsurge or spontaneous resistance movement, it is the handiwork of a tightly-controlled outfit with the component of total conspiratorial military brute violent efforts. People are still divided about the issue whether it is a mere local problem, a mere irritation rather than a deadly threat to the nation. Grave misperceptions of Naxalites' strategic intents occur at various levels.

Everything without State Power is Illusion

For many people, an understanding of the problem is incomplete and full of ambiguities, inconsistencies and paradoxes. Therefore, in dealing with Naxalism, one must examine its essence and consider its appearance. Understanding any problem is more important than solving the problem. Unfortunately at the early stage nobody recognizes the problem. The evil comes masquerading and at the late stage most of the time prevention becomes difficult. Unless one understands its true nature counter-measures cannot be planned. Understanding is a pre-requisite before prescription. Understanding of LWE can be achieved through careful analysis of its objective, activity, organisation. Analysis of seized documents, literature, pronouncements, and interrogation reports give insights into their objectives.

The General Secretary of the Communist Party of India – Maoist (CPI-Maoist) in an interview to the journal, Peoples March, has mentioned: "Everything without state power is illusion—Hence, our party's basic line is formulated based on the Maoist principle—the seizure of power by armed force the settlement of the issue by war, is the central task and highest form of revolution".[2]

The above statements show the correct perspective of the problem and also prove the long-range objectives of CPI Maoists. The aims and objectives of Naxalites gleaned from their documents and interviews are:

1. New Democratic Revolution.
2. Over throwing the Government by violence which, according to them, is of the big landlord classes.
3. Ending feudal and imperialist exploitation.
4. Ushering in an agrarian revolution with the slogan of land to the tillers.
5. Take over all industries.
6. Take over all imperialist capital.

With a view to achieve the above objectives they have formulated an all-India perspective plan, and chalked out meticulous strategies. It leads to the notion that Naxalism is creating a piquant situation of cataclysmic armed rebellion and simultaneous political turmoil and paranoia. With this basic objective of overthrowing of the Government by violence, the

Naxalites have started their campaign of people's protracted war which is virtually a protracted war against the people and against Indian democracy. Now, it is essential to discuss the various Naxalite outfits that operate in India.

Various Naxal Outfits

In furtherance of Maoist principles, few dozens of Naxal groups are operating in India. In spite of the process of unification of ultra-left groups, conservative estimates put the present number of LWE outfits in India at 39. Presently 17 outfits—Communist Party of India (Maoist), CPML-Jana Shakti/Kurra Rajanna-CPML-JS/KR, CPML-Shanti Pal, CPML-Naxalbari, Communist Party Marxist Leninist-Liberation, Tritiya Sammellan Prastuti Committee: TSPC, CPML—New Democracy, Jharkhand Liberation Tigers (renamed People's Liberation Front of India) JLT (PLFI), Communist Party Marxist Leninist-Phani Bagchi Faction CPML-PBF, Jharkhand Prastuti Committee: JPC, Revolutionary Communist Centre: RCC, CPI-ML, Jharkhand Sangharsh Jana Mukti Morcha: JSJMM, Shashastra Peoples Morcha: SPM, Communist Party of United State of India/Bahujan Communist Party: CPUSI/BCP, CPML-Peoples Lib, CPML—Praja Parti Ghatana, CPML-Red Tiger committed violent activities. About 6% of Naxal violence was caused by the CPML JS, TSPC, CPML LIB, and PLFI. However, the CPI (Maoist) remains the most active left wing outfit being responsible for a majority of violence (90%) and resultant deaths (91%) in the country.

Genesis and Growth of Naxalism in India

When history is understood it is less likely that the errors will be repeated. Understanding of past events will give the real picture. Present knowledge of any problem can be gleaned to some extent from its history. How did these groups start arming themselves with leftist revolutionary ideas, weapons and continue their destructive, disruptive and violent activities? 'The outlines of the Naxalite movement can only be defined through its history not through geography or statistics.[3] Therefore it is imperative to delve into the genesis and growth of Naxalism.

Charu Majumdar sparked the Naxalbari flame and set further fires of the Naxalite movement in Srikakulam, Birbhum, Debra-Gopiballabhpur, Mushahari and Lakhimpur Kheri. The states of West Bengal, Andhra Pradesh, Bihar, Punjab, Uttar Pradesh, Tamil Nadu and Tripura saw a big spurt in Naxalite struggles, and Maoist formations sprouted in many states of India. At the 7th Congress of the CPM in 1964 Charu Mazumdar (after being defeated in the Assembly elections) opposed the official line and began putting forward a new line for the Indian revolution. Comrade Charu through his eight documents laid the ideological-political basis for the new revolutionary line. The first document, 'Our tasks in the present situation' stressed upon the need for a secret organisation and on carrying forward the agrarian revolution by boldly arousing the peasant masses.

Formation of All India Coordination Committee of Communist Revolutionaries (AICCCR)

On 12th and 13th November 1967 the All India Coordination Committee was formed with revolutionary comrades from seven states who met in Calcutta. In 1968 it was changed to All India Coordination Committee of Communist Revolutionaries (AICCCR) and Sushital Roy Chowdhury was its convener. Under the leadership of the AICCCR, State Coordination Committees were formed in about 13 states to coordinate and lead the growing waves of armed agrarian struggles in their respective states.

The AICCCR met in its plenary session in Calcutta from April 19 to 22, 1969 and formed the Communist Party of India (Marxist-Leninist) [(CPI (ML)] and announced the dissolution of the AICCCR after setting up a Central Organising Committee of CPI (ML). The formal announcement regarding the launching of the party came a few days later on 1 May 1969 at a public meeting in Calcutta.

Formation of Maoist Communist Centre (MCC)

At the same time Comrades Kanai Chatterjee, Amulya Sen and Chandra Sekhar Das raised another revolutionary movement under the banner of revolt against the line of the CPM 7th Congress. The 'Chinta' group was formed in 1965 as a secret revolutionary centre. The Chinta magazine was closed down and a new magazine 'Dakshin Desh' was brought out openly. Kanai Chatterjee discussed the development of a close relationship with Charu Mazumdar but the relationship did not grow. They did not agree with Charu's emphasis on squad action by small guerrilla groups. They were in favour of mass mobilisation and also front organisational activities. From 1967 to 1969 the then 'Dakshin Desh' group built up the movement in Kolkata, Howrah, Hooghly, Midnapur, Burdhwan, Birbum, 24 Parganas, Assam, Tripura and some portion of Bihar. In 1969 the Maoist Communist Centre (MCC) was created.

The activities of the MCC remained primarily confined to the limited area of Burdwan district known as Jungalmahal during 1971-76. 'Burdwan-Birbhum Regional Committee' and several local committees under it, constituted the underground party. Using Jungalmahal as a springboard, the MCC spread to neighbouring Bihar from 1973-74 onwards. He formed an apex body known as 'Bengal-Bihar Special Area Committee' to look after the budding organisation. The MCC has a slow but steady growth in Bihar, till a bitter rivalry over territorial expansion broke out with other contenders like the Liberation Group and the CPI-ML (Party Unity).

Birth of CPI-ML

Under the leadership of Comrade Charu Mazumdar, who guided these movements, the AICCCR passed a resolution on Party Organisation for the building of a Party of a new type. The CPI-ML took birth on 22 April 1969—the hundredth birth anniversary of Comrade Lenin. A coordination committee was formed to draft the Party Constitution and prepare for the Party Congress. The Party's formation was announced at a mammoth rally held in Calcutta. Left Extremist units from

West Bengal, Tamil Nadu, Kerala, Tripura, Assam, Bihar, Uttar Pradesh, Jammu and Kashmir, Punjab, Delhi, Odisha, and Karnataka joined the new party. However, the MCC and T. Nagi Reddy group of Andhra Pradesh did not join it.

The formation of such a mammoth party was a major success for Charu Mazumdar. Just before the formation of the Party, the Maoist student wing—the Progressive Students Coordination Committee (PSCC)—captured almost all the student unions of the institutions in and around Calcutta. In Andhra Pradesh, the students of Guntur Medical College were the first to come out in support of Naxalism and form the Naxalbari Solidarity Committee. After conducting several rallies in various parts of the country and acquiring an all-India character, the Party held the 8th Congress in May 1970. It was attended by Shrikakulam leaders Vempatap and Kailasham, and Satyanarayan Singh of Bihar. They stressed the need for a united front and emphasised the importance of guerrilla warfare. Charu Mazumdar became the Secretary of the Central Committee. Comrade Charu introduced the Political and Organisational Report in his introductory speech.

A concrete structure was given to the party by electing a central committee to lead the revolution. 35 delegates from all over the country attended the Congress and elected a 21-member Central Committee, which further elected a nine-member Politburo and formed Regional Bureaus. The party congress divided the country into four zones e.g. West Zone (Delhi, Punjab and Kashmir), Central Zone (Uttar Pradesh and Bihar), Eastern Zone (West Bengal and Assam,) and Southern Zone (Andhra Pradesh, Kerala and Tamil Nadu).

The railway workers of Kharagpur division, and adjacent struggling areas, were organised leading to a workers' movement. A section of the workers also participated in the peasant struggle. These revolutionary struggles and activities also influenced a number of drama groups, novelists, writers, composers and intellectuals. Hundreds of revolutionary dramas were enacted; songs were composed; novels and stories were written and published, and the revolutionary culture pervaded throughout the state. A section of these cultural activists went to rural areas and strengthened the revolutionary peasant struggles. Seizure of arms from the class enemies and the police was taken up as a big campaign. After Charu's arrest and death, the CPI-ML deteriorated. In December 1972 a new Central Committee of CPI-ML (Charu group) was formed with Jagjit Singh Sohala as general secretary.

Disintegration of the Naxalite Movement after 1972

The inner inconsistencies in the party came to the fore before the formation of the CPI-ML by Charu Majumdar when T. Nagi Reddy opposed offensive action. The second major difference was raised by convener Sushital Roy Chaudhury on the issue of Charu asking students to leave colleges and schools and jump into the revolutionary struggle. The third major difference was raised by S.N. Singh on the issue of the leadership style of Charu Majumdar. A fourth major inconsistency pertained to the tactics of the war of annihilation. Asim Chatterjee wanted that annihilation should be integrated with mass struggle. The inner inconsistencies and the 1972 setback of the Naxalites caused the disintegration of the party into several splinter groups. The absence of a central body due to the disruption of the Central Committee naturally gave rise to isolated groups and parties which were confined to limited areas/states until 1980.

Formation of People's War Group

On 2 March 1969, Kondapalli Seetaramiah joined the AICCCR as member of the state coordination committee. Later on he continued with Charu's CPI-ML. After Charu's death he organised a Central Organising Committee meeting in December 1972 along with Suniti Ghosh, K.G. Satyamurthy and Jagjit Singh Chouhan stressing mass work and mass organisation and eschewing militancy and violence till the party units became strong. Kondapalli Seetaramiah mobilised the Andhra Pradesh state committee by taking lessons of Naxalbari. In the three years from 1977 to 1980, the APSC of the CPI

(ML) built a strong mass movement which spread to most of Andhra Pradesh, particularly in the districts of Karimnagar and Adilabad. It created a base among the peasantry in Telangana and among the students, youth and intellectuals all over Andhra Pradesh. Later, Kondapalli Seetaramiah developed differences with the Central Organising Committee of the CPIML on the issue of adopting a more militant posture following Charu's line, and broke away from the Central Organising Committee CPIML. Kondapalli Seetaramiah then formed the CPI (ML) (People's War Group) on 22 April 1980 by merging the Andhra Pradesh and Tamil Nadu State Committees. In May a group of revolutionary forces of Maharashtra joined the CPI (ML) (PWG). The Party also had a few members from Karnataka.

After the initiation of the Naxal violence Jagityal and Siricilla taluqs were declared as 'Disturbed Areas' in October 1978. Keeping in view the prospects of offensive action by the security forces, the Naxalites drew up first the Jagtyal Perspective and later the Guerrilla zone perspective entitled, *"Get prepared to take the Karimnagar and Adilabad peasant struggles into a newer stage"*. They expanded the armed struggle over a wide contiguous area and developed three guerrilla zones in NT, DK and AOB regions in the process. As part of the efforts to implement the plan of building the four districts of Karimnagar, Adilabad, Warangal, and Khammam districts (northern Telangana) into a guerrilla zone, seven armed peasant guerrilla squads were sent to the strategic area (Dandakaranya) on the borders of Andhra Pradesh, Maharashtra and Madhya Pradesh in 1980. The armed struggle also spread to the South Telangana region, Rayalaseema and later to some backward parts of the South Coastal district in Andhra Pradesh. Guerrilla zones also came into existence in the South Telangana and Nallamala regions. Gradually an extensive mass base was built in Dandakaranya according to plan, and a separate Forest Committee was formed in February 1987 covering the forest regions of Adiḷabad and the East Division (comprising of the Districts Vishakhapatnam and East-Godavari) in Andhra Pradesh and parts of Maharashtra, M.P. and Orissa. The

CPIML developed four Forest Committees in Andhra Pradesh, Madhya Pradesh, Orissa and Maharashtra and four Regional Committees in plain areas.

In the mid-80s the Naxals suffered many losses as the security forces had an upper hand. Consequently, the Naxals formulated defensive tactics. In 1987-88, the Naxals tried to withstand the security force by attacking with arms in various forms and also by rebuilding the mass organisations and consolidating the mass base and squads as well as forming new squads in the plains and forests. Starting from the middle of 1988, the mass resistance and armed resistance movement gained intensity. In 1990, utilizing the contradiction among the ruling classes, the Naxalites changed tactics and consolidated their mass base, expanded and consolidated their armed units, and extended the movement.

From the end of 1990, the armed offensive by the security forces was stepped up throughout Andhra Pradesh and a ban was imposed on the CPI (ML) PWG in May 1992. The Naxals organised ambushes and raids, both opportunity and deliberate, and mobilised the people's militia units into armed actions, in some places, against the police and state property. Armed clashes with the police and paramilitary force became more intense and emerged as the main form of action, while the clashes with the social groups became secondary. The armed resistance by the guerrillas gave a fillip to the mass movements which increased after 1995. Class struggles on various issues and land occupation struggles became a common feature and various people's committees emerged in several villages of North Telengana. The successful holding of the All India Special Conference in 1995 in South Bastar and consolidation of the party in newly extended areas, gave the erstwhile PWG an all India stature. It had party units in Andhra Pradesh, Chhattisgarh (then Madhya Pradesh), Maharashtra, Orissa, West Bengal, Bihar (including present Jharkhand), and Haryana.

Formation of Party Unity and other LWE Groups

CPIML (Lin Biao faction) in its end of party congress in 1973 November decided to follow Charu's line. Towards the end of 1973 the anti-Lin Biao group led by Subrata Datta broke away from the CPI ML (Charu Mazumdar group) which adhered to the line of Lin Biao. The Andhra Pradesh Revolutionary Communist Party (APRCP) jointly with CPI-ML (SNS) issued an appeal, in May 1973, to the Communist Revolutionaries in India to unite on one platform. The initiative was taken by S.N. Singh, K. Vasudeva Rao and Chandra Pulla Reddy who issued an appeal for sinking their differences on ideological issues with a view to building up a revolutionary party. In pursuance of this appeal, a United CPI-ML was formed, merging the Andhra Pradesh RCP (Chandra Pulla Reddy), the Central Committee of Communist Revolutionaries (Phani Bagchi) and the State Party Committee of Maharashtra CPI-ML. The Central Committee of the United CPI-ML met at Nagpur, in April 1975, and sought to streamline the organisational functioning by creating centres from where organisational plans and party actions would be guided. Besides, a five-member trade union Sub-Committee was formed along with a mass front Sub-Committee to carry on the mass struggle.

Another viable group came into existence in Andhra Pradesh after the merger of three splinters Maoist group viz. Committee of Communist Revolutionaries (Mani Singh), Andhra Pradesh Communist Revolutionaries (Nagi Reddy) and Communist Unity Centre (COC-CPIML). All of them united in April 1975 to form the Unity Centre of Communist Revolutionaries of India-Marxist-Leninist (UCCRI-ML). They formed a Central Committee with Nagi Reddy as its Secretary.

The United CPI-ML (SNS-CP Reddy group) again merged with the United Committee of CPI-ML (Bhaskar Nandi-Khokan Mazumdar group) in December 1977 and formed a provincial Committee of CPI-ML. This group tried to entrench itself in some of the areas of influence of the former CPI-ML.

In April 1982, the COC CPI-ML (Appal Suri group) and

unity organisation CPIML (Bhabani Roy Choudhary group) formally merged and formed the CPI-ML (party unity). On 3 August 1992, the CPIML Jan Shakti was formed by the merger of CPIML (K. Ramchandra group), CPIML (Polia group), UCCRI-ML (T.N. Reddy group), CPIML (Khokan Majumdar group), and CCRI-ML (Parimal Dasgupta group).

Efforts to merge various LWE Groups and Unification Spree

Learning from history, some groups of Naxalites made efforts to unite and merge with various other groups. The first merger of Party Unity was with the Communist Kranthikari Sanghatan (CKS), a small organisation, which was one of the members of the AICCCR of Bihar. CKS did not join with the CPI (ML), because of the differences between CKS and SNS, who was the then secretary of the Bihar state committee. There was a split in the CKS and one section which had some work bordering Aurangabad and Palamau districts, merged with the CPI (ML) (PU) to form the CPI (ML) (UO) in 1980. Some more small organisations too merged with the PU. The Bihar faction of the CCRI (ML), a small organisation of West Bengal, united with PU in 1988. A fraction of CPI (ML) (CT), known as the Coordination Centre, (or Sangram group) Punjab united with the PU in 1990. During the 80s the Peoples War Group considered unity among the genuine ML parties and urgent task as explained in their Tactical Line: *"since building a strong, united party is the largest issue we are facing, it is the principal task of our party to unite the true ML parties, groups and individuals under one umbrella"*[4] *(Our Tactical Line)*

The PW and MCC met for the first time in 1981. Comrades Kondapalli Seeatramiah and Kanai Chatterjee initiated unity talks but did not succeed. Later, at the end of the 80s', when the PU took a firm stand on the question of China, regular contacts were resumed. It was only in 1991, that the PWG again decided to meet and exchange views with the PU on various ideological and political issues.

In 1993, the CC of erstwhile PW held talks with the

Maharashtra PW, which had separated since 1987 and completed the unity with Maharashtra PW in 1994. The AISC opined that had the all India Plenum been held to solve the internal crisis of 1985-87, history would have taken a different course. But in 1996, due to serious differences on how to build the all-India mass organisation, MCC withdrew from it and cordial relations deteriorated. Yet bilateral meetings continued between the two. Meanwhile, in this, joint activities and merger talks continued between the PW and PU. Even between the PU and MCC bilateral meetings continued, mainly to settle local problems developing in Bihar.

In 1998 Party Unity merged with Peoples War Group and formed Peoples War. The merger between PW and PU increased the unified party's stature. In March 2001 the 9th Congress of PW took place. In the Congress POR, PW correctly mentioned that "*we should hold talks with the MCC and strive to maintain fraternal relations*". On 24th August 2001 Central Committee (PW) and Central Committee (MCC) made a declaration to stop mutual clashes and to fight united. Before this declaration in January 2000 MCC and March 2000 PW had separately announced the cessation of clashes between these two groups.

In January 2003 MCC and RCC(I) merged together to form Maoist Communist Center India (MCCI). The unification spree of Naxalites continued in 2004 PW and MCC(I) merged to give birth to CPI (Maoist) and in 2007 CPML 2nd Coordination Committee/Ajit Chakravarty group merged with CPI Maoist. Now Janshakti is trying to merge with CPI Maoists. Naxalites after merger also faced problem of coordination which they have admitted in their documents as mentioned below:

> "Lack of proper education to the cadres of two erstwhile parties about what each had learnt from the other which creates some doubts and hesitancy in receiving new ideas such as the agreement on KKC. Influence of still-prevalent old weaknesses on present relations that are creating problems; Influence of the past remnants and differences in

each of the erstwhile Parties that had accrued and entered the unified Party; Influence of some problems dating back to the period of AICCCR and the formation of the two Parties, Com CM, etc.; There are also some real problems such as different standards in the selection, gradation and promotion of cadres basing on different levels of the movement, problems arising out of composition of some committees, and so on."

Formation of Guerrilla Zone

PWG started building squads in DK in 1980 as part of the Guerrilla Zone Perspective. From 1983 onwards they formed regular squads in North Telangana districts which were chosen as the Guerrilla Zone Perspective. These squads performed both organisational and military tasks. Since then PWG has been developing guerrilla squads and guerrilla warfare. Armed squads were formed in the Magadh region of Bihar from 1981.

In 1995, the Naxals made efforts to activate the organs of People's Political Power in NT and DK Guerrilla Zones and in the East Division with slogan: *"All power to the Revolutionary People's Committees."* Through these organs Naxalites attempted to control rural masses in a few villages. In the Guerrilla Zone of NT the GRCs became defunct due to severe government repression.

Although the Party Unity entered Palamu district in 1978 itself recognising its importance, it was only in 1985, that the Party's activities spread to three blocks of Palamu, and one block of Rohatas district in Koel-Kaimur region and two squads were functioning. Due to the arrest of a major section of the leadership, the movement entered a period of stagnation after 1991. In 2001 following the 9th Congress of the Party, they made concrete planning for the development of the guerrilla zone and guerrilla bases for Koel-Kaimur region.

Militarisation of the Outfit

In order to upgrade armed resistance Naxals of both streams PWG and MCC made efforts to specialize in the military sphere. In 1980 Naxals (PWG) reinitiated armed squads. In 1995 they developed military platoons. They could not take the decision to build the People's Guerrilla Army in 1995. As part of the Special efforts to specialize and concentrate on the military, a separate sub-committee on military affairs (SCOMA) was formed in 1996; state SCOMAs were also formed in some states. They tried to apply military theory to the practice and to develop the fighting capacities, techniques and skills of guerrilla forces. However, in 1995 the Naxals did not have the required understanding and capability to develop a People's Guerrilla Army; it is clear from their document:

> "LGSs, CGSs and platoons were also formed since 1995 but they were not brought under a separate military command. In the guidelines drawn up for developing NT and DK to higher-level guerrilla zones, we laid down certain conditions that platoons should assume the general form and that centralised military command should be formed from bottom to top. We did not have an in-depth understanding about the plan to be implemented to fulfil the above conditions such as to develop the guerrilla forces into regular military formations; forming the required command; relation between the two; relation between the regular army and the militia; relation between the base area and the army; the relation between the army and political power etc. *Yet, we did not have clarity on how to build the PGA and separate command structures. Hence, although the situation was ripe by the time of 1995 Special Conference itself, the task of forming the PGA was not taken up due to subjectivism and spontaneity in the CC*".[5]

> "Special Guerrilla squads were formed to fight against the state from 1994-95 but we did not give them a generalised form at that time. The military formations increased further after the separation of the organisational and military squads in May 1999. We dissolved the CGS system in 1999, and the formation of platoons, SGSs and LGSs was taken up. Thus, by undertaking specialisation, separate squads were formed for military and organisational tasks."[6]

In 2000 they developed Peoples Guerrilla Army. In 2004 after merger they converted the PGA into Peoples Liberation Guerrilla Army. Now, the Naxals are trying to transform the PLGA into Peoples' Liberation Army. They have the same view as Mao about PLGA, and consider PLGA as the main instrument of Naxalites for the seizure of political power. They developed primary, secondary and base forces. The People's Liberation Guerrilla Army became a major force by its close integration with the militia and masses.

The above observations mentioned in the documents of the CPI Maoists made it crystal clear that in the late 90s, the Peoples War Group was not conceptually clear about militarizing its organisation. The decision to form the PGA was taken by the Coordination Committee of PW in August 2000 and was implemented on 2 December 2000. Same was the case with MCC.

Many top cadres of CPI Maoists admitted that PWG was militarily superior to MCC and other groups of Naxalites. However efforts to militarise Naxals started early in Bihar; in the erstwhile PU areas, "Commanders Committees" were formed in 1987 under the leadership of the RCs, and later transformed into the "Sainik Sanchalan Teams (SST)" in 1993. They fulfilled the military and fatigue needs of the squads and coordinated the armed attacks. This was formed first in Magadh and later in Koel-Kaimur. Although they were formed with the understanding of command, they did not develop in the direction of command due to lack of concrete study and planning.

Formation of PGA and Subsequent Transformation into PLGA

In fact, the CC of the erstwhile PW had correctly summed up the political, organisational and military situation and made the following assessment in the document "*Guerrilla Zones-our Perspective*".

> "The People's Militia is the Base force in the PGA. Without the People's Militia the PGA cannot develop. If our regular armed forces have to effectively counter the enemy the help

of the militia is indispensable. When the militia, local squads and the regional forces are engaged in guerrilla actions against the enemy indulge in acts of harassment, it will be difficult for the enemy to directly concentrate on our regular armed force and inflict losses. It is the principal source for the recruitment into the regular army. Although we recognised the role of people's militia, we did not make much headway in building and extensive network of People's Militia due to which our resistance too did not become extensive."

"In the present situation, along with the military task, the political-organisational tasks too are acquiring importance. We have to develop armed organisations which are sufficiently trained and skilled enough to face the enemy offensive. In order to efficiently carry out the political and organisational tasks on the one hand, and military tasks on the other, it is essential to form separate organisations for each and pay special attention for developing them".[7]

"However in the course of development we acquired knowledge through direct and indirect knowledge and experience, which culminated in the formation of the PGA and a separate full-fledged CMC to guide and lead the People's army directly. This final clarity came to us through study and practice which was enriched in the 9th congress."[8]

The Naxals have developed a Central Military Commission. They decided to develop it in the Congress of 2001. The CMC is in-charge of intelligence, logistics, weaponry, medical wing; it coordinates, organizes the activities of all commands, sub-commands, primary, secondary and base force. They have also developed military instructor teams to provide *in situ* training to the effective and have taken the struggle beyond the guerrilla stage and initiated into mobile warfare stage. The Koraput (2004), G. Udayagiri (2006), Ranibodli (2007), Nayagarh (2008), Tadmetla (2010) incidents highlight the features of mobile warfare—bigger well trained and rehearsed formations fighting for longer duration of time. Naxalites also planned and conducted special operations with high political impact which could cause rabid reaction in urban areas. The Naxalites were precipitately regularised into sections, facsimile companies, and one small battalion (in Bastar only). They have even committed themselves to multi-layer defence in their base areas. The Naxalites have developed many hideouts in their base areas which may be termed as '*points d' appui*'—strongly occupied ground and only to be approached with difficulty

Naxalites of 1967 vis-a-vis Recent Phase of CPI Maoist

The context, contour, means and methods of conflict of Naxalites have altered over the decades. However, first generation Naxalism and the present phase-third generation Naxalism have much similarity and many contrasts. Charu advocated a People's democratic revolution, while the CPI Maoists advocated a new democratic revolution.[9] CPIML started a war of annihilation and subversion. CPI Maoist continued political war, war of annihilation, attrition, political and physical subversion.

The first phase of Naxalism was the handiwork of great ideologues; and their ideological line is still followed by Naxalites. In spite of the fact that Naxalites were ideological turbo-charged, yet ideological controversies were tremendous, they were floundering in a welter of confusion over some polemical issues. The spectre of schism was hanging high over CPIML and very soon the Naxalite groups splintered into dozens of small groups. Mukti Yuddha group used to dub Charu's political line as an admixture of Narodism[10] and Guevara's petty-bourgeois romantic theory of revolution. In contrast to the problem of disintegration of first phase, the neo-Naxalites have achieved merger of many splinter groups even though many differences among them persist.

1967 and 1969 are the important milestones of first phase of Naxalism, and Charu Mazumdar set 1975 as the target of liberating the entire country and achieving a people's revolution. The Naxalites of third phase are better strategists than the first phase who have learned from the old mistakes, and have kept 2060 as the flag post to liberate the entire country. The First phase Naxalites had a direct link with Mao and some visited China to garner support for their activities and sought directions from Mao. They even coordinated with CPIML Pakistan. The Maoists through CCOMPOSA and RIM are coordinating with LWE groups of other countries.

First phase Naxalites were weak in tactics and their strategies were lacking. However, the present day Naxal leaders have many shrewd strategists and astute tacticians who have to some extent mastered guerrilla warfare, mine warfare and mobile warfare. However, the neo–Naxalites draw inspirations and ideas from the writings of Charu Majumdar (our tasks in the present situation, take forward the people's democratic revolution to success). Internet is the greatest teacher of the present day Maoists. They are studying the situations of Nepal, Peru, Chechnya, Philippines to gain insight into various experiences of revolutions.

First phase Naxals did not have the support of civil liberty groups. Only in 1974 top intellectuals including Dr. Amartya Sen, Chomsky and others started supporting the Naxalites. But, recently Naxals have developed collaboration with some civil liberty groups and foreign intellectuals. Recently, in Dr. Binayak Sen's case, 22 Nobel laureates (many of whom received Nobel prizes in 70s) who had probably not protested against even Nelson Mandela's case made protests without understanding the merit of the case. Naxalites take advantage of the tendency that 'people love popularity to truth'. They feel propaganda can mould public opinion. The neo-Naxalites have both sword and shining shields. They attack with sword, save themselves with shields and dazzle the opponent into inaction through information operations and civil liberty interventions.

Charu wanted his CPIML to destroy state machinery and liberate the areas, so also the Maoists. In the first phase more peasants and students were involved in developing peasant armed power. Charu Majumdar wanted the working class to lead the peasantry; many workers participated in many violent Naxalite activities.

The first phase Naxalites did not target industries or

industrialists. The new phase is milking some industrialists and industries; they are preventing further industrialisation of the country. Whether in Lohandiguda, Nandigram or Kalingnagar they are opposing industrialisation.

Initially Charu was dismissive of mass line and mass organisations; later on he stressed their importance. However, mass organisations were not active in the first phase, as the importance of politics was not well understood. Charu Majumdar had negative views about the role of mass organisations and mass movements in rousing and mobilising millions of people in revolutionary struggles, Charu Mentioned: 'The revolutionary peasants have demonstrated through their struggle that neither mass movement nor mass organisation is indispensable for waging guerrilla warfare. ... Mass organisation and mass movement increase the tendency towards open and economic movement and expose the revolutionary workers before the enemy, which makes it easier for the enemy to launch attacks. Therefore, open mass movement and mass organisation are obstacles in the way of the development and expansion of guerrilla warfare.'

Charu Majumdar ignored the fact that it was at the call of the Siliguri Sub-divisional Krishak Samiti, a mass organisation of the peasants (which had roused and mobilised them) that the Naxalbari peasant uprising took place. So also the Girijan Sangham and Mahila Sangam rouse and organize the peasants in Srikakulam. In other areas of struggle also, mass organisations and mass movements played their important roles until they were banned by Charu Majumdar. At first all these struggles had a mass character.[11] In eight documents Charu spoke about setting up an underground organisation, and secret combat groups were raised but not well organised.

Many uneducated and unemployed jumped into the bandwagon, and lumpen elements led the rural groups, mainly led by the Presidency College student leaders. The CPI (M) held a meeting in the Ram Mohan Library hall of Calcutta and formed the Naxalbari peasants struggle aid committee which became the nucleus of CPIML of the future. The present phase

Naxalites have developed a Revolutionary United Front with number of frontal organisations. Initial Naxalite upsurges occurred without developing much roots. Present day Naxalism is making a sinister design to radicalise people and grow its roots in many remote and urban areas. First phase Naxalites had made preparations for years to start offensive 'spring thunder'. The first phase Naxalites started massive annihilation campaigns. Besides killing the so called class enemies they indulged in wanton destruction of infrastructures, railway stations, coaches, office buildings. Many statues of renowned freedom fighters, national celebrities including the statues of Gandhiji, Tagore, Swami Vivekananda were destroyed and vandalized, schools and libraries were set to fire, infrastructures were destroyed in the same line as the Cultural Revolution of China. To some extent first phase Naxal actions were the cloned action of the Cultural Revolution of China. Here it is worthwhile to mention the words of Charu Majumdar recorded in his central committee report:

> "The CPI (ML) considers attacks on educational institutions as a first step towards a cultural revolution and a revolt against the bourgeois-controlled education system. Burning of portraits of so-called national leaders, kings and military rulers and books written by them and on them should be intensified in all the districts, such as those of and on Gandhi, Nehru, Tagore, Vivekananda, Rammohan Roy, Netaji, and this task should particularly be continued by Naxalite students and youths without being deceived by any illusion of careerism and the movement should be carried on with double vigour following the examples set by our Chinese and Vietnamese comrades, the Red Guard followers of out Great Chairman Mao Tse-tung." [12]

In January 1971 CPIML prisoners made a jail break from Kurseong jail in Darjeeling and 11 top cadres of CPIML escaped from Siliguri central jail. In line with their avowed objective to escape from the jail, the Naxalite detainees and UT Prisoners made a bid to escape from the Dum Dum Central

Jail on May 14, 1971. In all, 45 Naxalite detainees and UTPs escaped from the jail but 13 of them were recaptured by jail staff and eight fugitives were arrested by police while 24 imprisoned Naxalites could remain at large. While escaping the Naxalites were intercepted by the jail staff and a clash ensued between them and imprisoned Naxalites resulting in injuries to 72 Naxalites and 43 jail staff including one Deputy Jailor. Charu Mazumdar wrote in Liberation; "Today the prison is a centre of revolt; today the comrades in prison are repeatedly making a mockery of it by escaping from it." Present phase Maoists in their 9th merger congress document have mentioned the method of prisoner's struggle:

> "*The congress urges to* form secret Party units even in prison and carry on the task of running them regularly through secret methods.
>
> Build action committees such as "*Jail Bandi Sanghursh Samiti*" behind bars. In case comrades are kept in separate prison barracks, then form barrack committees, and press with demands to keep all revolutionaries in the same barrack depending upon the concrete situation. Such action committees are quite helpful in further enhancement of the spirit of unity and sacrifice, and in identifying vacillators and coverts.
>
> Transform the prisons into political universities.
>
> In order to enhance your own theoretical-ideological and political levels, continue holding a series of study and political classes as far as possible.
>
> Arouse and mobilize common prison inmates, forming cultural teams, aid committees and various types of organisations.
>
> Develop the prisons as centres of struggle against the ongoing widespread extortion, corruption and atrocities as well as against the attacks on democratic rights. At the same time, unite and create a huge outcry in support of the revolutionary struggles being waged on the work scale, and against the repression campaigns aimed at them.

This Congress hereby adopts a resolution to take up every possible programme so as to express solidarity with the *'struggles of prison inmates'* to lend strength to their struggles; and to form suitable organisations. The Congress resolves to:

Form organisations, such as 'Committee to Release Prisoners' along with intellectuals, democracy—lovers and members of the families of imprisoned comrades, in solidarity with prisoners' struggles and to lend them strength. Such an organisation shall conduct struggles on various demands related to the jail by establishing coordination between various Prisoners' Action Committees. Employing different means, such committees shall help create public opinion about the assault upon the civil rights of the prison inmates. In this direction efforts are already underway.

Organize progressive lawyers to provide legal support to the prisoners. Some efforts have been made in this direction. Yet we shall lay stress upon forming such organisations in different cities. These organisations shall provide legal support to imprisoned comrades as well as generate public opinion against draconian laws.

Mobilize 'Committee to Release Prisoners,' lawyers organisations, civil liberty organisations and the common masses against 'Fast Track Trials' and such other outright anti-people provisions.

Pay special attention to raise protest against and organize resistance to atrocities perpetrated upon women prisoners.[13]

Rope in various means of propaganda in order to highlight the inhuman conditions in prisons.

Conduct signature campaigns on various demands of the prisoners and in support of their struggles issues in order to arouse and mobilize the masses.

Strive to punish the prison officials who carry out atrocities upon the prisoners.

Constitute a Prisoners' Fund to help secure their release.

This Congress resolves to strive to carry out every possible means to free our comrades from the jails besides waging different forms of struggle within constitutional limits. With support from the masses, we had carried out historic actions such as the Jehanabad and R Udaigiri Jail breaks. The Congress calls upon the entire Party ranks and the mass organisation rank and file to prepare in this direction and educate the masses."

On 21 February 1971, guerrilla squads raided the police camp at Behala airstrip; the RPF post was attacked at Santoshpur Railway Station near Calcutta; With the capture of rifles from policemen in Magurjan in Purnea district by Naxalbari guerrillas Charu Majumdar declared that the Peoples Liberation Army had been formed. But it was for name sake only. In the recent phase the Naxalites have developed Peoples Liberation Guerrilla Army, with dozens of military companies and one small guerrilla battalion. On many occasions Maoists have exhibited second, third and fourth generation warfare in their offensive campaigns.

Ideologically, the CPIML's objective was an agrarian revolution, but 65 percent of student revolutionaries from Calcutta who went to the countryside were overwhelmed by the physical difficulties encountered in rural areas. They returned back to Calcutta and mixing with lumpen elements they harboured in about 3000 clubs of Calcutta and started an urban annihilation campaign. Their main target was the police, police informers and large number of political cadres of The Congress and CPM. In the first phase urban guerrillas became a force to reckon with and 50 per cent of revolutionaries centred in the greater Calcutta area; about ten thousand Naxalites were present in greater Calcutta and about double that number in other areas. The present phase Naxalites are planning to start urban movement, though they have some presence in few urban centres.

First phase Naxalites introduced Deshbarti, Liberation as the party literature. Present phase Maoists publish many journals, Awam-E-Jung, Peoples March, Lal Pataka, Chingari, Biyukka, Prabhat, Maoist Bulletin. It has a printing press and Central Propaganda Bureau to look after this work. Maoists have developed their organisation with a central technical wing to conduct research and development in weaponry and communications. They also have a counter intelligence wing, military commission and training wing with military instructors. Naxalites in the first phase used to destroy schools in urban and remote areas; the present-day Maoists are destroying schools, public buildings, hospitals, banks, communication towers, roads, bridges, transmission towers, railway lines and infrastructure in remote rural areas.

Explosives and mines as well as sophisticated weapons were not available with the Maoists earlier. Mine warfare has now become an integral part of the neo–Naxalites tactical arsenal. Recently, the Naxals are also able to hit helicopters. Unlike the first phase, the present outfit has organised large militias; more diversified and flexible tactical moves and also dispersed its actions to disguise its intentions.

There were no base areas in the first phase till Asim Charterjee in a document of the Bengal-Bihar-Orissa Border Committee emphasised the need of a base area in hilly areas, as developed by Mao in 1927 in Chungking Mountains. In the late 70s and early 80s Naxalites developed their bases in Telengana and adjacent Bastar area and Bhojpur district of Bihar and sustained many of their bases. In 1971 Charu directed his followers to create base area in those areas where no Railway lines or national high way passes. Later on Naxalites developed many guerrilla zones and base areas. The Maoists have achieved depth due to various base areas and also revolutionary politics.

Both the phases exhibited revolutionary barbarism. Both were swayed by Mao's ideology and showed lack of patriotism. Supporting Pakistan and China's stance during 1971 Indo-Pak war Charu had mentioned in Naxal document:

> "Crush Indian Expansionists' attack on Pakistan and their anti-China clique. Support the Government of Pakistan and Pakistani people in their anti-imperialist struggle to defend their National Sovereignty and Independence. Ensure defeat of the Indian Expansionists by all possible means. Long live the glorious CPI (M-L)"[14]

The first phase did not have a correct perspective of revolutionary warfare; they were not able to raise the armed struggle to a higher level; they had not militarised their cadres, there were no military commissions. Neo-Naxalites considered it a failure not to establish a powerful mass base, and developed the idea of building a large people's army right from the beginning. Not following rules of guerrilla warfare were the reasons which brought failure for the first phase. First phase Naxalites' upsurge is considered an abortive attempt and now it has evolved as a serious attempt. Charu's efforts started as the final convulsions of the revolutionary movement, whereas the present-day Maoists are conducting nibbling operations. The spokesperson of the first phase of Naxalism—late Kanu Sanyal—in an interview, a few days before his death in 2010, mentioned that the plan of the Naxalites to liberate India is nonsense.

Spread and Surge of CPI Maoists

Some people try to estimate the surge or decline of LWE only from violent incidents reported and registered in police stations, which is not accurate. Violence reported is one important parameter to assess the LWE surge. But sometimes it can be ineffective; when the underground groups absolutely dominate any area then the rate of reported crime in that area goes down due to terror of the members of the outfit. If terror is administered in a large enough dose, over a long enough period, it has an anaesthetic effect on the public and society. In many areas the Naxals have systematically improved their position unopposed. Spatial spread and surge of any LWE group can be assessed from its presence both over ground and underground; from its influence due to over ground activities, and underground activities due to violence. It's over ground activities in recent years has tremendously multiplied. Surge and decline of threat is the outcome of the equation of capability, intent and activities of the extremists group. It can be put into following mathematical formula:

LWE Threat = LWE Capability + LWE Strategic Intent + LWE Activities. (T= C+I+A)

The activities and capability of CPI Maoists and its strategic intent makes it crystal clear that it is surging. The above parameters reveal that CPI Maoist is the one LWE group which has the largest arc of influence, presence and engagement in India, which spreads to 18 states. The Naxals have organised themselves into nine guerrilla zones and four red resistance areas. The Naxal problem is inchoate form in many states. In 212 districts Naxals have showed their footprint. In Naxal parlance 129 districts are in the strategic defensive stage which means these districts are mildly affected; fifty districts are in strategic equilibrium (highly affected) stage; 33 districts are in strategic offensive (extremely affected) phase. The Naxals have formed about a dozen guerrilla zones, and in the last category of districts they have formed about two dozen base areas. Naxalites are also making efforts to expand bases all along the western coast. In some pockets of one guerrilla zone they are graduating from banditry to Janathana Sarkar (parallel administration through peoples committees). In the areas of three guerrilla zones of Dandakaranya and Bihar-Jharkhand, Andhra-Orissa-Border they have launched high intensity guerrilla warfare. The guerrilla zones have turned into crisis zones which have increased.

In these guerrilla zones Naxals are making calculated moves to cut off the area, make the area inaccessible and make the administrative developmental institutions dysfunctional. It has a honeycomb network of organisation. In 2007, the CPI (Maoists) Congress elected a fresh Central Committee, General Secretary and Politbureau. Five regional bureaus i.e. Eastern Regional Bureau, Northern Regional Bureau, (almost dysfunctional) Central Regional Bureau and South Western Regional Bureau (now dissolved) operate under Politbureau/ Central Committee. Special Zonal Committees/State Committees, Special Area Committees, Divisional Committees/ Regional Committees operate under regional bureaus. Naxals have a combination of predators and parasites in their outfit. They are the cadres of conspirators and killers. In the entire country Naxalites have about twenty thousand armed cadres and about sixty thousand sympathizers. However, making a total estimate of the total Naxalites strength of the entire country is a difficult proposition. But the Naxalites' order of battle can be computed by totalling the primary force, secondary force, base force of Naxalites, the part timers and the professional revolutionaries of various Guerrilla zones, Special Area Committees and Red Influence Region. Desertion from Naxal outfit and continuous recruitment is also there. Therefore, there may be 5 to 10% variation in the naxal order of battle. However the number uncertainty of LWE was so much there in Vietnam that, it was referred to U.S. Supreme Court. American Supreme Court conducted trial of Gen. Westmoreland to find out North Vietnamese troops.

Naxals are networking with ULFA, PLA, and NSCN. This has been vividly described in South Asia's Intelligence Review: 'gravest internal security threat' is methodically expanding its spheres of influence into the traditionally unstable regions of the country's troubled Northeast. The Communist Party of India-Maoist (CPI-Maoist), under a strategy to rope in sub-national armed groupings in the country's 'periphery', is widening its campaign for a pan-Indian consolidation of violent anti state movements. As the locus of India's earliest and multiple insurrections, most of which are now degraded, the Northeast frontier constitutes a strategic space for Left Wing Extremist (LWE Expansion. At the first 'Unity Congress' after its formation in September 2004, the CPI-Maoist declared its sympathy and support to insurgencies by 'various nationalities', including those in Jammu and Kashmir (J&K), Assam, Manipur and Nagaland, declaring: "This Congress reaffirms its wholehearted support to all these nationality movements and their right to self-determination, including their right to secede from the autocratic Indian state." Indicating an intention to form closer alliances with various insurgent groups, the Congress noted, further, "it may be necessary to form a separate organisation to take up the nationality issue, and we should form such organisations in accordance with the concrete situation."[15]

They are trying to utilize their networking with these groups for both strategic and tactical purposes. The tactical purpose consists of the objectives of arms supply and training; and the strategic purpose is of creating more storm centres for Indian forces by supporting the causes of North eastern and Kashmir terrorists. Naxalites have mobilized tremendous amount of resources and manpower. A perverse confluence of underworld, few publicity-seeking intellectuals, and vested interests have also been noticed in the bandwagon of Naxalites. The above surrogate mothers are also nourishing Naxalism.

Statistical Analysis of Naxal Violence and Incidents

LWE phenomenon cannot be encapsulated into tables, figures and statistics. All the killings and destructions are not same. The timing of some killing incidents has more impact than others. However, it is pertinent to make a statistical analysis of Naxal violence, incidents and attacks against security forces and also death of Naxals in encounters and the recovery of their dead bodies. Naxalites follow a tactics of taking away the dead bodies of their comrades with a view to deny credit to the security force. Therefore the figure of death of Naxals in encounters is inexact; it depicts only the number of recovered dead bodies by security force. However, the real death of Naxalites due to encounter may be double or triple the numbers. Sometimes the injured naxalites succumb later on.

A pattern emerges out of the data. Analysis of LWE violent incidents and killings since 1971 to 2009 shows that 1971 had seen the greatest violent upsurge and highest killings. Year 1971 was highest watermark of Naxal violence. From 1990 the killings and incidents started shooting up. 1991 and 1992 also marked sizable violent incidents and killings. 1991, 1996, 1998, 2004, 2008, and 2009 have shown rise in Naxal activities. These years are the years of Lok Sabha general election and Vidhan Sabha elections in affected states. During the election period Naxal violent activities increase. After merger and formation of CPI Maoist in 2004 continuously violent incidents and killings graph went high.

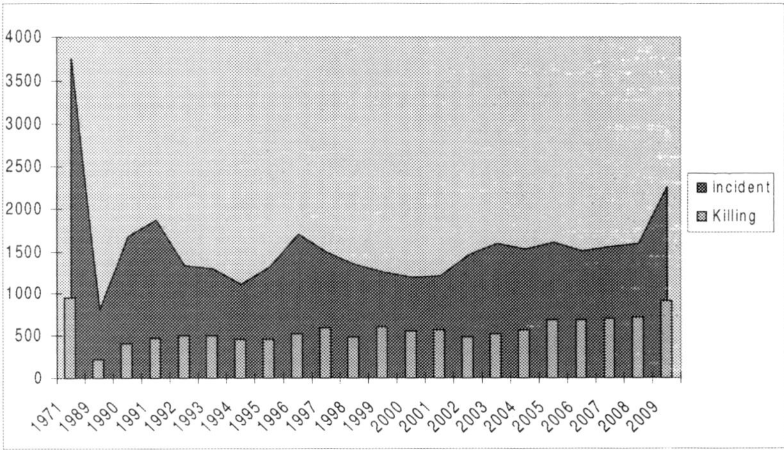

Figure 1: LWE Violence over Four Decades

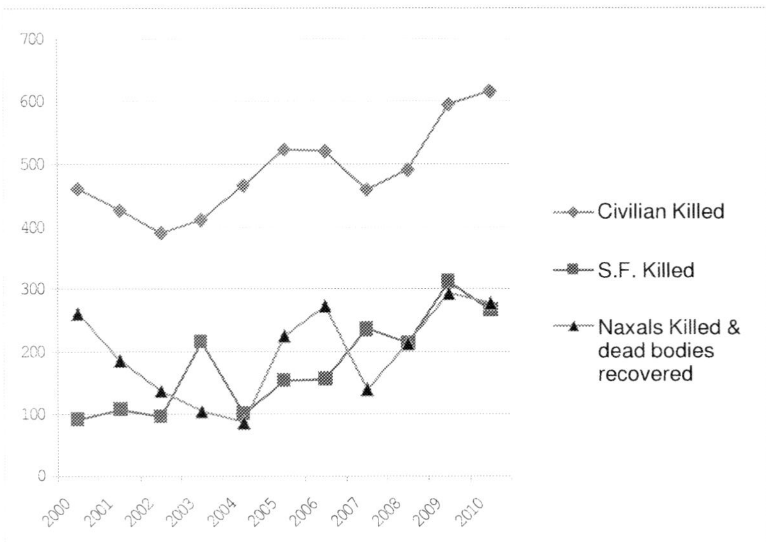

Figure 2: Civilians Killed, S.F. Killed, Naxals Killed and Dead Bodies Recovered in the Millennium Decade.

The reading between these tricolour lines are quite revealing and startling. Initial two years of millennium decade was marked by more security force successes and less S.F. losses, credit goes to A.P. Police and Grey Hound for this initial trend. 2003 was the election year of many Naxal infested States; the newly formed People's Guerrilla Army started their adventures in Chhattisgarh, Jharkhand, Bihar, Odisha resulting in more losses to security forces. 2004 Naxals suffered minimum loss due to the reason that due to peace talk ceasefire occurred in A.P. In 2005 and 2006 the reconfigured PLGA started major offensives in Chhattisgarh, Jharkhand, Bihar, Odisha, West Bengal. 2006 on wards, security forces of Chhattisgarh, Jharkhand, Bihar, A.P. also intensified major offensives against Naxals. In 2009 and 2010 West Bengal and Odisha also launched serious operations. In a number of operations security force killed many Naxalites in encounters including their leaders. It shows that the lethality, tempo of operations has tremendously increased.

The increase in killing of civilians by Naxalites is only the reflection of their desperateness. After almost every successful encounter they blame some civilians or even the militia, brand them as police informers and kill them. In remote areas the villagers who refuse to provide Naxalites rice or money as demanded by their local men after consecutive 2/3 refusals are branded enemy of the party and then they are killed by Naxals.

Naxalites *Modus Operandi* of Political and Guerrilla Warfare

The Naxalites conduct political war and guerrilla war in tandem with the strategy to confuse and disorganize by politics and defeat by guerrilla warfare. Naxalite modus operandi consists of both political manoeuvring and military action. They have designed a Revolutionary United Front to organize revolutionary politics and save their movement from government repression. They have developed sub-committees on mass organisation (SUCOMO) to organize mass movements; Nandigram, Singur, Kalingnagar are recent examples. They have formed urban sub-committees (USCO) on the pattern of the Peruvian Communist party,[16] with the purpose to start an urban Naxalite movement. They have prepared an urban perspective plan complementary to peoples' protracted war. Naxalites exploit the grievances, deprivation and exploitation of the masses, cause agitations and mass movement. Through various frontal organisations like Peoples Democratic Front of India Revolutionary students union and many more organisations, they are trying to exploit various issues like displacement, students', farmers' issues, and cause mass movement. They use the tactics of propagate, agitate and act to convert mass movement into armed struggle. Naxals use military power through political means and gain political space through military means. Naxalites use hit and run offensive to induce over reaction and then to cause public agitation and in the process wear security force down and demoralise. On the military front, they conduct operations on the pattern of copy book guerrilla warfare of Mao and Giap; these operations basically consist of ambush, landmine blasts, and short raid and action team attacks. They follow all manner of dirty tricks to inflict casualties. They follow messier low-tech methods of classic guerrilla conflict and also some novel methods. Naxalites attack isolated security forces first, and attack concentrated and strong force later; they strike to wipe out the when he is on the move. When security force enter a village or their base area Naxals fight S.F. for a short time and then vanish. But, when he retreats exhausted then they pursue him absolutely. Naxals make themselves alternately visible and invisible so that the S.F does not know where to march and how to attack.

Naxals plan to annihilate security forces and gradually liberate areas. In base areas they continue constant pin-pricking. They initially fight with smaller units and later on with bigger units. Naxals conduct harassing operations ***ad infinitum***. They perpetrate small protracted harassments punctuated by a few major actions with extremely subtle, flexible tactics designed to wear down the security forces. Naxal offensives follow the pattern of attack-lull-attack-lull. They make good use of the intervals between tactical counter offensive campaigns and other campaigns of short raid, ambush to rest, train, and consolidate troops. This period is generally short so that they do not give breathing space to security force. They systematically reconnoitre their target, they study routine of security force or the target, conduct extensive rehearsals with sand model and when they become sure of victory after last minute reconnaissance, they raid. Naxals conduct diversionary and harassing attacks in order to disturb and wear out security forces encircle and split up his positions. Naxals cut trees and roads and block road by disrupting the line of communication they force security force to come out to repair them and then they attack the security force. Instead of widespread isolated attacks, they are making efforts to dominate village by village in remote areas and forcing villagers to give one member to naxalite outfit in some remote areas. They take away orphans form remote villages, and grown up boys and girls from remote Bal Ashrams. They form Krantikari Bal Sanghs out of these children, later on use them as child soldiers. In due course of time these kids graduate to hard core Naxalites. The movement continues to disrupt the forested areas and the countryside. They make occasional forays into urban areas adding to the complexity of the problem. They are progressively increasing their spheres of influence and activity. Rather than being the result of a spontaneous popular upsurge or spontaneous resistance movement, it is the handiwork of a tightly-controlled component of total brute violent effort.

Naxalism is Evil *per se*

Naxalism is evil per se. It is anti-democratic, anti-national, and anti-people. Naxalites in 1971 decided to support the Government of Pakistan in their struggle in Bangladesh. Charu Mazumdar's emissary, Soren Bose, left for China on 25 August 1970 to get ideological direction. The Naxalites celebrate India's Independence and Republic days as black days. They do not have faith in the democratic system. During every election not only do the CPI Maoists boycott them and try to damage electoral process, but they also try to destroy the roots of democracy by preventing people's participation. They obstruct the election process through violence and threatening people not to cast votes. They are against development; damaged railway lines, cause train accidents and death of hundreds of innocents. They have extensively damaged roads, schools, bridges, hospitals, government buildings and infrastructure. In the entire country till date, the Naxalites have taken a toll of about 18,000 killings and 50,000 maiming. The killings include the assassination of two ministers of A.P. and M.P., one Member of Parliament, few Members of Legislative Assembly, and hundreds of members of various political parties. Even the Naxalites in the past had attempted to assassinate two Chief Ministers of A.P. and West Bengal. They set fire to a relief camp and village of Errabore in district Dantewada and even burnt alive two-year old children. They killed a scholar who visited Kanker to research on tribal society, a doctor in Midnapore, and 10 members of a marriage party by blasting their vehicles by landmines. In November 2010 they blew up an ambulance carrying patients and a medical team. They killed commuters on the Kaktiya Express in Andhra Pradesh, in the early-90s by setting fire to the coaches of the train; they killed hundreds of innocent people on the Gyaneshwari Express in West Bengal recently. After their atrocious brutality they become effusive in apology. Nevertheless, the various real or imagined reasons proffered by them to justify their actions are meaningless. The Naxalite movement has degenerated into a frenzy of violence. They indulge in widespread violence, sabotage and continuous terror in several infested areas. By their violent and destructive conduct they are taking the country in a new disastrous direction.

Chaotic conditions have emerged due to the vicissitudes of Naxalite activities. They plunder ruthlessly and destroy wantonly. They have plundered many banks, ransacked many homes and many PDS godowns, and destroyed hundreds of schools, hostels, panchayat buildings, roads, bridges, railway stations and railway lines. Every year they destroy public property worth few billions of rupees, causing extensive damage to economic and social infrastructure and reduction in Government's prestige, thereby gradually cause disintegration in society. The systematic and continuous Naxalite activities are breaking the local economy and society. Their depredations have a cumulative and corrosive effect on security, development and administration. It comprises a continuum from sabotage-terror-violence-guerrilla warfare-mobile warfare.

Naxalism from Incipient Extremism Stage is reaching Strategic Proportion Stage

Naxalism has gained much of its momentum; in some areas, from the stage of incipient extremism to reach a strategic proportion stage. By killing SFs and destroying infrastructure they are injuring and weakening the nation and the situation is deteriorating. Targets attacked by them have expanded enormously. The capability of the Maoists to recruit new members and their ability to organize significant offensive actions has enhanced, numerically and materially. A gradual expansion of the Naxals areas of operations and influence is taking place. Volatility, uncertainty, complexity, ambiguity characterize the conflict and in return affect the operational environment.

Levels of violence have accentuated. Deterioration of public services in some remote areas has occurred due to wanton destruction by Naxalites. They are attacking Government targets to undermine the credibility of administration and developmental measures. LWE has become more lethal, more tenacious, more sophisticated in tactics and in use of weaponry and mines. They have turned some guerrilla zones into veritable minefields. Through their central technical teams they continue weapon, mine and rocket fabricating efforts, through their research and development activities. The Naxals have also developed an intelligence wing—People's Security Service—to support their military activities to develop greater combat power. The map of the pathways of LWE show that in 1980s it rose as a non-entity with 12 bore gun. Now, they have about two hundred AK-47 rifles, few dozens of light machine guns, few hundreds of SLRs, few thousands of .303 rifles and twelve-bore guns. At a rough estimate, they have around twenty thousand armed cadres.

Their method of communication ranges from the use of drums to digital means. They have many printing units and are gradually becoming organisationally formidable and technically savvy. A steady escalation in the means of violence has also taken place. Though the problem is surging and spreading in many states, yet they have also suffered many setbacks on the ground. Many of their arms-manufacturing units have been raided by the security forces. Many Naxalites, including one central committee member, have surrendered and one-fourth of their central committee and Polit Bureau members have been killed in encounters and a similar numbers are in jail. The North-Chhattisgarh State Committee and the South West Regional Bureau have been disbanded, after the NTSZC retreated to Bastar. However, like a balloon the movement reacts to a squeeze from one side by spreading to the other side.

Total War of Naxals Vs Limited War of Security Force

The Naxals are fighting a full-spectrum guerrilla warfare whereas the security force is fighting a limited war. Naxals fight a no-inhibition war. In order to conduct a reign of terror in their area of operations they raise the level of brutality to great extent. Guerrilla warfare is far more exhausting and brutal than regular warfare. Naxalites try to wear down the security force while building up their own strength. The concept of protracted war has been brought about over a long period of time, with a gradual, yet fundamental shift in their ratio of power between the two constants. The Security Force is trying to 'fight the guerrilla like a guerrilla'; which seems to be a good quote rather than a good commitment. Besides guerrilla warfare, Naxals are waging full scale political and information warfare which seems innocuous, but highly damaging. PLGA and other armed cadres also fight to agitate local public through information operations.

Naxals are translating their aims and ideas into tangible results by physical, political, and information offensives. They conduct operations scattered in area and concentrated in time. Success of LWE in one area often prompts them to replicate their action in other areas. Problem mutation rather than steady state improvement is the more realistic scenario. Moreover, the security force has to fight Naxalites not only in the sharp black and white area of formal combat, but also in grey, fuzzy obscurity where politics affects tactics and economics influences strategy. Therefore, the anti-Naxalite operation is a total war, its political psychological, socio-economic aspect must be given proper consideration and a solution to it must be sought through systematic, long term planning. There is no point in agonizing, but a great need to organize speedily. The Government should figure out the solutions, coordinate and implement.

Naxalism Remains the Biggest Challenge

The Naxalite problem has attained the biggest theatre in terms of spatial spread, subversion and violent incidents, including killings. During the last few years, the maximum number of violent incidents and killings of civilians and security forces have been in Chhattisgarh, Jharkhand and Bihar; but of late violent incidents in West Bengal, Orissa have also shown considerable increase. During a press conference on 23 May 2010, in New Delhi, Prime Minister of India Shri Manmohan Singh mentioned "I have been saying for the last three years that Naxalism remains the biggest challenge facing our country. It is imperative to control Left Wing Extremism for the country's growth".[17] LWE has become public issue number one. It is causing a cumulative erosion of national economy. LWE is accelerating turmoil and the problem appears immense. The statement correctly portrays the threat as more than elemental.

Conclusion

The Naxalites are trying to take the struggle beyond the guerrilla stage and into a mobile warfare stage. Naxalism has become a mindless monster now moving under its own momentum. The problem got a new spin with the activities of it's over ground activists. Over time Naxalism is surging due to the joint activities of underground and over ground activists. They are trying to conduct their game plan with Bolshevik tactics and Maoist strategy and tactics. In some pockets the syndrome has brought about a hepatitis-like coma of local administration leading to its multi-organ failure. Naxalites are attacking on the vital organs of the state. The challenge of Naxalism is a dangerous epidemic affecting the socio-politico-administrative system whose remedy has not yet been achieved. Naxalism has raised and aggravated many problems rather than solving any. It is a disease not a cure. It is evil and anathema; as a result issues and problems that once seemed remote now appear on the doorsteps of the nation.

NOTES

1. Albert Camus, The Rebel, London: Penguin, 2000 p.19. Albert Camus worked in Algeria during disturbances. He was the member of resistance group in 40s. He contributed as a journalist to the underground news paper combat. In 1957 he got Nobel Prize for literature.
2. Ganpati's Interview Peoples March July 2005: It contains Lenin's statement-'Every thing without state power is illusion' and 'Seizure of power by armed force' from p. 36 of Strategy Tactics of Indian revolution CPI Maoist (P), 2004.
3. Regis Debray; The Revolution on Trial, New York: Penguin Books, 1974.
4. Naxalites Document.
5. Ibid.
6. Ibid.
7. Ibid.
8. Ibid.
9. Ibid. In order to understand new democratic revolution, it is essential to know Maoist scheme of revolution. A revolution is not a dinner party, or writing an essay, or painting a picture, or doing

embroidery; it cannot be so refined, so leisurely and gentle, so temperate, kind, courteous, restrained and magnanimous. A revolution is an insurrection, an act of violence by which one class overthrows another.

10. Narodism: In the late 1890s the word links in Russia held that the Principal revolutionary force was the peasantry, not the working class. When the peasants did not respond to their call, they adopted the tactics of secretly killing enemies; they assassinated even Tsar II. Lenin demolished Narodism ideologically.
11. Suniti Kumar Ghosh, Naxalbari Before and After Reminiscences and Appraisal, New Age Publishers (P) Ltd. Kolkata (2009). Suniti Ghosh is the lone surviving member of Central Committee. He is M.A. in English. He was a member of AICCCR.
12. Naxal Document.
13. Naxals' 9th Congress document. 9th All India Naxalite Congress of Naxalites was held in Paralkot forest in Abuzmarh of Bastar in March 2001. This Congress was conducted after 3 decades. But after merger the other groups did not recognise this congress. They had organised another 9th Congress merger in 2007 December in Jharkhand. As per their party constitution they should have congress in every five years.
14. Sandipani Dash, Research Associate, Institute for Conflict Management, South Asia Intelligence Review (SAIR), Weekly Assessments and Briefings, August 2010.
15. Nayak Nihar Geo-politics vol. 2 (2010).
16. UNI May 23rd 2010.

2

Revolutionary Unified Front Through Revolutionary Politics

Protects and Spearheads Naxal Movement

In the Naxals' scheme of things the concept of revolutionary politics is the key to understand protracted people's war[1] which is the main idea behind revolution. The protracted people's war is 30 percent guerrilla warfare, 70 percent revolutionary politics. Political offensive takes precedence over military offensives; through political offensive strategic paralysis can occur. Revolutionary politics further constitutes 30 percent information warfare and 40 percent political warfare. Naxals conceptualise their campaign as an integrated political military effort, and they take tactical kinetic operations in the broader political context. Revolutionary politics and Revolutionary war are two engines which drive LWE conflict with the motto to smash the state machinery and control the targeted population. They often change gears from guerrilla warfare to political manoeuvre and sometimes conduct both activities in tandem to maintain tactical initiative. They use brute force and clever political manipulation, organising political and military effort under one combined command. Politics in command is their tenet. Political activities are more important than military activities, fighting less important than propaganda.[2]

Potential Danger of Revolutionary Politics

Naxalites through revolutionary politics cause political order to fade into irrelevance and drive it into disrepute and bring severe social dislocation and tension. They try to cause deep fragmentation of state power through a collaborative effort of diverse over ground and underground groups. Through politics of discredit, disintegration, disruption, and destruction they cause conceptual confusion and create political pandemonium. The real challenge of revolutionary politics to the regime is its coalitions in armed rebellion. The political context of conflict is the key to understand the potential dangers of conflict. Revolutionary politics is the outcome of Marxist ideology, Maoist strategy and Leninist tactics of organisation politics. Marxism and Maoism provided the strategic template while Leninism provides the operational/tactical component. Confuse and disorganize by politics and defeat by physical force is the main strategy of LWE which they have borrowed from Lenin and Mao. This strategy propagated by Mao to create confusion in the enemy camp over the proper policy to be followed by exhaustion of resources, disintegration of morale, and the alienation of public opinion. Lenin propagated the tactics of creating a revolutionary party. Naxalites are also trying to Bolshevise the party. They follow Leninist tactical principle:

> "To put in the forefront precisely those forms of struggle and organisation which are best suited to the conditions prevailing during the flow or ebb of the movement at a given moment, and which therefore can facilitate and ensure the bringing of the masses to the revolutionary positions, the bringing of the millions to the revolutionary front, and their disposition at the revolutionary front."[3]

Even, Charu Mazumdar in the article 'Carry forward the peasant struggle' mentioned:

"The main cause of success of the Russian revolution was the correct application of the united front. The questions of united front tactics are equally important in India too."[4]

Revolutionary United Front through Revolutionary Politics Protects Naxal Movement

The main aim of revolutionary politics is to create a revolutionary front. What they fail to win on the battlefield, they try to gain through the revolutionary politics of mass organisations. Through information war revolutionary politics transforms defeat of Naxals into victory. They force the government not to take harsh actions against them. By opening many proxy war fronts (media and legal) they force inaction. In their document of Strategy and Tactics of Indian Revolution Naxals the aim for the revolutionary united front is:

"This revolutionary united front is the real bastion that protects the revolutionary movement from suppression and annihilation campaigns. The aim of the united front is to isolate, weaken and destroy the main enemies one by one and win over the maximum possible forces opposed to the main enemies."[5]

Urban Movement through Revolutionary Politics

After the great debacle of 1972 the Naxals had left urban centres which they are now trying to occupy in a different manner. Naxals desire to build a strong urban revolutionary movement oriented towards people's war. Their urban plan aims at giving political orientation to the work in urban areas and is complementary to the all-India perspective for Guerrilla zones. The plan also focuses on urban areas where the working class is numerically strong and politically conscious and which have economic and political importance for the ruling class, in key industries like the railway, airports, telecommunication, posts, coal and textiles and identified military centres, including ordnance factory units in urban areas. They have identified three key potential areas for concentration of its 'subjective force' which include the raw material belt from Singreni

(Andhra Pradesh) to Asansol (West Bengal) the Pune-Ahmadabad corridor and the Delhi-Faridabad, Ghaziabad belt. Their Urban Sub Committee has been upgraded to the level of a Regional Bureau and tasked with the responsibility of further operationalising the plan. They want to develop the secret network in the urban areas and build a powerful movement of the workers; specifically in the core sector. In their language violent agitations are the fiercest cats' paw to every revolutionary storm in urban areas; the importance of urban movement is highlighted in the following paragraph of Naxalites document:

> "The urban movement is one of the main sources, which provides cadres and leadership having various types of capabilities essential for the people's war and for the establishment of liberated areas. Moreover, the responsibility for the provision of supplies, technology-expertise, information and other such things, to the people's war, too lies on the shoulders of the urban revolutionary movement itself. In the absence of a strong revolutionary urban movement, the growth of the people's war will face limitations and difficulties in its advancement". [6]

Urban activities have started in Andhra Pradesh, Maharashtra, West Bengal, Delhi and Uttar Pradesh. The Mumbai resistance in 2004 and Kolkata convention in 2005 are efforts to organize the masses. The urban movement performs tasks complementary to the rural armed struggle. They believe strongly that without widely mobilizing the masses it is not possible to perform any of the other tasks such as building of a united front and performing military tasks. The urban centres serve as the dens of their top cadres, which also facilitate the supply and storing of arms, ammunition and equipment. Some Politbureau members like Khobad Gandhy, Tushar Kanti Bhattacharya were arrested from urban areas. Urban centres also help to create propaganda centres because of their access to intellectuals and the media. They have organised research and development of arms and ammunitions centres. The security forces had raided their urban hideouts in Bhopal, Chennai and Rourkela in the past and recovered rocket manufacturing and gun manufacturing units.

Economic Social Disruption

Naxals are growing political power for their organisation by creating maximum economic and civil disruption. By creating maximum economic and civil disruption they are trying to gain political influence. They feel that, with the advance of the people's war, the pressing need is for entering into key industries and establishing a strong base there. Some industries like transport, communications, rail, dock, power, oil and natural gas, defence production, etc. can play a crucial role in their scheme of revolution. In the course of war, the disruption of production in these industries has an immediate impact on the regime's ability to fight the war.

Political Propaganda

An extremist movement needs a platform for propaganda. Naxals wage a propaganda campaign to support political warfare. The concept of guerrilla warfare as political war turns psychological operations into a decisive factor. The target then, is the minds of the population including Naxal cadres, the security force and the civilian population. Their documents have mentioned:

> "Attention must be paid on conducting wide political propaganda of the revolutionary politics through various means-open, and secret concentrating the anti-people nature of the parliament and the government, the attacks and atrocities on women, Dalits and Adivasis, the persecution of the religious minorities, the oppression and suppression of the rights of the nationalities".[7]

Popular Mobilisation to Support Guerrilla War

Political setting through the revolutionary front provides the incubator to guerrilla warfare. In Andhra Pradesh, through the radical students and workers movement in Hyderabad and

Vishakhapatnam, and the Singareni collieries trade unions the Naxalites have spread their party activities and guerrilla warfare. In Andhra Pradesh these movements provided sustenance to Peoples War in the early 80s. Offensive action by the government in 1985 and 1991 eliminated the Naxalites from urban areas. Again in the mid-1990s, by utilizing the contradictions of Indian democracy and among the ruling classes, the Naxalites changed tactics and consolidated their mass base, expanded and consolidated the armed units and extended the movement. Land occupation struggle is a common feature.

The post-1995 period has seen a resurgence of mass movements in several states led by revolutionary mass organisations or by various cover organisations formed through Naxalite initiatives. In their documents they have mentioned that struggles of peasantry were taken up on a big scale in Andhra Pradesh, N.T., AOB, DK and Bihar and to a lesser extent in West Bengal; struggles of students and women were taken in Andhra Pradesh, N.T., Delhi, Haryana Karnataka, Punjab, AOB, DK, Tamil Nadu; struggles for remunerative prices of agricultural produce, against rise in fertilizer prices, against spurious seeds, pesticides power cuts etc. in DK, Orissa struggles against minerals, against SEZ in West Bengal, D.K., Orissa. PW and CPI Maoist followed the mass line to organize political mobilisation:

> "In the respect of political mobilisation, CPI Maoists functioned very much as has other Maoist groups (e.g. Thailand, the Philippines, Sri Lanka, Peru) especially Sendero Luminoso prior to its own 1980 declaration of People's War in Peru".[8]

Revolutionary Politics Targets the Special Groups

Revolutionary politics constitutes a sort of common ground between masses, frontal organisations and ideology, between political struggle and revolutionary Utopia. In order to intensify struggle and conflict the Naxals, through revolutionary politics, are trying to involve more people. They are creating broad-based militant mass movements on political issues with a view to build and strengthen the united front. They are also making efforts to organize the working class, the semi-proletariat, students, middle class employees, intellectuals, etc. It also has the task of dealing with the problems of special social groups like women, *dalits*, and religious minorities and mobilizing them for the revolutionary movement.

Naxals are mobilising women against class oppression but also against all types of patriarchy, male domination, and discrimination. They are trying to bring more and more women into the revolutionary movements by imbuing them with the politics of new democratic revolution. Naxalites have organised All India women's organisation (AW1 and AW2): revolutionary organisation and open organisation where UG cadres meet over ground activists and organize activities of mass organisation and agitation.

Taking benefit of the obnoxious caste system of Indian society, Naxalites are trying to organise *dalit* masses and exploit Khairlanjhi type situation. Not only in Maharashtra they are exploiting the caste fault line, but also in Haryana they are trying to exploit the Jat and *Dalits* conflict upper castes and lower caste conflict in Bihar. In other parts of the country also they are trying to exploit the caste issues and issue of discrimination. Maoists are making efforts to mobilise *Adivasis* with the slogans, "Right over the forest belongs to people and *Adivasis*". "Political Autonomy to the *Adivasi* territories" and transform the territory as exploitation free territory i.e. 'red land' fight for land, water forest and minerals. They have distributed thousands of forest land to tribals to marshal their support.

Naxalites are also propagating the politics of new democratic revolution among the people of the religious minorities. They are also in the forefront of every democratic demand of the nationalities whether it is for autonomy like Kashmir; for equal status for their languages; for separate statehood Bodo. Naxalites support the sub-national movement.[9] Naxals in their strategy and tactics document have narrated the reasons for support of sub nationalism in following words:

The book provides details of why the party should support sub-national movements in India. It says, "Lakhs of enemy's armed troops have been deployed since long in Kashmir and the North-Eastern States alone. More and more nationalities may come into armed confrontation with the reactionary Indian state… as a considerable part of the enemy's armed forces will inevitably be engaged against the growing tide of struggles by the various nationalities; it will be difficult for the Indian ruling classes to mobilize all their armed forces against our revolutionary war"[10]

Efforts of Revolutionary Front to Create/Hijack Mass Organisations

Through Politics of discredit they are trying to spread political paranoia, wide spread disturbance and unrest. They are secretly conducting social engineering to cause political subversion of democracy. They are planning and preparing to make democracy bankrupt by hijacking many mass organisations. Soon after the setback in 1972 Naxalites realised the importance of mass organisations. From mid 1980s they are trying to create various mass organisations or hijack the mass organisations. The Revolutionary United Front is a conglomerate of legal, illegal, open, semi-open, cover, underground mass organisations.

Underground Mass Organisations

They give preference to mass organisations which secretly organise the masses into struggles, and directly serve at the base for recruitment for the Party and the people's war. Those mass organisations remain strictly underground and propagate the Party's revolutionary line among the masses rousing them for armed struggle. They openly call upon the masses to participate in the people's war, propagate the central task drawn up by the Party at any given time. These mass organisations are built clandestinely and conduct secret propaganda. Examples of such mass organisations are Adiwasi Kisan Mazdoor Sangh, Krantikari Adiwasi Mahila Sangha, Student-Youth Leagues,

Chetana Natya Mandali, Jana Natya Mandali, armed cultural organisations, Red Guard organisations, etc.

Cover Mass Organisations, Open, semi-open and Legal Democratic Organisations

The second type of mass organisations is the open and semi-open mass organisations which openly propagate the politics of New Democratic Revolution and prepare the people for armed struggle. Thus, these mass organisations too directly serve the people's war as long as scope for open revolutionary work exists. Revolutionary Women Organisation, Revolutionary Student and Youth organisations, Revolutionary Art and Cultural Associations, Revolutionary writer's Associations. These mass organisations are not directly linked to the Party and work under some cover with a limited programme. Naxals also use cover organisations to keep their members unexposed to the security force while carrying on open mass work. In A.P./N.T./AOB Naxals made efforts to create cover organisations since 1985 and after 1995 they got some success.

Considering the importance of legal democratic organisations they mentioned in their document:

> "We must keep in mind that cover organisations are not a substitute for the legal or underground mass organisation. We must form the Party units within the cover organisations and direct them."[11]

Legal democratic organisations formed on an explicit political basis with a program of action and forms of struggle are also hijacked by Naxals. These serve as the Naxals' attempts at the political mobilisation of the vast masses. Such organisations can be formed at various levels—town/city level, district level, state level, regional level, all-India level, or even at the international level. The views of Naxals are clearly mentioned in their document which is mentioned below:

> "The principle underlying the legal-illegal coordination is to form the widest possible legal organisations inside which

the party operates secretly. Com. Lenin remarkably pointed this out:

'The legal organisations are the points of support which allow taking to the masses the ideas of clandestine cells. That is to say that we modify the form of influence to the objective of which the prior influences continue in the sense of clandestine orientation."[12]

The Party, through its members or other activists, penetrates such traditional mass organisations normally set up by the masses to fight for their sectional interests without exposing any links with the Party. Through the activities of the organisation, the masses, while being mobilised for their sectional interests, are attempted to be drawn towards the revolution. The best organisations are those which are more oriented to struggle, like trade unions, slum and other locality based organisation, youth organisations, unemployed organisations, students associations and unions, women's organisations, cultural organisations, sports clubs and gymnasiums, libraries, *bhajan mandals*, non-governmental welfare organisations, welfare organisations for oppressed castes, nationalities and minorities etc.

Special Mechanism of Revolutionary Politics

As a corollary to Marx's assertion 'Religion is opium of masses', it can be said that revolutionary politics is the poison for the political system. Naxals are trying through disruptive technique to make political point, mobilise people, create right political condition for mass insurrection and advance armed struggle. Their scheme consists of arousing masses to revolutionary work only by ideological political work. They want to alter the political landscape of the country and cause political crisis by revolutionary politics. Naxals try to achieve their goal through various high level sub-committees headed by central committee members and Politbureau members e.g. Sub-committee on mass organisation (SUCOMO), Urban sub-committee (USCO), AIMCC. CPI Maoists through their different organisational network organize, conduct, manipulate revolutionary politics, SUCOMO (Sub Committee on Mass Organisation) USCO, CMSC are the units of CPI Maoists headed by top cadre Naxalites who organize revolutionary politics. There are two types of mass organisations (1) with MLM programmes (2) broad base organisations.

SUCOMO, USCO, and AIMCC Control, Coordinate Mass Organisations

SUCOMO is headed by three Politbureau members of CPI Maoists who liaise with the leaders of different front bodies of the outfit who, in turn, mobilize the support of organisations, people's movement, spearheading agitation against various issues including SEZ/displacement etc. in different states. SUCOMO guides the activities of various mass organisations e.g. All India League for Revolutionary Culture, Student organisations, RDF, Legal Front, *Visthapan Virodhi* Front, *Visthapan Virodhi Jan Vikas Andolan*. Any coordination problem between various frontal organisations is resolved by SUCOMO. The urban subcommittee makes efforts to mobilize the working class industrial workers.

They are also developing town committees to start the urban Naxalite movement. All India Mahila Coordination Committee (AIMCC) is organizing both underground women and over ground women of trade unions and intellectual groups. Two women central committee members were looking after its tasks, now some top cadre women Maoists are in-charge of AIMCC. They coordinate with all legal women organisations to use the masses for the benefit of the CPI Maoists. Even state level SUCOMOs and Mahila subcommittees of the CPI Maoists were formed and are functioning. *Mahila morchas* and organisations in slums are being built up. State Committee members of the CPI (Maoists) coordinate with mass organisations directly and also through professional revolutionary and part time members. Their role and process is described:

> "Thus the first principle in building the united front is that the Naxalites should play the vanguard role in this united front. There cannot be a revolutionary united front without the basic worker-peasant alliance and the urban petty bourgeoisie from whom the ruling classes gain credibility and strength".[13]

Building the United Front

The Naxals are striving to form Revolutionary United Fronts at the village, area, regional and state/special zonal/special area levels. This involves unifying the working class first, and then building worker-peasant solidarity and alliances, uniting with other classes in the cities, building the fronts against exploitation and oppression. They have developed a special mechanism to turn the human terrain through revolutionary politics. They mobilise the masses through political activism, political opportunism and ideological commitment. They consider mass organisations as absolutely indispensable for the victory of the Red revolution. The principal aim of building mass organisations is to organise the masses for revolution. Without mobilising the masses into innumerable struggles and raising their political consciousness in the course of those struggles, they cannot realise their aim to overthrow the state power.

The Naxalites concentrate on organizing the masses into revolutionary mass organisations. It is in the process of organising the various sections of the population and giving leadership to their struggles, and transforming them into an armed struggle for the seizure of state power. The Revolutionary United Front mobilizes the masses politically for the capture of state power. They act not only as organs of power, but also as organs of armed uprisings of the masses. They politically rouse, arm and lead the masses to defend their power to make political gains.

Role of Professional Revolutionary and Part Timers

In the Polit Bureau documents, the Naxals are urged to build a strong underground party with a stable nucleus of professional revolutionaries and an extensive network of part timers. Special emphasis is laid on recruiting and promoting party cadres from the working class, poor and landless peasants, and the most oppressed social sections—Dalits, adivasis, women and Muslims. They are making great efforts to Bolshevize the Party ideologically, politically and organisationally and achieve unity of thought, will and action. It is the organised activity of conscious revolutionaries and conspirators who are known as Professional Revolutionaries and part timers. In their document Strategy and Tactics they mention:

> "Only when the two components of the Party organisation- the professional revolutionaries and part-time members- are strong, will the Party be really strengthened. Among them the professional revolutionaries are the core of the Party while part-timers are the base. At the same time, the part-timers should maintain lively relations with the people to the maximum extent and while continuing their professions be vigilant not to get exposed to the enemy".[14]

Party factions with members have been set up in the executive committees of the mass organisations. These factions under the party leadership coordinate the activities of members. Thereby the mass organisation under working class leadership serves as conveyor belts between the vast oppressed masses and the Party. The fractions will help establish party leadership over the mass organisations and through these over the oppressed masses.

The majority of the members of trade unions, employees, students, women, youth, and organisations are brought under the leadership of the revolutionary party by taking up their demands, raising their political consciousness and dispelling whatever illusions they may have through incessant political exposure of these parties and ideological-political education of the masses.

Formation of TUF and SUF

The TUF's main responsibility is to form broad fronts on various issues. The basic job is to search for allies. All tactical alliances or UFs in the form of joint activity with various organisations belonging to the anti-imperialist anti-feudal class, at whatever level, are subordinate to the aim of building the strategic UF i.e. the NDF. The orientation in UF activity is to accelerate this process by rallying these classes on the basis of the New Democratic programme. All this activity serves to intensify and extend the armed struggle further.

> "All our Party committees should concentrate on building a strong mass base without which it is impossible to strengthen the Party, Army and UF or to intensify the war. Our entire orientation should be to mobilise the masses into the people's war directly and indirectly. There is also the need to put in special effort to develop cadres with the abilities to work in the urban areas. All the mass work must be oriented to building solid organisations of the masses, oriented towards strengthening the armed struggle and strategic united front."

> "Every advance made in armed struggle helps the mass organisations to expand and deepen their base and to advance the mass movement further. And, conversely, every advance in the mass movement, particularly the political mobilisation or arousal of the masses boldly against the principal enemies of our revolution, will contribute to the deepening and expansion of the armed struggle."[15]

The area of operations of revolutionary politics exceeds the territorial limits of guerrilla warfare with the intention to penetrate, discredit and dislocate regular politics. Established professionals of different calling are recruited initially as "social crusaders" in typically "innocuous" movements in the area of operations. Slowly they are introduced to the Maoist party. When the cadres are placed or recruitment in organisations such as labour unions, youth groups, agrarian organisations or professional associations, they begin to manipulate the objective of the groups. The psychological apparatus of the movement through inside cadres prepares a mental attitude which at the crucial moment can be turned into a fury of justified violence.

Naxalites employ violence and threat to sabotage the functioning of the *panchayati raj* system in some parts of Chhattisgarh, Maharashtra, Jharkhand and Bihar. They forced some *sarpanches* to resign in Chhattisgarh. During the last election in Gadhchiroli and some areas of Bastar and in Bihar the Naxals used these tactics to field their supporters unopposed in *panchayat* elections.

Naxals conspire to cause cumulative destruction of political forces by engaging in violent confrontations with the cadres of rival political parties. CPI Maoist cadres are killing members of the main political parties in various areas of West Bengal, Chhattisgarh, Bihar, and Jharkhand with the aim to dominate the areas by finishing local key political leaders. Sometimes local members of some political parties support them, and some also try to co-opt them for political, electoral gains. However, the Naxals consider electoral struggle as class struggle and they try to consolidate themselves during various elections. Crises are precipitated by challenging institutional legitimacy and governing capacity of the regime. Political force in tandem with military force aggravates the situation (e.g. in Nandigram).

Exploit Causes and Cause Chaos

Through manipulation of facts and subtle propaganda the Naxals turn some small issues to large problems. Through frontal organisations they exploit the weakness and mistakes of the regime or various branches of administration. In the process they manipulate various issues of displacements. In the first phase, the main issue for the Naxals was to provide land to the tiller to garner mass support. Land is a very potent issue; it was exploited by activists in the Russian revolution, and also by the left wing extremists in Nepal, Philippines, Mexico and Peru. In various parts of India, Naxalites have distributed government land, forest land and have also grabbed land of villagers. Subsequently, Naxals started raking up the issues of jungle, mineral, SEZ, displacement, forest rights, and reorganisation of states along with the issue of land.

Exploitation of issues gives a semblance that the causes gave birth to Naxalites in an area. However, the fact is that the crafty manipulation of the environment gave them a platform to operate. Revolutionary politics cause issues to give rise to conflict. Disputes evolve into crisis and violence. Political ambiguities are exploited by LWE. Naxals along with their frontal organisations try to raise latent disputes and disagreements into conflicts. Nandigram, Singur, Khairlanji, Kalinganagar are recent examples. By stressing economic distress of local people they try to breed political radicalism. Revolutionary politics help LWE in a sustained and systematic attempt to regroup.

Current Situation of RUF

Naxals are trying to get various forums to widen the conflict. In AOB, DK, Orissa, BJ, West Bengal, Kerala and Andhra Pradesh, propaganda and agitation was conducted on the issue of SEZs, mining and displacement. These were taken up under the leadership to united front forums or mass organisations creating a good impact. Subsequently they strengthen these organisations politically and organisationally and give them a struggle orientation.

PDFI, as the main frontal organisation of Naxals, works to mobilise, tribal's, women, religious minorities, backward castes and people on displacement issue. PDFI worked to create platforms for farmers' fronts in Uttar Pradesh, Punjab, and Haryana; to oppose displacement in West Bengal, Orissa; and for backward castes in Maharashtra. The central committee of CPI Maoists coordinates with RDF and PDF.

Krantikari Kamgar Union is an underground revolutionary organisation run by PRs of CPI Maoist. PRs are organizing workers in Ahmadabad, Surat, Pune, Mumbai, Ranchi, Dhanbad, and Calcutta. Vidyarthi Pragati Sanghatana is a student revolutionary organisation run by PRs of CPI Maoist.

The anti-displacement organisations are spearheading agitations against different industrial/mining projects. VVJVA is spearheading the agitation against POSCO at Paradip, Khandadhar Sundargah, Rourkela, Vedant at Kalahandi, UICL at Nalgonda, Tata Lohandiguda/Jagdalpur, Polavaram project in Andhra Pradesh. The Naxals have identified SEZ and industrialisation areas in Jharkhand and are chalking out plans to start agitations in the Manoharpur area against the Tata steel plant at Jamshedpur and the satellite town of Tata expanding towards Ghatshila; at Chandil against the Jindal steel plant, Dumka-power plant, and Latehar aluminium factory.

A committee for release of political prisoners was floated after a special initiative was taken by Khobad Gandhy PBM In the 2nd Central Committee Meeting it was decided to float a political prisoner's organisation. Committee for Release of Political Prisoners (CRPP) and IAPL are making efforts to exploit the criminal justice system. CRPP had also taken the lead in the formation of an umbrella organisation of 22 organisations to protest against anti-Maoist operations by the security forces:

> "In the mass front, there has been modest activity during the two years. We achieved some results in building broad-based fronts and made some progress in united front work. We succeeded to some extent in politically intervening in the burning issues of the day but more concerted effort is needed. When we organised the first mass struggles, we could only mobilise a few hundred, and later for meetings and demonstrations when calls were given by the Party and mass organisations people gained more confidence in the Party and revolution and began to participate in numerous struggles in thousands."[16]

Efforts to Counter RUF

The Revolutionary United Front looks deceptively democratic and innocuous, but performs divisive, dangerous activities. Union Home Minister Shri Chavan stated in the Rajya Sabha in 1968:

> 'It is the inconvenient children of Marxist ideology thinking in terms of certain classic revolutionary methods pregnant with dangerous potentialities'.[17]

Understanding of the revolutionary politics of the Naxalites provides an insight into their present and future political game plan. Guerrilla warfare is essentially a political war. It is basically the struggle for the support of uncommitted people; the conflict is fought with political instruments. Therefore, it has to be confronted politically. Naxals use military power through political means and political power through military means. Reduction of the political space of the Naxalites will automatically reduce their depth.

Perception Management Required

Revolutionary politics is important for the Naxalites; because it changes the perception of the public. It is a façade for subversive mobilisation. Through politics they are trying to manipulate and propagate acts of terror. The resilience of society and the administration to extremism can be gradually diminished by the aggressive propaganda by Naxalites. It must be countered vigorously. The challenge of propaganda is not merely a matter of words. One can repudiate it in words and yet be victim to it. Its hold is subtle. It affects people even unwittingly and against their will, even when they think they repudiate it. The regime has to organise information war. Television, internet, and other forms of mass media must be used to inform the masses. Perception management efforts should focus to undercut the Naxalites appeal by discrediting their propaganda, exposing their motives, and convincing the people to reject their intimidation. Propaganda narratives must initially target local populations. Care should be taken to inform and influence local masses. They should get the message of hope and prosperity. Ideas are far cheaper than bullets and much more effective in defeating Naxalism.

Prevent the Spread of Naxals' Influence in the Civil Population

Revolutionary politics develops complicated political geometry, which multiplies centres and extremes ad infinitum. They cause extensive proliferation of animosity, alienation, disappointment and disillusionment. Feeding on popular despair, the Naxals spread their influence among the masses. A prime Naxal objective is to turn the population against the government. They try to translate initial vague sympathies into conscious collaboration with the public. They continuously conduct socio–economic surveys to find out public irritants and then exploit those issues. The regime should protect the civilians from Naxals activity and influence.

Fight the Ideology at Ideas Level: Some intellectuals for some remuneration and some for recognitions are working for the Naxalites. By espousing Naxal ideology through their writings they are propagating Naxal causes. Their ideology has to be fought at the ideas level. The administration should make efforts to marginalise the Naxals' agenda. Estrangement of the population from the government and administration should be checked. The people have to be convinced rather than coerced.

Unite Political Forces: Naxals use a political cobweb to confuse and disorganize the security forces; the government and the masses. They have an agenda of marginalizing by mobilizing mass organisations, strategically manipulating political institutions. The decline and de-legitimisation of political institutions jeopardizes political order. The Naxals will cause political order to fade into irrelevance and to drive it into disrepute. Political forces should unite. Democratic forces should be mobilized to protect the political order and civil population from Naxals' activities and influence. Preventive political action is expected to be sophisticated and avoid media visibility. Politically correct measures must be taken.

Fight Trust Deficit: Naxals bring tremendous psychological tension among the public which causes a serious trust deficit. Efforts should be made to fight this. Progressive discrediting of public institutions erodes the basic public trust in the Government. Real demands of the public provide most of the impetus for Naxalism, it must be undercut. There should be grievances audit and a redressal system which can look after local population and restore faith in the system.

Strong Law: Naxals cause the economic-political decay of an area by wanton destruction and mass agitation. Not only they massacre people but also they dispossess and dehumanize people. They create political turmoil and take it to a crisis point. Strong law acts as a great antidote to mass agitation, divisive, destructive politics and anti-national activities. Therefore, strong laws should be enacted to deal with extremists, their supporters and abettors.

Break the Urban Network: In Andhra Pradesh, a ban on mass organisations and intelligence operations had an adverse impact on revolutionary activities of mass organisations. Intelligence operations should be launched to locate the urban network and strict legal action should be taken against them.

Conclusion

Naxals are bent to perpetrate pre-planned political disaster. They want to overthrow the democratic process and replace it by a Maoist undemocratic regime. They whittle away at the foundations of democratic institutions, mobilizing people to intensify their struggle, cause unrest, distort democratic processes, and dominate the political landscape. Accumulating tensions and escalating violence sometimes leads to breakdown of the political process. Political narratives are used by them to obscure their intentions and cause conflict to mutate and degenerate. The political context of the conflict is the key to understanding the political dangers of conflict escalation. The developments in

Russia during the Bolshevik revolution and in Nepal bear witness to this. The Government must give priority to defeating the political subversion.[18]

The Naxals have launched an uninhibited military/political crusade against Indian democracy. Some people believe that the regime has never taken their political campaign seriously. Through politics they can stultify the nation's offensive capability before it can be put into operation. Nevertheless, preventive physical action is always politically conditional. "What is at stake is the country's political regime and to defend it is a political affair. Even if this requires military action, the action is constantly directed toward a political goal'.[19] The country does not have substantial scope for committing mistakes.

NOTES

1. Mao Tse-Tung On War, Natraj Publication, Dehradun (2008). The doctrine of Protracted war in the Naxalites scheme of things have many characteristics, which are: (1) constantly shifting of the battle ground, weapon system and operational practices for the purpose confusing the opponent, (2) keeping him off balance, (3) wearing down his resistance.
2. Vo Nguyen Giap; People's War People's Army: The Viet-Cong Instruction Manual For Under Developed Countries; (Dehradun: Natraj Publications, 2002).
3. Strategy Tactics of Indian Revolution CPI Maoist (P), 2004, p. 124.
4. 'Carry Forward the Peasant Struggle' by Charu Majumdar 1970.
5. Strategy Tactics of Indian Revolution CPI Maoist (P), 2004, p. 80.
6. Ibid., p. 135.
7. Ibid., p. 124.
8. Thomas Marks, The Maoists in Nepal, Strategies of Subversion and Subterfuge, Fault lines Vol. 19, April 2008.
9. Pioneer, Sept. 2, 2008.
10. Naxalites Documents.
11. Strategy Tactics of Indian revolution CPI Maoist (P), 2004, pp. 1-3.
12. Ibid.
13. Ibid.
14. Ibid.
15. Naxal Documents.
16. Ibid.

17. *Times of India* (New Delhi) 12 December 1968.
18. Robert F. Thompson, Defeating Communist Insurgency: Experiences from Malaya and Vietnam (London: Chatto and Windus, 1972) p. 50.
19. David Galula, Counterinsurgency Warfare Theory and Practice, (New Delhi: Pentagon Press, 2008).

3

Peoples' Resistance Movement: A Community Initiative Against Left Wing Extremism in Bastar

'Mass and movement generate force'; this physical law proved itself in the public resistance movement of Bastar against the Naxalites. With the onset of the public resistance movement in south and west Bastar, in June 2005, the world woke up suddenly and found it is no longer the same region of red influence in large areas of west Bastar. The hothouse of extremism received showers of public awakening and public resistance against Red terror. Public resistance against LWE is historical[1] and it catapulted Bastar into the national spotlight when the tribals started a resistance movement against Naxalites. Thousands of young men and even women with infants in their laps congregated at various villages, discussed their miseries and expressed their resolve[2] to make the supreme sacrifice for fighting the Maoist menace[3]. The masses understand that raising their voice against the Naxalites might mean brutal death for them.

However, the people are not afraid of the consequences. More than 250 meetings and peace marches have taken place where thousands of villagers from more than one hundred villages have participated voluntarily.[4] The Naxalites tried their best to disrupt a few of the congregations by firing at the crowd and by blasting landmines at the meeting places. In order to foil the resistance movement, Naxalites attacked more than two dozen times various relief camps, and massacred poor unarmed tribals at Errabore, Gangalur and a few other places in Dantewada and Bijapur districts. Nevertheless, the Naxalites were unable to suppress and subdue the spirit of the masses by violence. The civic impulse of the public showed its vigour. Even Sangham (Militia) members, part time Maoists and few hardcore Naxalites surrendered before the public and the police.

It took the country in a new and hopeful direction, and surprised and baffled every strategist and tactician concerned with left wing extremism by the questions of why and how the so-called Maoist 'water'—the public, disowned the Maoist fishes-the guerrillas? The development of the extremist situation and public response is complicated and confusing; even now different players, strategists and tacticians, imperfectly understand the dynamics of the conflict and the situation. However, any attempt at serious analysis will point to the fact that the situation did not arise overnight. It was the outcome of simmering discontent supported by favourable circumstances. The biggest question is what favoured the public upsurge? What motivated thousands of poor people to stand up, raise their axes and pull the strings of their bows? To read the situation perfectly one must consider the facts.

Situation Analysis

The public awakening and resistance resulted from a gradual building up of resentment. The concrete empirical enquiry reveals the futility of Naxalite tenets, vulgarity of their actions, the barbarism and the enormity of the sins of Naxalites and Sangham members (militia men). The emergence of the consciousness of being exploited and dehumanised by the Naxalites caused a large-scale mobilisation of people. The wanton destruction caused by them, the denial of development, the intensification of counter-extremist operations caused the radicalisation of the poor and ultimately created the ground for a public upsurge.

Rejection of Naxalite Tenets

The public upsurge in Bastar represented a radical opposition to Naxalite tenets and the denunciation of their classic schema of controlling masses by terror. It was the rejection of the Naxalites so-called grand objective of democratic revolution and the grand design of the "Janathana Sarkar" (the rule of Maoist cadres in villages and districts); and it proved that the Naxalites have lost their *raison d'etre*. It proves that Naxalism is not a meaningful public-oriented movement, but a destructive anti-people, anti-national, anti-democratic movement. It unmasked the Maoists and started proving the fact that the extremists have intolerably oppressed the masses and deprived them of the necessities of human existence.

Phenomena of Alienation and Dehumanisation

Multifarious manifestations of alienation are apparent in local society. Here, it opens the manifold phenomena of alienation and dehumanisation. The locals are alienated from the human essence, tantamount to negating human existence and seriously disturbed by the schema of Naxalite activities. The Naxalites' method of conscription of young boys and girls, the closure of *ghotuls*, and the destruction of religious rites and religious places disturbed the psyche of poor tribals. Their action of damaging a number of hand pumps and destruction of roads caused great hardship for the poor. Their policy of closure of markets, not allowing construction of roads and other works, the denial of developmental activities, the siphoning of developmental funds and not allowing *tendupatta* plucking, destroyed economic lives. The very existence of the tribals faced a serious crisis. Forced cooperative farming, forcible distribution of poor peoples' land agitated the tribals. The absolute pauperisation of the masses due to the Naxalite policy of denial of development, destruction of roads, and closure of local markets radicalised the masses.

Impact of Intensification of Counter Extremist Operations

The fact must not be lost that the intensification of counter extremist operations instilled confidence in the minds of tribals. A series of successive combat actions, raids on temporary Maoist camps, the successful defence of police posts and police stations, the huge loss of Naxalite cadres during their offensive against the security forces proved the inferiority of the Naxalites before the public. The ineffectiveness of the Peoples Liberation Guerrilla Army against the Special Task Force of Chhattisgarh emboldened the public. The use of helicopters and induction of C.R.P.F. and Naga battalions tilted the balance of power in favour of the security forces. As a result, the public rose openly against the Naxalite oppression. People pointed fingers at the malafide intentions and wrong anti-national, anti-democratic, anti-public objectives and activities of the Maoists.

Old Templates of Jan Jagran

Historical reckoning puts forth few stages when extensive sporadic *Jan Jagran* and small-localised *Jan Jagrans* had taken place. The first *Jan Jagran*, which lasted from 1990 till 1991, was a massive one; people in large numbers came out openly against Naxalites. More than one thousand Naxalites and Sangham members had surrendered in 1991, and huge caches of arms and ammunition were seized. The Naxalites had to retreat, but after some time they regrouped and selectively liquidated leaders and suppressed the public. In 1998 and 1999 at Bijapur at Koilibera in Kanker district public awakening had taken place. In 2001, people of 42 villages took out processions against Naxalites of *Jan Jagran* and killed each member. On each occasion the selective violence by Naxalites, the liquidation of key public leaders, the inability to provide area security had smothered the movement.

Naxalites' Assessment of Peoples' Resistance Movement (Salwa Judum)

Naxalites in their fourth Polit Bureau meeting in 2006 mentioned:

> "The scale and magnitude of the enemy's military onslaught unleashed in the name of Salwa Judum is unprecedented in the history of the Indian revolution after the setback of 1972. This cruel, divisive campaign should be defeated in order to advance the task of transforming PLGA into PLA and establishing Base Area."[5]

The PB noted with grave concern that they had not taken up propaganda and solidarity campaigns in the various states to the extent possible corresponding to their strength.

> At this critical juncture when the Central and State governments, with the full backing of the imperialists, CBB and feudal forces, have unleashed a brutal encirclement and suppression campaign in Bastar region of Chhattisgarh, and are quite determined to ruthlessly carry out their heinous plans of destroying the Party PLGA, RPCs, revolutionary mass organisations, and terrorize the masses through gory bloodbaths, the main focus of our entire Party should be to build strong support to the ongoing armed resistance in DK in all possible ways.[6]

The PB decided to initiate the following steps in DK and in other states in order to defeat the enemy offensive unitedly and build a countrywide solidarity movement in support of the people's armed resistance under the party's leadership:

1. Central and State governments will intensify their brutal attack further this summer. Salwa Judum-para military's combined ongoing offensive is a springboard to facilitate the deployment of the Indian Army to capture our GBs particularly Maad. Already, in this direction the concerned officials have increased coordination.

2. Eviction of hundreds of villages and shifting them to new settlements is another plan initiated by the Chhattisgarh state government for which Rs. 500 crore is sought from the Centre. Already 70-80 villages were burnt, hundreds of villages were forcibly evacuated, and around 50,000 people had been shifted to government-organised camps.

   SJ leadership put forward alternative slogans to all our slogans reflecting the sharp polarisation into two camps —revolutionary and counter-revolutionary. Day-by-day offensive of these forces and counter offensive of our people and forces is increasing and a civil war situation now prevails in entire Bastar, which has now become the focal point of the bitter class conflict." Similarly Naxalites in their Central Committee meeting of January 2007 minutes said "Smash Salwa Judum". Naxalites in their DKSZC circular No.1 2005 have given a detailed description of the threat of Salwa Judum and tactics to counter it.

   "Party should treat this *Jana Jagran Abhiyan* as a country wide attack on the party introduced by the enemy after formation of CPI-Maoist. There is large mobilisation of armed forces and wide support from the public during the last two *Jana Jagran Abhiyans*. This time Rs. 2 lakh were allotted to each village, which participated in Jana Jagran Abhiyan. The government is also sanctioning Rs. 25,000 and one pair of bullocks to each family involved in Jana Jagran Abhiyan. The government is encouraging the people to become a part of the anti extremist activities.

   The repressive campaign laws renamed "Salwa Judum" took up the following programmes:

   1. In the first round, organize *Jana Jagran* meetings in all villages by threatening party committee members and asking them to surrender or to stop co-operation to Naxalites.

2. Attack, demolish and set ablaze the houses of party activists who have not surrendered.
3. Develop an informer network with surrendered party activists in villages and launch attacks on PLGA.

This is a three-dimensional attack of the government. They are giving extreme bad publicity against the party during the first round of *Jan Jagran* meetings by exposing that this is a revolt of Adivasis against the Naxalites. They are branding the people as Naxalites who are not joining the Salwa Judum (no exemption to shop keepers and employees). They are showing people support for this campaign by threatening and gathering the people. Create fear and divide one section of people to hit the majority of the people is the main object of this campaign.

1. Counter the bad publicity against our party during the meetings of *Jana Jagran* through media. Anti party publicity like Naxalites are stopping gathering *tendu* leaf, obstructing developmental activities, stopping of village exhibitions, destroying Adivasi culture and sentiments should be exposed by bringing out booklets and pamphlets and distributing them in the public. Party should expose that there is no people support behind this Adivasi revolt. This is nothing but an anti-people repressive programme. Publicity should be made by the party against this campaign by bringing out posters, pamphlets and giving press statements.
2. Take up people's struggles against CBBs, MNCs which are coming to loot the sources of DK by forming United Front with likeminded forces. Fight against Essar pipelines by taking support from all sections of people. Form a revolutionary movement with democratic forces on the negligence of Human Rights in Chhattisgarh due to State violence.
3. Take up substance of this circular and bulletins with the people in a place where Jana Jagran was started

and other places. Mobilize the party formations and people against Jan Jagran by conducting one or two public meeting at village level.

4. Eliminate important selected targets by targeting leadership of the *Jana Jagran Abhiyan*. Hit and cause severe losses to police forces which come to protect the *Jana Jagran gundas*.
5. Adopt day and night sentry system to protect the people's properties from enemy attacks. Implement the signal system, which can alert the villagers of the arriving enemy. After receiving the signal of enemy arriving, old men and children should be shifted to security areas. Youth should counter the enemy with available weapons.

- Encourage the people to carry weapons while they are going for work in struggle areas.
- Party should ask the people to make possible weapons (bow, arrow, spear, batti bombs, *burmars*, etc) on war footing to counter the enemy.
- Educate the people by telling them don't fear and surrender to the enemy.
- Boycott the meetings organised by the *Jana Jagran Abhiyans* in all villages.
- Ask the villagers not to attend the meetings. *Adivasis* should leave the villages and take shelter in forests along with old men and children while organizing *Jana Jagran* meetings. Encourage youth to lay ambushes for enemy forces while they are coming to the meetings of *Jana Jagran Abhiyan*.

1. Enemy is stopping village markets to avoid day-to-day requirements to the people in the area of party movement. Encourage and allow the businessmen who are having friendly relations with party workers to sell provisions secretly to the people.

2. As per the Resolutions of DKSZC in April 2005, counter tactics should be followed to counter the reforms implementing by the enemy after mobilizing all Government wings.
3. Resolutions of last DKSZC meeting should be implemented in new areas. Publicity should be made in spreading areas of the party by distributing circulars, books towards Jana Jagran. Follow suitable technical precautions to avoid losses from the party forces during that time."[7]

Why Naxalites are Afraid of Public Awakening

There is considerable evidence that the Naxalites are afraid of the peoples' resistance movement popularly known as *Salwa Judum* and are fearful of public awakening. In their documents, the Naxalites have mentioned that *Salwa Judum* is a three-dimensional attack and it is bringing bad publicity against them. In an interview Sekhar and Rajendra, Badranna—ex-combatants who were active as divisional committee members and squad commanders in 1991-92 in Bijapur and Dantewada said that, during the Jan Jagran of 1991-92 the Naxalites had faced a major crisis; their recruitment reduced, they did not get food from villagers, and they felt that they would die of starvation. Consequently, they resorted to heavy violence against villagers and killed members of *Jan Jagran* in 1991-92.

Reprisals of Naxalites

The memory of the Jan Jagran of 1990-91 became vivid again due to a sinister new scheme in the Naxalites' campaign of reprisals against public awakening. In 2005, the Naxalites attacked six Salwa Judum rallies and meetings and one relief camp. In 2006, the Naxalites attacked 13 meetings and rallies of Salwa Judum, killing 311 and injuring 206 villagers and police cadres. They did not allow villagers to cultivate their lands.

Civilians Killed by Naxalites at Relief Camps and other Places of Bijapur and Dantewada Districts (6 June 2005 to 30 April 2010)

Particulars	Bijapur	Dantewada	Total
Civilians killed in relief camps	09	33	**42**
Civilians killed in villages	252	93	**345**
Civilians killed in jungles and river banks	68	07	**75**
Civilians killed on the roads	85	67	**152**
Civilians killed at weekly markets	04	01	**05**
Total	**418**	**201**	**619**

Naxalites' False Propaganda against Salwa Judum

Soon after the Polit Bureau meeting in April 2006, the concerned citizens group visited Dantewada and Bijapur in June 2006; they started propaganda campaign against Salwa Judum. The Naxalites also resorted to false propaganda of human rights violations against Salwa Judum in various fora. They used newspapers and the electronics media. They took the help of frontal organisations of Naxalites and formed committees for the assistance of tribals affected by *Salwa Judum* (CATAS). They arranged with tribals of other states to stage dramas in the metropolitan cities of Hyderabad, Mumbai and Delhi. After getting information about this false propaganda, the victims of Naxal violence and *Salwa Judum* activists went to those places and clarified their stands. It is pertinent that the *Salwa Judum* movement was born due to gross violation of human rights by the Naxalites. This movement arose because thousands of people were forced to move away from their homes. It was felt that the genuine voices of thousands of tribals is meaningless because opinion-makers are not willing to listen, they are more interested in the simulated picture circulated by the elites connected to Naxalites. Basically, the *Salwa Judum* arose due to human rights violations by the Naxalites, which led to displacement of thousands of poor tribals. It is relevant to dig into historical facts to find the ground realities of this public resistance movement.

Fact File of Peoples' Resistance Movement against Naxalites in Bastar (June 2005 to June 2007)

Date	Incident
6 June 2005	Historic incident of about 500 villagers of 22 villages assembled at Ambaveli village against the oppressive acts of Naxalites.
18 June 2005	Matwada of P.S. Jangla (8000) villages. At Talmendri 3500 villagers of 45 villages gathered. Naxalites attacked the peaceful rally of Salwa Judum people. At Matwada 3000 people gathered; Naxalites attacked the peaceful rally of Salwa Judum while returning.
19 June 2005	Kotrapal (4000) villagers attended a meeting. Naxalites attacked the rally and killed one villager.
25 June 2005	Bijapur (3000) villagers under the leadership of MLA Shri Rajendra Pambhoi and Vice President of Janpad Shri Budhram Rana.
26 June 2005	Bhairamgarh (7000) villages. On 26 June 2005 Mr. Mahendra Karma, Leader of the Opposition joined the movement and it gathered momentum.
27 June 2005	2000 villagers of 21 villages gathered at Salwa Judum meeting at Bhairamgarh
29 June 2005	Kutru (3500) villages. Sangham members surrendered (10).
1 July 2005	Matwada (4000) villagers attended meeting at Matwada and Kotrapal. While the rallists were returning Naxalites attacked and killed two villagers.
5 July 2005	P.S. (3000) villagers attended meeting at Keshkutul of P.S. Bhairamgarh; while the rally was returning Naxalites attacked.
6 July 2005	54 villages (5000) villagers attended meeting at Toynar P.S. Bijapur; while the rally was returning Naxalites attacked.
09 July 2005	8000 villagers from 60 villages collected at Bodeli, PS Nelesnar and vowed to oust the Naxalites from Bastar.
11 July 2005	5000 villagers from 50 villages assembled at Pinkonda PS Mirtoor. 24 Sangham members from villages Pinkonda, Bodeli, Chotepalli, Chinrapal, Kocholi and Nelasnar surrendered during the meeting.
17 July 2005	Over 2,000 villagers from 10 villages assembled at Jangala PS Jangala.

19 July 2005	5,000 villagers from 40 villages met at Bijapur PS Bijapur and took out a peace procession shouting slogans against Maoists.
24 July 2005	20,000 villagers assembled at PS Bhairamgarh; the meeting was addressed by Shri Mahendra Karma Opposition leader, In-charge Minister Shri Kedar Kashyap, MLA Shri Lachhu Kashyap. Many political leaders and top police officials attended the meeting. 119 Sangham members surrendered during the meeting.
24 July 2005	Villagers of Farsegarh Police Station came out from their houses and stayed near Farsegarh Police Station.
05 August 2005	"Padyatra" was organised by Shri Mahendra Karma in village Kerpe, PS Bedre area and another "padyatra" was organised in PS Farsegarh area under the leadership of Kamlesh Singh Poyam.
12 August 2005	"Padyatra" was organised from villages Munder via Bodeli and Farapal, which terminated at Mirtoor after two days.
17 August 2005	Jan Jagran meeting was organised at Nelasnaar attended by over 4000 villagers.
23 August 2005	Meeting was organised at village Bade Kodepal, which was attended by 5000-6000 villagers from 20-25 villages.
23 August 2005	Hundreds of villagers of nearby villages left their homes and came to Police Station Mirtur and stayed near the Police Station.
August 2005	Last week of August S.P.Os were selected under Police Act. They were trained for two months and from November their active service was utilized to safeguard the camps.
4th Sept. 2005	At Bhairamgarh 89 Militia surrendered before public.[8]
9 Sept. 2005	3000 villagers gathered at the meeting organised at Kodoli. 19 Sangham members surrendered.[9]
11 Sept. 2005	5000 villagers attended the meeting at Mirtur. 25 Sangham members surrendered.[10]
12 Sept. 2005	15000 villagers attended the meeting at Gangaloor. 17 Sangham members surrendered.
12 Sept. 2005	21000 villagers attended the meeting at Bijapur. 27 Sangham members surrendered.
16 Sept. 2005	700 villagers attended the meeting at Tumnar. 32 Sangham members surrendered.

20 Sept. 2005	600 villagers attended the meeting at Santoshpur. 30 Sangham members surrendered.
28 Sept. 2005	7000 villagers attended the meeting at Chinnakodepal. 44 Sangham members surrendered.
19 Nov. 2005	Chief Minister Dr. Raman Singh with his cabinet colleagues and opposition leader Shri Karma attended the huge gathering of about forty thousand Salwa Juddum activists at Farsegarh, the fort of Naxalites. Twenty-three activists surrendered there. They assured the public to look after their development.
30 Jan. 2006	Naxalites raided the relief camp of Gangalur and killed 8 villagers and three Naxals were killed there during the raid.
27 Feb. 2006	12000 Salwa Judum activists of thirty-five villages of Konta, Dornapal block congregated at Dornapal; 190 militia members of CPI Maoists surrendered at this camp.
28 Feb. 2006	Naxalites used landmines and killed 28 villagers at NH 221 at Darbhaguda of P.S. Errabore of Dantewada district while returning from Salwa Judum meeting.
March 2006	Govt. started providing tin sheets to people for construction of houses.
27 April 2006	Naxalites raided relief camp of Usoor of District Bijapur, which was effectively foiled by security forces.
19-24 June 2006	UNICEF REDR made inspection of all camps.
17 July 2006	Naxals, about 1000 in strength, raided Errabore camp and killed 33 villagers, kidnapped 42 villagers set fire to 300 houses of relief camp and Errabore village. They burnt two infants two years and four years age alive.
February 2007	Five thousand people were forced by Naxalites to leave their homes on the plea that if they would not go with Naxalites to attack police post, they must move out from their homes because it is the war zone. So, they came and stayed near Police Station Jagargunda.
March 2007	Similarly people of about 5000 villages were forced to leave their homes and stay near Police Station, Mariguda.
June 2007	Govt. for four months did not provide any help thinking that the villagers would go back to their homes. Govt. provided shelter and other help to these internally displaced persons only in June 2007.

Naxalite Attacks on Salwa Judum Rally Meetings and Raid on Relief Camps[11]

Year	Naxals Attacks on *Salwa Judum* Rally Meetings	Raid on Relief Camps
2005	6	1
2006	13	8
2007	1	11
2008	-	3
2009	-	1
2010	-	3

Till 31 March 2008, 272 peace marches were conducted wherein about 2,500 militiamen and a number of Naxalites surrendered[12] i.e. about 8 percent of the total strength of Naxalites and militiamen operating in Bastar area. A quote about a similar experience of villagers in Peru is relevant:

> "In at least several recorded instances, whole villages have risen up and, using homemade weapons, often no more than sharpened stakes, wiped out or chased away the Sendero cadre. They have then appealed to the security forces for assistance in meeting Sendero's inevitable attempt to exact retribution. Such help has often been slow in coming, but coordination and use of militias is improving."[13]

Human action and situations are not intelligible outside their socio-economic framework. But, the timeline of incidents and data portray a vivid picture of the *Salwa Judum* movement. Critical study of all these historical facts makes it clear as to actually what happened with the internally displaced tribals of Bastar. Various issues pertaining to Peoples' Resistance Movement/Salwa Judum can be explored from the historical data. It can clarify the perception, dispel the misperception and can help contemporary debates on continuation or discontinuation of the Peoples' Resistance Movement.

Government Agenda to Build Peace

The public plight and mood have a great bearing on

governmental concern. The Government of Chhattisgarh started a programme of development and security to deal with the grave situation. However, any agenda of action prepared and acted upon, must be periodically reviewed and monitored. The Maoist problem in the area is a conjunctional phenomena linked to the supposed exceptional character of conflict, development of the area and development of local population. Due to *Jan Jagran* by public, the Maoists' agenda with regard to the local population of the area has been marginalised. It demanded serious intervention of the government and of all political parties with more commitment, long-term vision, and more profound, political and administrative inputs. It signified a vital change of circumstances, which would require a sudden and fundamental deployment of political forces and administrative resources. The most important aspect of the issue is the proper tailoring of the concepts of security, development, peoples' participation, and then inter-weaving these concepts correctly.

Security for Displaced and Dispossessed People

Anti-Naxalite tactical bases were created at strategic locations to provide security to the displaced people and as well as to dominate the areas. About 3,500 able-bodied young people were recruited as Special Police Officers under provisions of the Police Act to augment security. The SPO's were trained by the police and they helped the security forces to a great extent. At times the valour shown by the SPO's equalled that of regular forces. Joint operations of SPOs, CPMF and Chhattisgarh Police uprooted Maoists from a large area. The Maoists were forced to retreat from an area of 4,000 square kilometres in southwest Bastar, which in the past used to be their stronghold. The security forces engaged the Maoists in a number of clashes in this core area and areas peripheral to it. The surrender of hundreds of part-time revolutionaries revealed that the tail of the Maoists had been caught. Now efforts have been made to pull the tail and catch hold of the Maoist movement by its horns. Digging into the exposed networks of the Naxalites, the security forces started the strategy of demolishing their networks. Their weapons and other assets were seized; their channels of communication and courier system busted. Their hideouts were continuously raided. A series of successive combat actions were taken to eliminate the hard core cadres and defeat them militarily. The task is difficult and it needs enormous effort and resources.

Development is the New Name of Peace

Plenty of developmental opportunities exist. The socio-economic grievances of people are being redressed, but much more needs to be done. The area is a development-deprived region, so various opportunity-enhancing programmes for the public have to be launched vigorously. Construction of strategic roads has to be taken up with utmost urgency. Creation of local markets, establishment of schools and hospitals are taking place. Large-scale health camps have been organised. About 50,000 people left their homes due to Naxal atrocities and camped near police stations and security posts. In order to help these internally displaced people the Government of Chhattisgarh came forward with various schemes of development like housing scheme, and livelihood creation scheme under the National Rural Employment Guarantee Scheme. Model villages have been set up alongside the National Highway, State Highway and other strategic locations with built-in security provisions. But, livelihood creation needs more emphasis, which will act as an antidote to violence and conflict in the area. Micro-economy of the area needs to be built so that stability returns. It should be done with urgency and priority.

Assessment by UNICEF of *Salwa Judum* Relief Camps

UNICEF-REDR conducted multi-sectoral assessments of internally displaced people's camps of District Dantewada Chhattisgarh India from 19 to 24 June 2006. Its assessment in brief is given below:

> At present, the reach of Government services (Water, Shelter, Health, Education, Food, Electrification, ICDS) is

comprehensive to the IDP relief camps and good results are evident. Food aid is also being provided and is generally found satisfactory by the beneficiaries.

Key Findings

The blend of security with participatory and developmental perspective touches a new horizon of human security. This interweaving of security, public participation and development can generate peace building. It creates a scene where hope and history of the Bastar people come together. When further study of these perspectives is done from an epistemic approach, a number of interesting findings are drawn which are:

- Peoples' Resistance Movement projected a common front of tribals against Naxalites. It provided the instrumental nature of participatory initiative with focus on empowerment. Its impulse originated from bottom-up initiatives, which is potential to reshape political network that embeds within themselves a discourse of rights and a fuller sense of citizenship.
- It is important to recognise that there are structural factors—prior experience, strong community mobilisation and institutional support—that promoted and encouraged the public resistance movement.
- People's Resistance Movement activists demonstrated substantial commitment among community members to act to improve collective well-being.
- It has opened a potential path for the progressive realisation of rights. Rights are not given unconditionally but contested, practised and secured. The voting percentage in this region used to remain considerably low; in more than 150 polling booths the percentage of voting used to be zero percent, in those polling centres in 2008 and 2009 the voting percentage was reported about 30%. Large number of people participated in the new elections; people elected two of the activists as members of the Legislative Assembly of Chhattisgarh in 2008.

- An equation between state responsiveness and citizen mobilisation led to a more participatory and responsive Government and the response from local administration improved.
- Peoples' Resistance Movement is a type of social mobilisation to fight terror and extremism. Participation is a form of power that is able to organize resistance. It provided empowered participatory resistance and opportunity to develop collective awareness among the public.
- Peoples' Resistance Movement became a contested space, which contains significant potential for development, peace and offers scope for conflict resolution. Peace building and democratic reconstruction can take place.
- False propaganda by frontier groups of Maoists created ambivalence about the Peoples' Resistance Movement of Bastar among some sections of intellectuals and hostility among some groups of civil liberty groups.
- Poor and resource-less people continue to look to the State to intervene and solve their problems when it comes to the fulfilling of basic needs, physical security and conditions of dignified living.
- Citizen action by the poor and marginalised entails many costs-reprisals by extremists is an important one; the killing of hundreds of peoples' resistance movement members by Naxals proved it. The peoples' war of Naxalites has virtually become the war against the people.
- On the contrary, participation served as a contingent outcome that produced collective action, facilitated security and better living of masses in the end.
- It considers the democratising effects and dimensions of the participatory sphere, with a focus both on engagement with the state and on substantive prospects for democratising governance.
- Naxalites are afraid that the peoples' resistance

movement gaining momentum will turn their outfit into a pale shell of its former self. Therefore, through their network they tried manipulation of facts to serve their strategic interests and discredit the movement at various forums.

- Some people condemned peoples' resistance movement as fight of warlords, some people condemned it as civil war. When the poor tribals were butchered by Naxalites none of the above intellectuals who condemned people's resistance movement raised any voice. When the poor tribals organised themselves to protect themselves by joining as special police officer those people condemned it; after all people should understand that local people have tremendous stake in their own security. The fight of local people against Naxalism can be termed as social struggle against revolutionary utopia.

Conclusion

The public along with security forces started riding into the future, ridding Naxalites from Bastar. Hope and events could still prove false. However, the road is terribly long and difficult, strewn with pitfalls. The public must not halt short of its goals. The public has to be empowered and enabled so that they do not stumble over Maoist impediments but surmount them and reach their goal. The beginning of the mission has started. In spite of a heavy toll, the public and security forces have shown results by driving out the Naxalites from a huge patch of west Bastar. The balance of advantage should not be reversed.

Many initiatives start well, but tend to fall victim to entropy. This local initiative must survive; and it must be sustained and strengthened. This precious peace building initiative of the poor masses must receive all-out support from the media, intelligentsia and society, so that the public can be disentangled from the Naxalite octopus. The Naxalites must not be allowed to trample upon the voice of peace, the sane voice to save democracy. Hope is still there that the embers of peace are neither smothered by the excesses and false propaganda of the Naxalites, nor put out by the neglect of the State or society.[14] At the end, it will not be an exaggeration to say that the consequences of extremists' winning are not only ominous for the people of Bastar but for human society as a whole.

NOTES

1. Amrit Sandesh, 12.7.2005.
2. *Hindustan Times* 28.6.2005.
3. *Frontline* (Peoples War) 24.3.2006.
4. *Haribhumi* 6.10.2005.
5. Polit Bureau 2006 report. After Polit Bureau decision in April 2006 to fight peoples resistance movement at all fronts the concerned citizens group PUCL started visiting the area with so-called fact-finding teams in June 2006. Subsequently, Human watch group also visited these areas and published reports blaming both naxals and security force for predicament without mentioning any particular incidents.
6. Ibid.
7. Naxal DKSZC report.(Ghotul is tribal dormitory of Gond tribe. Salwa Juddum is a Gondi phrase mean peace mission. Jan Jagran means public awakening.)
8. *Daink Bhaskar* 5.9.2005.
9. *Haribhumi* 10.9.2005.
10. *Deshbandhu* 13.9.2005.
11. *Dainik Bhaskar* 2.7.2005, *Haribhumi* 7.7.2005, *Hitvada* 5.12.2005, *Daink Bhaskar* 31.1.2006. Hundreds of News Paper reporting in favour of people's resistance movement are available, only few have been cited.
12. *Highway Channel*, 11.12.2005, *Deshbandhu* 20.12.2005, *Dainik Bhaskar* 2.2.2006.
13. Thomas A. Marks; *Maoist Insurgency since Vietnam*, p. 269.
14. *The Hindu*, 20.8.2005.

4

Shun Violence and Talk

The idea of carrying out talks with Maoists is the talk of the day. The nation is, thereby, giving a chance to underground elements for coming into the mainstream. However, the Maoists aspire and conspire to bring about the death of the democratic system. They do not have faith in the Indian constitution, democracy and way of life. Even then, following the Gandhian tradition, our top decision-makers have appealed for talks. It is the outcome of the magnanimity of the nation and its decision-makers. The Indian temperament is gregarious, humanist, tolerant and forbearing. Talk accommodates dissent, and it hopes it may resolve conflict. The issue of talks with the Maoists was first raised in 1971 and later in 1977. On 21 July 1971 the then Minister of State for Home Affairs, Mr. K.C. Pant, told the Lok Sabha that the Government was willing to have a dialogue. He said it is the responsibility of all of us to carry on such a dialogue and help them see the path of reason and restore their belief in democratic process.[1]

Naxalites' Heart and Mind in Violence and Tongue in Talks

Let reality replace impressions about talks. Historically talks have shown different experiences in China, Nepal, Andhra

Pradesh and Sri Lanka. Talk seems innocuous and the easiest way out; but, it has proved the saying 'the straw can break the camel's back'. Talks have been used to consolidate strength and used as a tactics by extremists. There is a famous episode in the history of China, known as the 'Chunking Negotiation' which was held between two warring parties—the Communist Party of China and the Kuomintang in October 1945. During the course of the negotiations, Chiang Kaishek of the Kuomintang put forward the demand of reducing the army of both sides. However, Mao Zedong instructed his party men that the 'arms of the people, every gun and every bullet, must all be kept, must not be handed over'.

Mao and Giap saw negotiation as simply another tool in the conflict. According to Mao, 'revolutions rarely compromise; compromises are made only to further the strategic design. Negotiation, then, is undertaken for the dual purpose of gaining time to buttress a position (military, political, social, and economic) and to wear down, frustrate, and harass the opponent'.[2]

Quoting the above incident the CPN Maoists refused to surrender arms in Nepal. After each round of talks the CPN Maoists emerged stronger. On negotiations they followed the precepts of Mao who explicitly stated: 'How to give tit for tat depends on the situation. Sometimes not going to negotiation is tit for tat, and sometimes going to negotiation is tit for tat'.

On 19 June 1989, Ganapati, the State Committee Secretary of the Andhra Pradesh People's War Group (PWG) rejected the offer of Andhra Pradesh Chief Minister for laying down arms. Later also, in Andhra Pradesh, the offer of amnesty by the Chenna Reddy Government was turned down by the Naxalites. The efforts of the NTR Government to resolve the LWE conflict by peaceful means also yielded no result. Again, formal peace talks had been arranged twice in 2002 by Shri Chandrababu Naidu and in 2004 by Late Shri Y.S. Rajasekhar Reddy. Since 2000 different PWG leaders have issued statements about cease fire and conditional talks with the Government. In 2001, the Central Committee members of the

PWG put forward the conditions: that (a) the ban on PW should be lifted; (b) open inquiries into all encounters; (c) legal activities of frontal organisations to be permitted; and (d) the Government should stop all combing operations. In 2002 three rounds of talks with PWG representatives on 5, 9 and 22 June were organised. Varvara Rao and Gaddar declared that the armed struggle was not negotiable and insisted on a lifting of ban and revoking of cash rewards on PWG cadres. Other Maoist leaders have also reiterated that armed rebellion is non-negotiable. However, the PWG and its mediators asked for a conducive atmosphere for talks; thereby they organised huge meetings in cities where many Naxalites participated. PWG cadres also intimidated Government servants.

The protracted conflict has been waged in a subtle but systematic manner since its inception. Their hostility towards the democratic system and the public is aggressive, fanatical and unprincipled disgusting brutality. Each time the extremists used the pause to recruit, train and widen the scope of conflict. Historically, it has been proved that Naxalites have their tongue in talk, mind and heart in violence.

What have the Talks Brought?

It is plausible and commendable thing that major conflicts can be settled by talk and peaceful means. But, unfortunately the issues remain un-reconciled. Destructive consequences of conflict had been furthered. LWE draws sustenance from the fact, 'conflict to the bitter end.' Negotiation/talk is merely a tactics/technique to consolidate. The cease fire tended to arrest conflict- induced exhaustion and set combatants to reconstitute and rearm their forces. Combat suspended momentarily but a state of hostility prolonged indefinitely and carried to the masses.

Talk artificially freeze conflict and perpetuate a state of conflict indefinitely by shielding the Naxalites. Naxals use ruses as truce talks. It glamorises the extremists. It intensifies and prolongs the struggle. It is an ad hoc conflict management effort. It is sabotage of peace. Talk is not real path to peace. It retards the advent of peace. Naxals deliberately buy time. Naxals used talk in 2004 as a shield; statistics shows that during 2004 the killing of Naxals by security force was lowest. Peace talk moves could be a diversionary tactics by the Maoists to buy time by persuading government to halt anti-Maoist operations so that they can regroup and also reassess their strategy to overcome relentless police attack on their bases. Government is aware that Maoists utilize peace talks as breathing time. Maoists have always taken advantage of the fault lines of Indian Federal structure and political dynamics of various states. Here it is pertinent to discuss fate of talk and its outcome in Nepal, CPN maiosts conducted talks with Nepal Government in 2001 and in 2003 its outcome has been nicely narrated by Thomas A. Marks in which is mentioned below:

"Earlier negotiations had been unilaterally terminated by the CPN (M) in November 2001 in order to go over to the offensive, yet link had never been completely served. The UML, in particular, because its stated ideology continued to incorporate the notion of "revolution," had kept channels of communication open as had any number of other actors. Human rights groups, for instance, tried to act as mediators. Eventually, the Palace and its appointed government used these channels to renew discussions. Just how they would fare remained anyone's guess, because neither side showed any sign of altering its basic positions. These, to be clear, were irreconcilable on such basics as the nature of the state and the position of the monarchy. Both sides continued to train, re-equip, and acquire armaments.

In this situation, it was the Maoist position that was of most moment. From the previous ceasefire, captured documents and pictures, to include video footage, together with interrogations of prisoners, showed cadre telling the mass base that negotiations were a tactical gambit, that the cause of the revolution would never be betrayed or given up until a "people's republic" was established. That such remained the CPN (M)'s position had been stated directly. The real question was whether the party saw the new talks as but a tactical pause for regrouping or a more strategic effort to gain by non-violent means that which until then it had been unable to gain through violence, the standard political warfare approach. The latter course seemed likely, with the CPN (M), in its own calculations, moving from a position of strength into fractured Nepali politics.

The CPN (M), in the circumstance of the moment, felt it could not lose and would be able to defeat the enemy in detail, much as Lenin had in the chaos between the ouster of the Czar and the final Bolshevik coup. Directly and through its front organisations, as in 2001, it aggressively used political space, in which it could operate freely, to divide its foes further. In closed-door meetings, it made common cause with both political parties and the monarchy (through its appointed government), the end-game to use one against the other, then to out-maneuver the survivor in the organisational contest to follow.

Crucial in this strategy was the "constituent assembly," through which the monarchy was to be neutralised, in particular separated from its armed base, the RNA, in the name of establishing a "republic." Integration of the CPN (M) combatants, as was being demanded, would further ensure the RNA's inability to respond to provocation. In such an environment, co-optation would serve in place of armed confrontation. Indeed, the CPN (M)'s "75 Points" were structured as such a multitude precisely so that no one or minor grouping was objectionable. It was the platform's totality, to be achieved by persistently emphasizing that the smaller, 'moderate" compromises provided the only route to a "lasting peace," that was intended to produce a totally transformed whole.

The CPN (M) had not changed its basic positions but, like the Provisional Irish Republican Army (PIRA) in Northern Ireland, saw the moment as ripe for pushing ahead with non-violent means even as violence was held in reserve. This formulation was theoretically of particular interest, because it advanced that a sub-state actor held the same rights as the state.

In particular, the state was no longer granted monopoly of legitimate force. To the country, having lost this status by illegitimate action, the state, it was claimed, had to negotiate with the sub-state actor, which had access to its own purportedly legitimate force.

The Maoists hence claimed to have emerged, through the use of violence, as an equal to the state. The state controlled the urban areas, argued the CPN (M), the sub-state actor controlled the rural ones. The clash between the thesis and antithesis, hitherto a violent affair, had given rise to the demand for the realisation of a new synthesis through non-violent negotiation. Violence had been necessary to arrive at the point of "political solution" but it could now be superseded by political warfare. The destruction wreaked principally in the hinterland, therefore, although having various tactical and operational goals, such as area domination, strategically was intended as political communication, irrefutable evidence for the old order that the CPN (M) was a force that could not be ignored.

None of this precluded the Maoists' inclusion of more immediate concerns, although Bhattarai, as the head of the Maoist negotiations team, had begun to emphasize the CPN (M)'s "75 Points" was a document of strategic goals rather than tactical demands. He claimed for the party a willingness of the movement to accept intermediate steps (e.g., a "bourgeois republic" with a constitutional monarchy), a determination to move beyond an early attraction for the approach of *Sendero Luminoso* or the Naxalites in order to arrive at a unique, situationally appropriate "Nepalese Maoism." Specifics of application, for the building of a new Nepal, were to be found in an expansion of Bhattarai's PhD dissertation released in May 2003.

Even if this formulation had been accepted at face value, there would have been grounds for pessimism. Maoist excessive rhetoric, especially attacks on the RNA, and a bargaining emphasis on broad, often utopian, declarations at the expense of specifics, led to a situation where the two sides were talking past each other. Undoubtedly, the RNA saw little but a cynical effort to weaken it. In the field, Maoist cadre and combatants had been briefed that the major goal of the round of talks was the "national army." Simultaneously, the Maoist representatives in Kathmandu focused on ending international assistance to the government (which, as indicated above, was crucial to enhancing the capabilities of the security forces), all the while demanding that the RNA "return to the barracks." Under no such restrictions themselves, Maoist forces continued to move and train, funded by undiminished criminal activity.

In such an environment, the only real surprise came when the Maoists on 27 August 2003 abruptly terminated the ceasefire and again resorted to a variety of armed actions, including targeted assassinations of important government personnel in Kathmandu. The surprise came from the obvious quarter: Government disorientation and lack of focus seemed to be providing the CPN (M) with ample leeway to make progress, through "political" means, progress that would surely be more difficult in a state of armed conflict. Indeed, faced with renewed assassination efforts, the government promptly restored legal prohibitions and asked international organisations to assist in apprehending leadership figures. Thus people's war was again in full swing."[3]

In June 2004 the PWG and Andhra Pradesh Government agreed to a ceasefire for three months.

In order to create congenial atmosphere for talks with the Naxalites, on June 16, 2004 the Andhra Pradesh Government officially declared a three-month cease-fire against the PWG, with immediate effect. It also accepted the remaining three PWG proposals-constitution of a supervisory committee, initial dialogue with mediators and find discussions between ministerial representatives and PWG 'State committee' representatives. The peace talks between Andhra Pradesh Government and the PWG and CPI(ML) Janashakthi representatives in Hyderabad on October 15-18, 2004 failed to deliver the desired result as the Naxalites put forth demands that included withdrawal of criminal cases against participants in 'people's struggles', release of political prisoners, scrapping of rewards on the heads of 'revolutionaries.' In October 2004 Maoists underground leaders addressed a huge rally for the first time in three and half decades.

Further, taking interest in the peace process in Andhra Pradesh, many important persons in letters to the Maoist mediators in December 2004, stated that there had been a virtual collapse of law and order in view of extortion demands, display of arms, encroachments on public and private property and the militant rhetoric of naxal leaders at rallies and meetings in Andhra Pradesh.

Amidst repeated reports of forcible occupation of private and forest lands by the Communist Party of India-Maoist (CPI-Maoist), with whom the Andhra Pradesh Government was that time in negotiations, State Home Minister K. Jana Reddy asserted, on November 7, 2004, "Only an elected government can control surplus lands and distribute them to the poor. . . Nobody else would be allowed to take the law into their hands." On November 27, Naxalite mediator, S.R. Sankaran, expressed his concern over rising incidents of Naxalites grabbing private and Government lands. Earlier, on November 8, the People s Union for civil liberties (PUCL) President, Keshava Rao Jadhav, and its general secretary, Jaya Vindhyala, accused the Naxalites of endangering the peace process by destroying forests for the sake of land distribution. Illegal timber felling, incidentally, is also a lucrative source of Naxalite revenues.

On April 4, 2005, Maoist emissaries announced in Hyderabad their decision to pull out of the peace process. This announcement did not come as a surprise as earlier on January 17, Ramakrishna and Amar, state secretaries of the CPI-Maoist and Janashakthi respectively, had already declared they were no longer keen to continue talks. The charade of peace talk finally ended in Andhra Pradesh.

Precautions need to be taken for Fruitful Talk

Talk seems simple. But, execution of everything simple on

ground is difficult. Even with intention to do well to the system, if one is not careful, worse may happen. Before talk decision-makers should understand and study Naxals' mind; what is in Mao's kit is in their mind. People conducting talks should be well aware of LWE concept and LWE semantics. Therefore, the Government negotiators should study Mao, Lenin, Vietnam problem, Nepal problem before starting talk. Right people with adequate knowledge of LWE and skill of negotiation should be selected for talks. Precaution should be taken for selecting mediators; highly ambitious people who think that they will be worshipped for conducting talks should not be included in the team.

There are more than a dozen splinter Maoist groups active in India and there is no Pan- Indian group; talk with a group may not be binding on the other groups. In the post-Emergency period after 1977, the ban on the Naxalites was lifted. The Central Committee of the United CPI-ML under S.N. Singh, one of the larger left extremist outfits, met at Hardwar (April 15, 1977) and proclaimed to end violence and also decided to participate in elections as they felt that total boycott of election was incorrect in the context of the changed political situation in the country. Thereafter, S.N. Singh parleyed with the then Union Home Minister and urged the Govt. to release all communist revolutionaries including those convicted in criminal cases. He emphasised that his party, though believed in Marxism-Leninism, would shun violence which they would not accept as a part of their creed. Large number of under trials and convicted Naxals were released; unfortunately many LWE groups strengthened their outfit. Some people view the need to talk to Naxalites, but the above release of large number of Naxalites and talk with them had proved that in case of the diehard LWE and ideologically hard boiled groups this view will not hold water.

Some people think ballot box is the coffin of left wing extremists. But, in the past many LWE groups had contested elections. In the Lok Sabha election in January 1980, PCC/PPI-ML (C.P. Reddy), PCC/CPI-ML (S.N. Singh) Central team of CPI ML and coordination Committee of Communist Revolutionaries Contested 24 seats and won nothing. December 24-27th 1984 Extremist contested 16 constituencies —Wests Bengal (4), Bihar (3), AP (5), Kerala, Orissa, Tripura, UP (1 each) in the Lok Sabha elections and won no seat. March 1987 IPF, PCC CPI-ML (Santosh Rana group), CPI-ML (Sadhan Sarkar group), and COI-ML (Kanu Sanyal group) participated in Assembly Election in West Bengal. They set up 40 candidates in different constituencies but none could win. IPF, PCC CPI-ML COI-ML and CPI-ML (Sadhan Sarkar group) participated in Lok Sabha and Assembly Elections held in May 20, 1991. The IPF and PCC, CPI-ML fielded one candidate each to contest Assembly Bye-Election from Alipurduar Constituency in Jalpaiguri district held on February 27, 1990. Both of them, however, lost their security deposits. Six left wing extremist parties contested 39Parliamentary constituencies throughout the country in November, 1989. The IPF contested 16 seats (Bihar-11, UP-2, AP-1, Punjab-1 and WB-1), COI-ML contested 9 seats (Kerala-4, Bihar-2, UP-1, Rajasthan-1 and WB-1), CPI-ML (C P Reddy group) contested 5 seats (Punjab-2, UP-1, WB-1 and AP-1), UCCRI-ML contested 4 seats (AP-4), PCC, CPI-ML contested 3 seats (WB-3) and CPI-ML (PV Rao group) contest 2 seats (AP/2), The IPF contested 86 Assembly seats in Bihar held in February 27 and 28, 1990. The party could secure one (1) Parliamentary seat (Arrah) out of 16 contested and seven (7) Assembly seats, in Bihar. No other group could win any parliamentary seat. In spite of the efforts of some of the LWE groups many of the groups have shown their animosity towards the democratic system and electoral process.

Talk intervention on humanitarian and peace ground should not be allowed to worsen the chances of a stable long-term resolution of conflict. Talk should not be construed as weakness of the system. Generally, talk has been used by Naxals as a scheme to paralyse the will of the regime to take any resolute stand. They will exploit security force relaxing their ground. Talk should be for a very limited period of 15 days so that the combatants should not consolidate their strength during this period. During the period of talk in 2004 Naxals did merger and formed CPI Maoist party and made propaganda that it is a political party. Talk should be confidential and beyond media glare. Naxals try to glamorize them through media coverage. Only after final negotiation talk should be made open to public. Naxals like Nagas should deposit their arms in designated camp.

Third party mediation is of no value. Talk should be held directly with Naxal leaders. In the name of a conducive atmosphere for peace they should not be allowed to strengthen their bases in urban areas. In the name of talks Naxals are more interested for lifting of ban against Naxals and their frontal organisations. The ban of almost all the Naxalite groups in 1975 stifled the growth and spread of Naxalite movement for some period in the country. Even in Andhra Pradesh it was seen that during period of ban Naxal violence remained low.

Allied Issues Raised by Naxals

Talk should be within the parameters of the constitution. People should understand that generally, the policy of the limited objective in talk as in tactics at the beginning is achievable. The more people digress, the more they go away from achieving peace. However, in the past following issues were raised by Maoists:

- Equitable distribution of land to the tillers.
- Statehood to various regions.
- Re-imposition of total prohibition.
- Unconditional release of arrested Maoists or on suspicion of aiding the Maoists.
- Repeal of all draconian laws and Acts such as the Unlawful Activities Prevention Act (UAPA), Armed Forces Special Powers Act (AFSPA), etc.
- All the MOUs signed with the MNCs, and big business houses should be scrapped.
- Policy of Special Economic Zones should be

immediately scrapped along with the colonial policy of land acquisition.

- Mining and other so-called development projects that lead to displacement of the tribals and destruction of their way of life should be immediately disbanded.

Again CC member Azad in his writing has categorically mentioned central committees view about laying down arms in following manner:

> "The central committee (CC), CPI (Maoist), makes it crystal clear that laying down arms means a betrayal of the people's interests. We have taken up arms for the defence of people's rights and for achieving their liberation from all types of exploitation and oppression. As long as these exist, people will continue to be armed."[4]

Constructive Problem Solving Talk to Defeat Dagger behind Dialogue

Similarly more issues will be raised by Naxalites. Practical political concerns invoke talk but consequent political outcome should guide its continuation. People should see what lies beyond dialogue. These issues are raised by Naxalites to agitate the public, organize mass movements gain public sympathy and cadres. Basically the Naxals draw their dagger behind dialogue to hit democracy. The new issues will shift conflict to a new dimension. Politics and ideological impulses can spur talks, but there remains nevertheless an urgent need for constructive problem solving dialogue. The think-tank of Government should discuss the problems, issues, and well calibrated response should be prepared beforehand. The argument framework must be prepared thoroughly considering the issues. So, that during talk the response of regime to various issues raised by Maoists may be proper. The think tank should have nuanced understanding of the game to be played by the other side. The moment Naxals play to the gallery and show intention to damage national interest then they should be shown the door.

Less Intention of Peace and more Pretension to Peace

'I will be judge', 'I will be jury', said cunning old fury, 'I will try the whole case and condemn you to death.' The above quote from Alice Adventures in wonderland ch.-3 rightly paraphrases the scheme of Naxals in the above words. Naxals believe in monologue, but they play dialogue game. They use double talk, play win-lose politics and try to convert talk in to trial of the system.

Hindsight should be useful for more than regret. In the past talk failed to achieve its ostensible aim, although the consequences are with the pretence of ending conflict. Extremists feed off instability; extremists try to occupy the places of vacuum or instability. Naxals wanted to shift their battlegrounds to urban areas and transform the population into battlegrounds. Because, they knew that combat fought within these populations ultimately determine success or failure. They tried to protract the conflict by controlling human terrain. The theory of protracted war is so structured that they will not give up armed rebellion. Talk by Maoists seems to be a symbolic assurance showing less intention of peace and more pretension to peace.

Genie out of the Bottle

Talks will bring the genie out of bottle. Talk shouldn't be allowed to transform into maligned expression of divisive forces. If the talk is not handled effectively it will drastically change the contours of conflict. Long-term capability of resistance of Naxals will enhance. The means available to Naxals will increase and so also their strength of will because their mass base will widen. Revolutionary politics help LWE in sustained, systematic attempt to regroup. Political fallout of talks can be portentous. A campaign of misinformation wrong propaganda will be unleashed. The extremists' ability to live and operate freely among the urban population will increase. Politicising and radicalizing of public by LWE in large scale will continue. Political cadres of extremist outfits are like termites; they will unleash larger divisive forces and spread of political cynicism.

Taking benefit of political opportunity they will purposefully exploit issues. It will vitiate political environment of already overheated polity. It is only self deception induced by the statements of the Naxals and their frontal organisations. Naxals play the game of dialogue to discredit the Government and the system and confuse the people and get legitimacy in the eyes of the public.

Conclusion

In the war of wits and will the destiny of dialogue seems to be murky. Naxals believe in manipulative monologue, not in fruitful constructive dialogue. In the *past* talks have failed to achieve its ostensible aim; negotiation has become pointless. The precious time that still remains shall not be lost. In International arena it is diplomacy and in democratic field it is talk which can solve conflict to some extent. Peace talks, generally, hold after war become effective. Talk is a tool to de-escalate situations. By making realistic responses the decision-makers should make talk strategically purposeful. This can be done by opening channels to many underground members who want to surrender, by telling public the sordid activities of violence. Talk is nice, but delicate, fragile and at times treacherous. Even then people should hope for the best. Shun violence, come to the table to talk, and surrender of weapons is the ideal outcome every Indian cherishes.

NOTES

1. Samer Sen, Debabrata Panda, Ashish Lahiri; Naxalbari: A Frontier Anthology, Volume One, Calcutta: Kathashilpa, June 1978.
2. Naxal Document.
3. Thomas A. Marks, Maoist People's War in Post-Vietnam Asia, Studies in Insurgency and Terrorism No. 1, White Lotus Press, Thailand (2007), pp. 321-23.
4. Azad, Maoists in India Writings and Interviews, Friends of Azad, 2010.

5

Preemptive Development: A Great Tool for Conflict

Prevention, Resolution and Peace Building

Adopting the Millennium Declaration in the year 2000 India took the pledge to, "spare no effort to free our fellow men, women and children from the abject and dehumanizing conditions of extreme poverty". It is now more than halfway towards the target date of 2015 by which the Millennium Development goals are to be achieved. However, development is a process full of uncertainties; conflict breeds a climate of existential uncertainty. Eclipsed by conflict, development creates a hopeless situation; because development in an atmosphere of uncertainty becomes difficult and becomes the first casualty with the onset of conflict.

It is the practice among insurgents and extremists to not only target security personnel and the public, but also destroy infrastructure and development in an area. They try to create a situation of hepatitis polity which has the symptoms of initially making the area lose its capacity to develop, then the area goes into hepatitis coma with multiple organ failures, meaning thereby the gradual failure of the education system, health facilities, PDS system, banking system, transportation facilities, electric power transmission, water supply etc. This creates a piquant situation of a precarious local economy, and failed development and administration.

A recent study (2009) of the country's 33 districts hardest hit by Naxalites, shows an abysmal record of Government expenditure on basic amenities, including health, education, roads, electricity and child care. In fact, the evidence couldn't be starker: the expenditure in a state's Naxal-affected districts is merely a fraction of the figure for the rest of the state.

Percentage of Funds Spent in the Naxal Zone*

State	Water	Education	Electricity	Health	Child Care	NREGA	Rural Roads
Bihar	20	15	39	76	43	13	17
	(15)	(37)	(84)	(87)	(101)	(70)	(110)
Chhattisgarh	15	45	58	32	10	17	46
	(83)	(65)	(28)	(52)	(43)	(60)	(115)
Jharkhand	30	17	65	34	15	20	48
	(14)	(77)	(93)	(52)	(86)	(61)	(127)
Maharashtra	7	16	141	10	29	5	20
	(54)	(82)	(47)	(64)	(N.A.)	(42)	(99)
Odisha	45	18	36	38	41	41	53
	(43)	(61)	(44)	(76)	(145)	(64)	(118)

Figures in brackets are overall state average (Water: Drinking Water Scheme; Education: SSA; Health: NRHM; Child care: ICDS; Rural roads: PMGSY)
Source: Planning Commission.

The worst figures are in four states which account for 28 of 33 the worst-affected LWE districts: Jharkhand (10 districts), Chhattisgarh (seven), Odisha (five) and Bihar (six). The Naxal situation in these districts is the key hurdle to government schemes. Because these schemes cannot be implemented, there is lack of development and governance which, in turn, helps the Naxalites to step in and use the situation to their advantage.

**Indian Express*, January 24, 2010.

There is slow or no development due to armed conflict. In one district, Bijapur, of Chhattisgarh State none of the agencies came forward to construct an important road. 22 kilometres of the road were constructed by the Superintendent of Police in 2008 at the cost of 56 precious lives of security men in various operations supporting the road construction. In such situations, security intervention may provide a short-term result, but in the long run the system will not improve. It poses a greater question of there being any other method to ameliorate the situation? Before answering one should understand the situation, which is like the door of development being locked with the key of security and public participation. The answer is 'yes'. It implies an integrated and holistic approach, which is overdue. Radical rethinking and overhauling the entire system is required. Development intervention has to start with public participation and security in tandem. The answer is to develop the area, isolate the extremists socially, politically and as well defeat them physically.

Merging of Security, Development and Public Participation

Developmental operations and security operations with public participation have to be started. Merging of development with security is essential and this merger should carry public participation with it. This can be graphically represented as:

Fig. 1: Merging of Security, Development and Public Participation

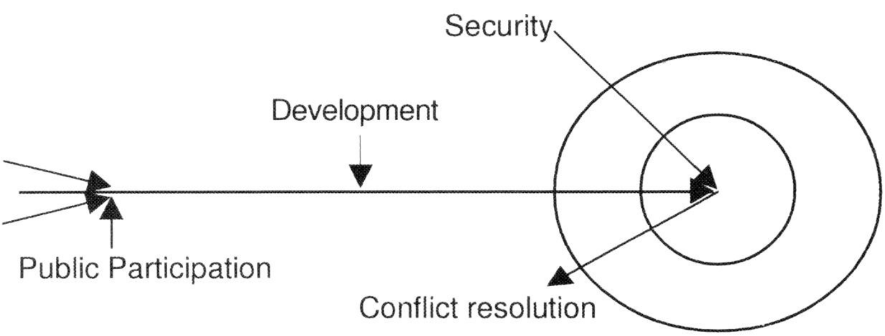

It falsifies the presupposition that the area has to be initially cleared and then only it can be developed. The whole subject is beset by confusion and misunderstanding. Security will complain that it is not sustaining due to lack of development and development will complain that it is not taking place due to lack of security. This precipitates an egg-and-chicken syndrome. Security should start in extremely infested areas as, in mildly infested areas, development does not face many hurdles. But, to facilitate smooth functioning it can be arranged in such a manner that development moves fast in that area. In that case development should be aided by security. Development and security has to go side-by-side. Collaboration between development and security is the urgent need.

From where should the Developmental Trajectory Start?

Initially development should start from pockets of security. It must move along the trajectory of security. As security is the precondition, so security should assure developmental authorities and developmental activities. The development activities can benefit a large number of people. Security cannot be arranged at all the places. But, even in areas of extreme conflict, security pocket exists; these are the places near police stations, police posts, police headquarters and district head quarters. Long persistent developmental challenges can be taken at these places vigorously. The outcomes will be self-evident. Naxalites in the 1990s did not allow agricultural activities in a few areas of Andhra Pradesh; now they do not allow public agricultural activities in few areas of Chhattisgarh, Orissa and Jharkhand.

Development should start from such area, like district head quarter, sub divisional head quarter or village where police stations/police posts exist. The infrastructure developed can be easily protected as the extremists cannot easily damage or destroy these facilities. Due to the presence of security forces they cannot easily hijack the benefits by terrorising people. They cannot loot the godowns of the public distribution system, if it is juxtaposed with the police station. They cannot recruit children from hostels, if the hostels are located near police posts. Therefore, the security posts should be the hub around which all the facilities should be located.

Requirement of Sustainable Pattern of Human Settlement

Cluster localities are also essential in remote areas. In most of the remote areas development is not sustainable because pattern of human settlement is not sustainable. If one house is located in the jungle in an area of 1.5 square kilometres with another two houses at a distance of another three square kilometres, it is not economical and almost impossible to create power sub-stations, schools, and colleges, hospitals to serve a spread-out population as the benefits of development cannot be taken to all the houses. Schools, electricity, and roads cannot reach isolated hamlets. Therefore, there is a need to establish clusters of houses at strategic places. Thought this type of settlement will cause deforestation and total denudation of some areas; its adverse impact on climate change will have to be accepted. Sometimes people argue that tribals like to stay in the forest why should development traumatise them?

Another argument people offered is that the culture of tribals should not be disturbed. The author had the opportunity to ask some old tribal people from relief camps of Bijapur, "why don't they go back to forest from the relief camp? They retorted "why do not you go back to forest? Your father, grandfather might not have come from forest; but 20 or 25 generations back somebody in the genealogy tree must have come from the forest. People do not get education, medical and other facilities in jungle." Human civilisation has advanced from hunting—gathering stage to the new scientific age. In every stage of civilisation human settlement has advanced. Therefore, there is urgent need to make the pattern of human settlement sustainable.

Development is the Solution, Security is the Precondition

It presupposes a fact that development can solve conflict and the vice versa is also true. In areas with extremely infestation of LWE of insurgency the first postulate applies, in mildly infested areas the reverse of the postulate i.e. development is the precondition and security is the solution can be applied. It is a fact that immoderation and systematic underdevelopment fuels conflict. Therefore it can be said that there is an inter-linkage between development and security.

Fig. 2: Inter-linkage between Development and Security

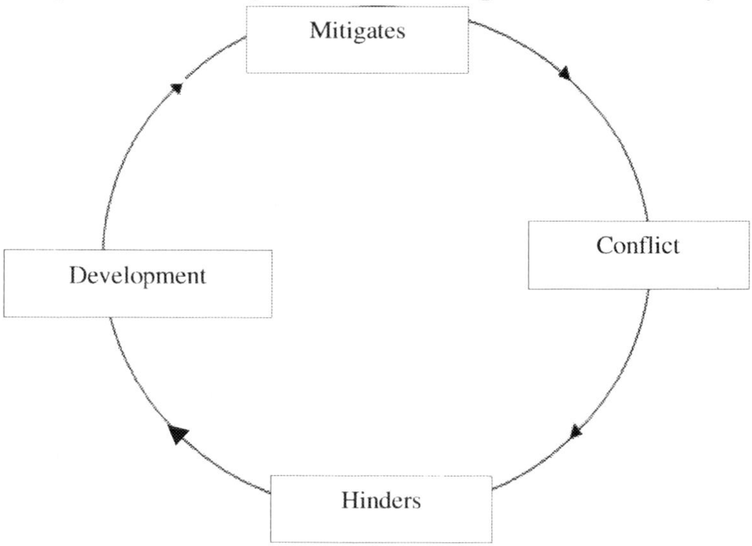

Development without security is untenable and security without development is unsustainable. Development is dependent on security and vice versa.

The Agenda of Development

Development objectives also encompass universally excepted human values and rights such as freedom from hunger, the right to education, the right to health and a responsibility to future generation. Initially development agenda should be meticulously prepared; otherwise haphazard development will not contribute to peace building. The administration must satisfy them with following important questions:

(1) What initiatives can most effectively address the underlying local and structural causes of the conflict?
(2) What type of development project can contribute to micro-economic reconstruction of the area and local market with local resources?
(3) What projects can lead to the consolidation of the peace process and long term peace building in the area?
(4) How more employment generation can take place in a local area so that the younger generation does not get channelised into extremism?
(5) How popular participation in these projects can be achieved?
(6) How the projects and population can be protected?
(7) What is the time frame for the effective implementation of a sustainable development agenda?

Creation of Livelihood for the People

Without combating poverty in remote areas where Naxalites have spread their tentacles or are planning to spread, it will not be possible to fight the Naxal menace. In many areas extremism becomes an illegal industry. In some areas Naxalites pay their cadres. Therefore, simply kinetic operations cannot eradicate Naxal menace. Because, of kinetic operations any area may be cleared, but to hold that area and make that area free from the scourge of Naxalism it is most important to promote economic and social revitalisation of the area. Youth unemployment is an important issue for mitigating conflict. Successful employment generation cannot take place, unless human resource development of the area is done seriously. This cannot spread without spreading education, higher education and vocational education among the affected people. MNREGA and other projects of Government should be able to complete these urgent tasks.

Panchayat Raj Revitalisation in Naxal Affected Areas

In mildly affected areas *panchayat* revitalisation is easier. Continuous movement of security forces and officials of developmental agencies and continuous monitoring of activities of local bodies can improve the system. Effective counter measures should be taken to prevent siphoning of *panchayat* funds by Naxals in highly affected areas.

Pre-emptive Reconstruction

Pre-emptive reconstruction of any disturbed area is required like pre-emptive action against extremist groups. Both generate hope of survival. Pre-emptive reconstruction necessitates well formulated projects with finances, motivated work force, and public participation. This helps in reconstruction of the micro-economy of the area by creation of local markets, improved livelihood of poor people, and creation of local infrastructures. The Government has so many schemes pertaining to improvement of watershed management, fisheries, utilisation of forest produces, rural unemployment, rural infrastructure, animal husbandry, rural human resource developments. These should be implemented vigorously with public participation in the affected areas. Utilisation of local resources for implementation of these schemes should get top priority. Public participation is not only required for developing infrastructure of the area but also for protecting the existing ones with public assistance.

Implementing Vigorously various Schemes

The district administration must vigorously implement various developmental schemes in affected areas which are mentioned below:

- Under the Backward Districts Initiative (BDI) component of the Rashtriya Sam Vikas Yojana (RSVY), which covered 147 districts, an amount of Rs. 45 crores per district had been allocated on a non-lapsable basis. The scheme of Backward Regions Grand

Fund (BRGF) has now been initiated in 250 districts (replacing BDI).

- Pradhan Mantri Gram Sadak Yojana (PMGSY) offers enormous opportunity for rural road connectivity. For certain naxalite affected areas, it has been decided that 3-year perspective plans would be prepared for covering all eligible habitations under PMGSY. The State Governments have been requested to identify and prioritize unconnected habitations having population of 500 and above in plain areas and 250 and above in tribal areas for preparing detailed project reports as per PMGSY programme guidelines.
- Mahatma Gandhi National Rural Employment Guarantee Programme (MNREGP), which was originally being implemented in 200 districts, and was extended to 330 districts in April 2007, is now being extended to all districts in the country (except metropolises), having regard to the need to universalize this demand-driven programme for wage-employment.
- The above schemes are in addition to schemes like Bharat Nirman, National Rural Health Mission (NRHM), Sarva Shiksha Abhiyan (SSA), Integrated child Development Services (ICDS) Scheme and various income-generating, public-utility and social-security schemes of Ministries like Rural Development, Agriculture, Panchayati Raj and tribal Affairs.
- In totality, these provide an immense opportunity to address all development aspects relevant to naxalism, provided the implementation is done in a systematic and qualitative manner and closely monitored.
- A major step has been the enactment of 'The Scheduled Tribes and other Traditional Forest Dwellers (Recognition of Forest Rights) Act, 2006' on 02.01.2007. It seeks to recognise and vest the forest rights and occupation in forest land in forest dwelling scheduled tribes and other traditional forest dwellers who have been residing in such forests for generations.

- A new scheme for special infrastructure in naxalite affected areas, with Rs. 500 crores in the XI plan period, is being finalised to provide critical mobility to the police by upgrading existing roads/tracks in inaccessible areas, provide secure camping grounds and helipads at strategic locations in remote and interior areas, provide secure police station/outposts by strengthening those at risk of attack due to their dilapidated condition, upgrade and strengthen approach roads to police station/outposts where there is risk of attack by improvised explosive devices (IEDs) and landmines and provide for critical needs, specific to the areas/districts where holistic anti-naxalite measures are being taken in a focused manner.

Establishing Model Villages

Emphasis should be put on creation of model villages by developing infrastructure and implementing various schemes of government. Provision of irrigation facilities will improve overall economy of the villagers. Master Plans to exploit entire Minor Irrigation potential in the identified villages in a phased manner should be prepared. Bus connectivity through BT roads to all the gram panchayats should be established. All quality-affected villages should be provided quality water supply scheme. Every eligible family should be provided a house. 100% institutional deliveries, 100% birth registration and HIV/AIDS awareness and prevention/Malaria/T.B. treatment/Regular medical services should be ensured. Anganwadi centre should be run in every village. Old age, widow, disabled and other schemes of financial help should be properly provided to the eligible villagers. In A.P. and Maharashtra village development has hit at the root of Naxalism up to some extent. Now all the affected districts must give more importance to develop model villages to eliminate the menace by building peace.

Exposing False Propaganda of LWE and Denying the Scope for Token Development

Naxalites are trying to transform their role and image from bandits to *Jananthana Sarkar* by developing some token facilities in remote areas. For example, by siphoning off Government money of some projects they constructed few ponds in South Bastar; and by hijacking few remote schools in interior places they claim by propaganda that they have established alternate development action in the remote areas. The romantic propaganda of LWE needs to be countered properly.

The ultimate goal of development is to improve and enhance human well-being and the quality of life of all people. The need is to fight poverty, hunger and lack of education and after education proper livelihood. The sustainable developmental reconstruction of areas infested with Naxalite problem is a challenge we ignore it at our own peril.

NOTE

1. *Indian Express*, January 24, 2010.

6

How Much is Sufficient to Fight LWE Conflict (Operational Capacity Requirements)

Combat in any region and a forest fire have many things in common: (i) it spreads very fast to other areas; (ii) fire cannot be extinguished by mere talk; (iii) failing in combat and fire fights will be disastrous; (iv) being simply an onlooker will not help, and (v) fast mobilisation of resources is required. Problems will not go away on their own. On the contrary, inadequate resources cause great handicaps. Before the problem overwhelms, overwhelming efforts must be made to control, contain and eradicate the problem. Being analytical enhances capability in system reorganisation. Transcending from the abstract to the concrete, it can be said that a greater alignment between priorities and capabilities is needed.

Resource Crunch Emboldens Naxals

Interventions to be meaningful need teeth and tail. It is a well-known fact that full spectrum operations cannot be launched if the security force does not have optimum operational capacity. It is further needed because paucity of resources emboldens combatants. The post-election review of CPI Maoist Polit Bureau meeting of June 2009 has mentioned:

> "Though the enemy is itching to suppress our Party and movement by deploying a huge force in all our areas, he has severe difficulties in implementing this at present; he has plans to increase the number of central forces in the next few years, to set up and train special forces like the Cobras, but in the immediate context it is quite difficult for the Centre to send the forces required by each state to control our movement. Keeping this in mind, we have to further aggravate the situation and create more difficulties to the enemy forces by expanding our guerrilla war to new areas on the one hand and intensifying the mass resistance in the existing areas so as to disperse the enemy forces over a sufficiently wider area on the other; hence the foremost task in every state is to intensify the war in the respective states while in areas of intense enemy repression there is need to expand the area of struggle by proper planning by the concerned committees; tactical counter-offensives should be stepped up and also taken up in new areas so as to divert a section of the enemy forces from attacking our guerrilla bases and organs of political power."[1]

Testing the current circumstances with an ends-ways-means construct will help to assess capacity requirements. Critical requirements and critical capabilities are needed to sustain the fight. Demands of conflict show that without improving operational capacity there is every possibility of the response becoming irrelevant and ineffective.

Performance Gap Due to Use of Second versus Fourth Generation Warfare[2]

Some of the security forces in their battle against left-wing extremists generally use second generation warfare which is based on tactics of fire and movement, whereas Naxalites have started third generation warfare which is based on manoeuvre and occasional fourth generation warfare i.e. asymmetrical warfare carrying the war to the rear of the security forces and to use the strength of security forces against them. Naxalites are using power fire and force against structures and vulnerabilities. Therefore, there is a great need of assets at the tactical-operational-strategic level to withstand the complexities of the current contemporary operations and asymmetric threats. Besides this, Naxalites operate by following the tactics of local superiority through fast mobilisation from various states. This the security forces cannot achieve quickly due to territorial jurisdiction of various forces. There are number of asymmetrical factors. Therefore, there is a need to assess the performance gap and, ultimately, the capacity gap. The security forces have to grow in capacity and resources. The first priority is to examine the critical gap depth.

Need to Define Needs

In some areas, steady state improvement has taken place; in some areas problem-mutation has taken place; in some areas spill-over effect has occurred. When the conflict has turned into a crisis in some areas, we should not waste much time; serious preparation should be made. The LWE problem has been defined, but the urgent need is to define the needs. Felt security needs and anticipated needs must be properly projected and fulfilled. Another point for consideration is that different areas have different needs; urban areas have different needs, while rural areas and forested areas have different needs, and coastal and river side areas have yet more different needs. Also, different stages of the problem have different needs. Mildly affected areas have different problems. Extremely affected areas have different problems. But, the ground situation indicates that a rigorous analysis and assessment is required to project the actual requirement. Resources have to be constructively applied to the tasks projected. In order to improve the current state of operations, it is necessary to focus and model immediate future state capacity requirements. This is critical to ensure that resource demands and potential risks are identified with enough advance notice so that they can be managed pro-actively. Half measures and piecemeal perspectives will not help. Full perspectives and worst case scenario analysis should be used for assessment.

Capacity Matrix of State Prepared by Naxals

In order to assess the capability of the security forces of different areas, the Naxals had made a study of resources available to security forces in the year 2000. They assessed the security forces capabilities and plans, and augmented their own strength. They had used many broad parameters while calculating the capacity of security forces. It included not only force and weapons, but also all a range of functions and institutions which support combat directly or indirectly.

Form	State			
	Andhra Pradesh	**NT**	**DK**	**Bihar**
Modernisation of force	Already modernised	Modernised	Going on	Going on
Construction of roads	Built	Well built	Process started	Process started
Communication network	Using modern equipment	Using modern equipment	In the process of acquiring	In the process of acquiring
Informers network	Well built	Well built	Infant stage	Infant stage
Stopped moving in vehicles	Yes	Yes	Yes	Not yet
Using auto weapons/ using grenades	Yes	Yes	Yes	Yes
Using helicopters	Yes	Yes	Yes	Yes
Achieved coordination, speed in action.	Yes	Yes	In the process	In the process
Announcing new reforms	Yes	Yes	Yes	Yes
Anti propaganda	Yes	Yes	Weak	Weak
Special action plan submitted to centre	Yes	Yes	Yes	Yes
PS fortified	Yes	Yes	In the process	In the process

July 2000, *Peoples March*.[3]

Capacity Matrix of Naxalites

The Naxals understand that striking power comes from operational capacity, which has a great bearing on the span of success. Naxalites with over-bearing numbers outgrow and overpower the security force. They have started developing their organisations extensively and meticulously. As a result, from a position of non-entity they are coming up as a formidable outfit.

In "Counter-Guerrilla Operations, the Philippines Experience" authors Valeriano and Bohnnan had aptly mentioned:

> "For strategic-planning purposes, a great deal about guerrilla capabilities can be correctly deduced from information readily available. His successful operations give very fair evidence of his minimum capacity. His unsuccessful operations, although a less reliable source, may give accurate evidence of his maximum capabilities."[4]

The factors considered are:

- Arms/Ammunitions/Mines/Manufacturing unit.
- Explosives procurement.
- Training area.
- Training team.
- Technical manpower.
- Money generation capacity.
- Use of modern gadgets.
- Mobility: use of vehicles.
- Guerrilla bases.
- Intellectual support.
- Recruitment base/per annum recruitment.
- Sophisticated arms/Ammunition available.
- Propaganda capability.
- Bunkers and other fortified positions.
- Linkages with other outfits.

The above capacity matrix of Naxalites reveals their organisational capability. They are using night vision devices, bullet-proof jackets and vehicles. They have military instructor teams, R&D facilities, network with other extremist outfits; and they have leadership development programmes. After merger every year they recruit about two thousand armed cadres out of which about two hundred leave the organisation, about two hundred are killed in encounters and about one thousand are arrested. The Naxalites use mines; they have LMG/automatic weapons. The resources employed by the Naxals show what an operational challenge they pose against the security forces of the country. Considering the war preparation of the Naxalites, the security force should have greater resources and greater sophistication. Operational challenges should reshape operational capacity requirements.

SWOT analysis of both organisations is necessary to fight the menace. Estimation of enemy capability helps in projecting operational requirement; another important factor—long range intention of extremists should also be considered. It is not just the numbers that matter; the right skills must also be available. History is littered with instances of poorly prepared troops failing to execute their assignment, bungling operations, deserting and committing atrocities. The incumbent regime should have not only combative but also preventive deployment of resources. Disproportionate resources contribute to fiasco. Steps should be taken to assess the security forces' capabilities and plan and augment their strength. Estimating effective force sizing for an area and estimating resources required are two important studies.

The process consists of a series of well-planned iterations, each adding to the capabilities of the system. The process provides sufficient latitude to allow the implementation of capabilities resulting from altering resources and advances in technologies. However, efforts should be made for the root and branch reconstruction of the force.

Model of Capacity Requirement Analysis

Determined enemies and inadequate resources create a precarious situation. Therefore, a good security infrastructure is required by committing adequate resources. The material basis of combativeness of any force is its equipment, which is the crucial element for organizing any security force. In order to achieve operational effectiveness it is desirable to make an assessment of operational capacity requirement of a system. Whereas it would be unwise not to calculate the operational capacity requirements to fight such menace; it is also a difficult notion to calculate exactly the operational capacity requirements. The system should be so structured that it can accommodate flexibility of requirements. The focus should be both on prioritisation and planning. Goal, objectives and tasks of different organisations should be well considered to make the assessment realistic. Instead of using isolated, ad hoc techniques, there is a need to use quantitative and qualitative parameters to specify desired operational capabilities. Instead of taking the wish list of any person or group or institution, first critical analysis of requirement is needed; this should presuppose problem analysis, capacity gap analysis and the capacity matrix of the opponent.

Allocation of resources is the first concrete decision for fighting any combat. In order to achieve efficiency of resources an analysis of misallocation of resources and no allocation of resources is required. Then priorities should be prepared and according to the priorities resources should be acquired and allocated. The principal prerequisite of any strategy is the projection of complete, correct and unambiguous specific requirements.

The organisations that shoulder the burden of conflict should be revitalized periodically. If the ground situation worsens in arithmetic progression, resources needed are in geometric progression and if the ground situation deteriorates in geometric progression the resources needed in quality, quantity and time are the square of geometric progression. Escalating security commitments need accelerated efforts which in turn need enhanced resources. Significant improvement in capability can be made by making force structure adjustments to correspond to the ground requirement.

Capacity Gap

Capacity gap puts the security force in an operational morass. Paucity of resources creates a precarious position for a security force. Sharply limited resources constrain authority. Tools for actions are needed for performing tasks. Sometimes operations lack punch and staying power due to lack of equipment, logistic support and forces. Large gap between resources needed and low resources provided and allocated demoralize the troops. More tasks with less resources lead to failure, frustration and demoralisation. Without operational capacity none of the strategies can be implemented. Urgent need is to explicate what needs to be done.

Capacity gap can be decided by calculating what is available and reducing it from the minimum required resources. Current needs forecasting and projecting can give a picture of capacity gap. It should be calculated initially for police stations and districts and then for the entire state. Minimum capacity requirement should be calculated which will help in saving resources. By using the law of averages, assessment for different organisations and for the entire country can be made. It will help in regional revitalisation of security and also revitalisation of national security. However, one-size-fits-all approach should not be applied in all cases.

Capacity Building

Limited resource causes a precarious position. Capacity building is a very slow and cumbersome process. It should have both human resource and material resources. Talent shortage at field level causes tremendous problems. Trained officers constitute the most vitally essential human resource in anti-Naxal operations, and the only one that under no circumstances can be improvised or extemporised. Leaders need to devote 40 percent of time and emotional energy to select, appraise and develop people. Minimum threshold of provisions should be considered first. Prioritize functions critical to the survival of the state. Low priority needs can be deferred. Addressing the range of urgent needs is essential.

Focus should be both on short term and long term needs, and also on high priority needs. Urgent operational requirements arise from the identification of previously un-provisioned and emergency gaps. Mobilisation should start early because gestation period for human resources and other resources for procurement are very high. The rational assessment of operational priorities has to be complemented by an emphasis on quality. Innovation is an incredibly effective tool in countering extremist situations. Provision should be there to procure newly innovated appropriate technology. "Build a little, test a little and field test products" principle should be adhered. Misguided decisions about resources can waste public resources. Again there should be planning for sustaining capabilities of security force during continuous operations in such high intensity situations.

Extraordinary Problems Need Extraordinary Resources

The security force has to fight on many fronts some very difficult battles. The problem has become a national problem. Extraordinary problems need extraordinary human and material resources. Punjab is a proven case. Punjab had human resource of security forces at 12:1 i.e. 12 security force per extremist. In international situations in Greece and Malaysia it was 15:1, i.e., 15 security persons per extremist, whereas in Naxal infested region, the ratio of security forces to Naxalites in many regions is 1:3, in some it is 1:5; i.e. one person of security force operates against 3 to 5 Naxalites. In combat, force is an objective reality in action. Therefore there is a great need for operational capacity. In order to make current interventions and initiatives more effective, operational capacity requirement should be realistic.

Conclusion

Inadequate resources in difficult circumstances become dangerous. Appropriateness is based on evaluation of alternatives. Only with the help of adequate resources can TINA (there is no alternative) situations be converted into

TATA (there are thousand alternatives) situations. No nation deprives its security force of material resources or moral support, so also ours. But, the crux of the problem is to quantify operational capacity requirements. Now the time has come for experts to use their brains and make serious rational assessments of operational capacity requirements to fight LWE, keeping in mind the operational goal and operational challenges. The decision makers must appreciate the realities and remain sensitive to the needs. They should recognize the problem, prioritise appropriately, and mobilize effectively. The shape-deter-respond construct can help in manipulating the strategic environment in favour of government strength and preferences and against Naxal weaknesses.

Conflict situations aggravate due to a critical gap. We should learn from the Chinese debacle of 1962. Without fundamentally overhauling requirements it will be unfair to be judgmental about outcomes. Sometimes security forces face power failure due to lack of resources. It is high time they should forget zero budget projects and minimum resources theory. A scattergun approach may not achieve the critical mass necessary. A fragmented approach may have the unintended consequences of weakening the security forces and governmental capacity. Massive commitment of resources is a vital element of any good strategy. Today, if the country spends a few billion rupees on operational capacity requirements, definitely it will save trillions tomorrow and solve the dangerous state of affairs.

NOTES

1. Naxalite Document.
2. Generations of Warfare: 1st generation warfare is force against force, power against power. 2nd generation warfare speaks about firepower on target. Third generation warfare speaks about Blitzkrieg or lightning Warfare: Fourth generation warfare is asymmetrical warfare unconventional power against unanticipated targets.
3. Peoples March July 2000. Defeat the First Offensive War of the Central Government.

4. Napolean D. Valeriano and Charles T.R. Bohannan, Counter-Guerrilla Operations, The Philippine Experience, Pentagon Press, New Delhi (2008), p. 44.
5. Capacity matrix of states: In May 2000 Naxals prepared the capacity matrix of DK means Dandakaranaya Zonal Committee area which consists of areas of Chhattisgarh, NT means NorthTelengana area. It had many other parameters. They prepared it with a view to conduct SWOT analysis of security force.

7

Combat Stories from the Field

Life and combat is never formulaic. Combat occurs and subsides; but life continues and stories of life and combat continue. In combat, the past conspires to shape the present and future. The battles of Panipat remind us that some places and some stratagems are repeated in combat. Past incidents condition many engagements many times. However, the scale and scope of combat stories vary wildly. Combat narratives provide a study of the dynamics and dimensions of combat with myriad patterns and designs of offensive and defensive operations.

A number of operations have been conducted against LWE in the battlegrounds of hinterland India i.e. various guerrilla zones and red-resistance regions in various phases by security forces. The Naxalites also have conducted a number of tactical offensive campaigns, raids, action team operations and mine warfare. These engagements merit a brief overview and, to make it interesting, the narrative as better to be presented as combat stories. These incidents deceptively resemble celluloid fiction because of the shock they create with surprise achieved through speedy and violent actions. It facilitates the provision of an analytical framework to deduce general principles and postulations, which can be applied to operational situations.

In this analytical framework there are some critical combat stories of success achieved by the security forces. The failures and near-miss situations experienced by the security forces are also discussed in order to provide pictures beyond the clichés and platitudes of regular operations against irregulars. The rich repository of combat stories and anecdotes of inspiration, aspiration, desperation, and prudence will help the security forces to draw relevant lessons and help navigate their way in combat. They would also enable the common people to understand the difficulties and deprivations and messiness of combat. People can, thus, realize how the security forces move from the impossible to the possible, from the jaws of death to the crown of victory, and sometimes from a position of comfort to a situation of death.

Stories of combat are numerous. Many are familiar, yet people want to hear them. Therefore, an effort is being made to present the overlooked and underappreciated factors of combat narrative, in a brief manner. The stories are different, varying in scope, scale, tone, tenor, intensity and subtlety. Basically they are sequential, short explanatory accounts of events and human actions, and what really happened. Every incident impels a discerning analyst to dig deeply and develop ideographic accounts. Effort has been to for not allow the complexity of the incident to obfuscate matters.

Police Post Attack

The Naxals have used tactical imagination in attacking police posts in various States. Sometimes they have conducted multiple attacks, sometime they have used deception and sometimes they have exploited the security weaknesses. There are some instances where the Naxals have had to make exhausting retreats. A few cases are narrated to present the scenario of attacks on police stations and posts vividly.

PS Tarlaguda (1998). Located at the Andhra Pradesh border, near the river Godavari, the police station was attacked from 19.00 hours till 01.30 hours in three successive waves by 66 Naxalites armed with AK-47, SLRs, .303 Rifles, G.F. Rifle and grenades. The Naxals made announcements through a microphone calling for the surrender of the police. However, the police personnel did not surrender and fought bravely and intelligently. They recovered the dead bodies of one divisional committee secretary, one DCM, one squad commander and two other members. They also seized two AK-47, three .303 Rifles and a huge cache of ammunition, including grenades. Effective firing by one section of CAF and 10 members of the police station staff yielded results. Effective firing, immediate reaction, and not falling into the trap of the Naxalites call to surrender arms helped to achieve victory.

PS Chhuria (1999). The Naxalites came in a Maruti van and other vehicles and attacked the police station located in Rajnandgaon district. The SHOs response saved the situation. He broke open the *malkhana* lock by firing a shot from his pistol and took away the weapons. Along with two other policemen, including the sentry, he fired at the Naxalites who were unable to blast landmines but engaged in a fire fight. Reinforcements from other police stations reached the spot quickly, in spite of Naxalites' roadblocks, which further caused panic among the Naxalites who carried the injured and dead, and fled.

Bedre (2002). Bedre is a police stations located at the border of Maharashtra in the forest region. The Naxalites had surveyed this one police station whose maximum number of staff had turned to be alcoholic. Five days before the incident, on the basis of intelligence input, the alcoholic members were shifted and fresh personnel were stationed at Bedre, who were put through a rehearsal. The Naxalites attacked the police station with automatic weapons and grenades and shouted, 'how come you policemen are not drunk tonight'. The police party gave a befitting reply by firing automatic weapons and 2" mortars. The Naxalites had to undertake a punishing retreat leaving two dead bodies.

Geedam (2003). Geedam is a roadside police station

located on National Highway 16. After blocking roads and disconnecting electricity, about 150 Naxalites approached the police station from three sides. On being challenged by the police station sentry they replied that they are policemen from Bijapur district. They entered the police station, shot dead the sentry, looted and then blew up the police station building.

Dhaudai (2005). The Dhaudai incident is a tactical and operational masterpiece against numerically and superior armed Naxalites. Dhoudai is a platoon post of district Narainpur. On 17 May 2005 at around 23.30 hours, the Naxalites consisting of two companies, ten local guerrilla squads and forty militia members (total about 300 strength) with four LMGs, few rocket launchers, 122 automatic and semi automatic rifles, and grenades attacked the post of the Chhattisgarh Armed Force. Naxalites documents mentioned that they had, in the assault group, four sentry capturing groups, three assault groups for capturing the camp, two groups for capturing the kitchen and other rooms. In the support group they had one diversion group, two other groups, one artillery team, two demolition teams, two relay teams, two groups for dummy raids on the nearby police station and police posts and four ambush parties to block reinforcements and one reserve group with a medical team. An extensive in situ rehearsal to confront the raid was organised by the IG himself. On the night of the raid, the entire platoon fought bravely using grenades, LMGs and SLRs effectively. They even replaced the injured sentries tactically. The Naxalites blasted an anti-landmine vehicle carrying reinforcements en route. The route to the post was blocked at 72 places by boulders, logs of wood and at few places by landmines. Police reinforcements cleared the road and reached after 12 hours. A helicopter was used to shift the injured policemen. The Naxalites suffered a punishing defeat. They lost their military chief and other four members. Timely intelligence, good rehearsal, brave execution of plan and effective firing, accomplished the mission.

Murkinar (2006). Murkinar is a temporary platoon post in Bijapur district. On the fateful morning, the Naxalites boarded a private bus whose passengers were asked to alight. The Naxals arranged a LMG post with sand bags on the top of the bus and reached Murkinar. At that time, the in-charge of the post along with staff were doing *shramdan* to repair the defences of the. There was only one sentry posted on the rooftop bunker of the building with one LMG. No sooner did the bus stop at the post the Naxalites started rapid fire from the LMG and other automatics. The LMG group engaged the sentry and in the meantime the irregulars rushed into the post, massacred the unarmed police party and looted away weapons. The post had no fencing, the lone sentry was unable to hold on for long and the unarmed police party were sitting ducks for the raiding parties. Had the *shramdan* personnel been armed they could have given some resistance. The defenses around the post did not have depth and as there was no layer of fencing, it became easy for Naxalites to rush in and loot weapons.

Ranibodli (2007). On the night of the attack, around 02.00 hours, about 500 to 600 Naxalites including three military companies, eight LOS and few militia platoons attacked the camp with LMGs, GF rifles and Molotov cocktails. The Naxalites engaged the sentries and police party in a gun battle. They put small ladders against the perimeter wall, and used it as a sentry post. Bigger ladders against trees were used as LMG posts. They lobbed petrol bombs, grenades and also sprayed petrol and set fire to the barracks. In the gun battle, the policemen were shot down and Naxalites also suffered six losses. The Naxalites blocked all approach roads by cutting trees, putting stop parties and land mining the roads. From the premises of the camp 560 empties were found. The walls of the building and bunkers had about 900 bullet marks. Reinforcements reached at 06.00 hours and found that even beneath dead bodies, the Naxalites had put 29 I.E.D.s, which had to be defused by bomb disposal squads; reinforcement made hit pursuit of Naxalites engaged them in gun battle and killed one Naxalite in encounter next day. The attack provided hard lessons, which enabled other police posts to face the onslaught of Naxalites' offensives.

Lessons Learnt from Police Post Attacks

- During any raid, the Naxalites are ready to take casualties. Effective use of area weapons, grenades and automatics can deter them.
- Contingency plan to intercept fleeing Naxalites is essential.
- Proper sentry posts with clear arc of fire are needed at each post.
- Sentries must operate on a 'buddy system'.
- Constant alertness and instant readiness of force must be maintained. This can be done through perimeter vigilance, proper task distribution, proper rehearsal and good discipline.
- One third of the force at remote areas must do guarding at any point of time. During an attack, the entire force must take up pre-determined positions. Odd time security must be carefully maintained.
- Immediate action drill with emphasis on proper warning system, arms carrying technique, reloading drill, rapid firing practice must be hammered into the minds of the force.
- The force must rehearse automatic reaction keeping in view various situations like arson, deception, and injuries to the sentries.
- Every month proper security review by supervisory officers must be carried out.

Wanton Destruction of Infrastructure by Naxalites

Not only do the Naxalites attack police posts, but also they vandalise and destroy infrastructure wantonly. Sometimes they damage or destroy the infrastructure like roads, bridges, railway lines, railway stations, forest guest houses, hospitals, and school buildings, hostels with the intention to damage the state machinery, show their strength and sometimes as diversionary tactics. Sometimes they give the excuse that due to the deployment of troops in these buildings they are damaging these structures. But ground realities shows that in 90s, and even in the early 70s they have extensively damaged infrastructures. Damaging infrastructure is one important tactics of MLM which Naxalites used for achieving their objectives.

Naxalites' Action Team Attack

A dozen action-team incidents by Naxalites have occurred in Bastar region. In one instance, the SHO of Police Station Pamed was killed only one hundred metres away from police station on a weekly market day by a Naxalite action-team hitting him on the neck with an axe. In another instance, two sentries performing helipad security duty were hacked to death by an action-team who also took away their rifles. A police patrolling party intercepted them 10 kilometres away on a jungle track but due to inaccurate firing were unable to get success.

In another incident, an action-team member of the PLGA spotted a weak constable and snatched his rifle from him. Another constable in civvies, who was purchasing vegetables, snatched the rifle back from the Naxalite. Before other members of the action-team could attack him, he shot dead the Naxalite in self defence and saved the situation. In a number of incidents Naxalite action-teams have killed informers and policemen in markets. They survey the habits, and movement of the target and the area. The action-team carries concealed small firearms, or a sword or axe, have a getaway motorcycle or sometimes they flee on foot. They shoot at their target point blank range or from a very close quarter and then flee. They select soft targets, survey their quarry thoroughly and then hit. Target hardening, inculcating self-defence, as well as access control can help in preventing action-team attacks.

Landmine Blasts and Ambushes by Naxalites

The maximum number of casualties suffered by the security force has been caused by landmine blasts and ambushes. Along with increased sophistication in landmines blasts, the Naxalites have improved their mine warfare. Now, they are using claymore mines, directional mines and pressure mines. During the 90s, every year there used to be a dozen of incidents, one or two of which were fatal. Since 2004 the average landmine blasts incidents per annum has increased exponentially to more than one hundred, out of which two or three are fatal. The amount of explosive used in the landmines is also increasing; some even weigh up to 85 kilogram's. In one incident during March 2005, a convoy of the security forces went ahead of the road opening party. The Naxalites blasted six landmines at one go but the vehicles halted only a few feet before the blasts. The Naxalites, through I-com radio sets, listen in to security force communication. On the basis of information gained, about the movement of security forces, they lay landmines and ambushes on roads. Ambush is the most intense form of combat and it is the most effective way to conduct counter insurgency operations.[1]

Madanwada Multiple Ambush of Superintendent of Police Rajnandgaon and his Teams by the Naxals (2009). On 12 July 2009 the Naxals laid an ambush for the Superintendent of Police (SP) of Rajnandgaon and his team after killing two CAF Jawans, at Madanwada post. The SP had received information about an injury to the driver of his escort vehicle at around 10.00 hours, near village Kohoka, 12 kilometres from the police station at Manpur. The SP and his team returned to organize medical help to the injured. In the meantime, the Naxals had killed the members of motorcycle party in the same ambush. Presuming the situation to be one of hit and run tactics, the SP assumed that, after killing the policemen and looting their weapons the Naxals would have left the scene, they started evacuating the injured and dead bodies. In the meantime the re-positioned and re-grouped Naxalites again ambushed the police party. The Naxalites felled trees and blasted off the road by a huge land mine, thus blocking the black top road from both sides, and started firing at the police party. The SP and the police personnel fought bravely, but succumbed to bullets of Naxalites. Subsequently, the Naxalites set off another land mine and killed 2 policemen of the reinforcement party. Two military companies of Naxalites along with four LOS of Naxalites, (total about 200) participated in this action involving multiple ambushes. They had dug up a BSNL tunnel to a depth of 5 feet deep to arrange standing firing position for their party. The undergrowth near the spot in the rainy season provided sufficient concealment to the ambush party. (The BSNL tunnel was only 25 yards from the main road). The road was so good that the vehicles could move at a speed of 80 to 100 kilometres per hour.

Tadmetla Incident (2010). On 6 April 2010, at about 04.00 hours one company of the security force reached near the village of Tadmetla in district Dantewada where it had camped on previous day for a long-duration operation. The Naxalites encircled the company from all sides and started firing at first light. The company fought desperately but the terrain favoured the Naxalites who later ambushed the reinforcement parties also and blasted one anti-landmine vehicle. The reinforcement parties finally reached the spot around 08.30 hours after breaking several ambushes and saved 7 policemen. Two companies of Naxals, two platoons of LGS and 50 local militia (total about 250 armed Naxalites) participated in the ambushes. 76 CPMF personnel lost their lives and 7 personnel were injured. 9 Naxalites were also killed including 2 section commanders and about a dozen were injured.

Lessons Learnt from Various Ambushes

- Naxals use the tactics of hit-hide-hit. They lure the security forces into traps; using small teams to disturb and large teams to annihilate.
- Line of communication to posts should be secured. The movement of the security forces must be tactical, and they must avoid rushing to the spot of danger.
- ROP should be placed before any force movement.
- BSNL tunnel has been used by Naxals for concealment and firing position.
- Motorcycle convoy drill needs improvement and practice with a scope for riposte.

- Causality evacuation drill has to be practiced taking into consideration the factor of enemy sniper and rapid fire.
- Inter-group communication and signals must be used during force movement.
- Reconnaissance and proper rehearsal are essential to counter the element of surprise.
- Ambush breaking drill, in various terrain conditions, must be rehearsed.
- Officers must be very careful about the use of informers.
- The operational and tactical environment must be properly studied by commanders.
- Each security force has to strengthen the section. Without this the conduct of manoeuvre cannot be done. Proper manoeuvres will help in countering the Naxals.
- Battle drills have to be perfected.
- Ground commanders and the security force must have focus on the terrain and enemy.
- The force should neither miss targets of Naxalites nor offer themselves as targets to Naxalites.
- The security force should improve its capability to use guns, grenades and ground.
- The company's deployed in anti-Naxal operations should improve their reconnaissance, scout, and manoeuvre capability.
- Besides training they need expert teams to draw relevant lessons and rectifying errors.

Use of Booby Traps

Now-a-days Naxalites are using IEDs with anti-handling mechanisms. When the policemen retrieves it and handles it then the device blasts; it results in death of persons gathered near the booby trap. In February 2007, (Fundri P.S. Bhairamgarh) the Assistant Commandant of 9th Naga Battalion and staff retrieved a landmine and while fiddling the device it blasted causing the death of 4 security personnel including the Assistant Commandant and 3 civilians. In another incident in March 2007 one SPO was killed due to mishandling of an IED.

Encounters

The quantum of encounters between the security forces and the Naxalites has increased over the years. In 2006, a company of security forces were marching, with an informer, in jungle terrain. Even after reaching the designated spot, the security forces did not have faith on the informer. At that point of time two scout constables between themselves decided on a bait to prove is firing capability by firing a shot at a mango on a nearby tree. No sooner did the constable shoot at the mango, the hidden Naxalites fired on the police party. In that encounter one Naxalite was killed and his dead body recovered.

In an encounter at Halainar, the Naxalites used abusive language against the police. When the company commander stood up and replied, he was shot at. In several instances police parties used to fire beyond a distance of 300 metres causing the Naxalites to disperse rather than pin them down. On number of occasions security forces have three or four encounters within a day. Retrieving the dead bodies of Naxalites while facing encounters and then crossing difficult terrain becomes a major problem.

Study of the military literature reveals an interesting insight that security forces are more worried about friendly fire rather than fire from the enemy. Fire and move techniques and proper manoeuvrability have to be imbibed in the security force as only intelligent pursuit of enemy can result in success.

On some occasions security forces have fallen prey to ruses and deception by the Naxalites. In the Seetapur encounter (in 1999 in Abuzmarh) the police party located a small group of Naxalites taking bath in a stream in hilly terrain near the Naxal camp. Some policemen tried to come closer to identify the target. In the meantime, the Naxal sentry alerted the Naxals taking bath by firing one round at the police party from a distance. The female and male Naxalites ran away in their birthday suits. The policemen kept staring instead of shooting, and the Naxals fled away. In another incident, a few Naxalites in the jungle showed themselves for a few seconds and then disappeared, thereby luring the security force to pursue them carelessly and, in the process, they fell into a trap (Tarmetla PS, Jagargunda 2007, Partapur 2004, PS Pakhanjur).

Cordon and Search Operations

Cordon and search operations do not yield much result because the security forces do not generally rehearse and practice this operation and the deployment pattern adopted is porous. One company force carried out a cordon of village Akabera in Abuzmarh in 2007 April where 60 Naxals were camping. But the cordon was so porous that Naxals observed one point, fired heavily at that point, broke the cordon and moved out. In this operation one Havildar was killed and also one Naxal.

In another situation, in February 2005, one platoon of the security forces had an encounter with the Naxals in the Jungle of Basaguda Police Station of Bijapur district. The police party had noticed that about six Naxals entering a village and cordoned off the village. While the cordon operation was underway, suddenly one young man came out from a house, ran and jumped into a pond. In reaction, the entire cordon party rushed towards the pond. Taking advantage of the break in the cordon, the Naxals fled away.

Jail Breaks and Escape from Police Custody

Naxalites think jailbreaks give them a sense of invincibility. They have conducted many jailbreaks starting from the days of 1971. Some of the jailbreaks have been organised from inside and some from outside. In January 1971, CPIML prisoners carried out a jail break from Kurseong jail near Darjeeling. On 21 February 1971, 11 top cadres of CPIML escaped from Siliguri central jail. On 2 November 1974, ten extremist under-trial prisoners escaped from the Central Jail, Bankipur, Patna (Bihar) at 10.00 hours through a conservancy passage. One of the escapees had earlier been arrested for aiding and abetting an unsuccessful jailbreak attempt in the Muzaffarpur jail on the night of 30-31 July 1974. CCMS Nishit Bhattacharjee and Azizul Haque with 40 other Naxalites escaped from Presidency jail Calcutta on 24 February1976. On 10 November 1979, 10 under trial Naxals escaped from the Central jail Bannipar near Patna, in Bihar. One of them had earlier attempted to break out from jail in Muzzafarpur. Prominent Naxal leader Ter Master and six other Naxalites escaped from Coochbehar jail after assaulting the warden on 16 May 1985. Three Naxalite cadres committed jail breaks in Jagdalpur district jail on 26.6.1989 and fled away. Besides the above jail breaks Jahanabad and Dantewada jail breaks are very important. There are number of near miss situations of jail break by Naxalites. In one jail break the jail inmates used a gate as ladder by leaning it against the wall, then climbing it and jumping to the other side. On another incident the jail inmates used two rifles thrown into the jail premises and fled away from jail. In another incident the jail inmates overpowered the sentries and fled away. Appalsuri, Kondapalli escaped from police custody. In 2009 central military commission secretary Sunirmal escaped from police custody.

Kidnappings: Like other terrorist and extremist organisations, Naxalites have also resorted to kidnappings. On some occasions they had killed the victims and on others they had released the victims. Whenever they had killed the victims it had created an adverse public opinion against them. In 2009 Naxals kidnapped one special branch inspector of Jharkhand and beheaded the officer. In Odisha, Bihar and also in Chhattisgarh naxals have committed dozens of kidnapping some cases they had killed the victims and in some cases they have released the victims after few days of keeping him in their hideouts. The most important is the kidnapping of 8 senior I.A.S. officers.

Kidnapping of 8 Senior Officials by CPI-ML (P.W.G.) Group (1987)

During the raids on December 15, 1987, the police arrested 8 prominent cadres of CPI-ML (PWG) and recovered substantial amounts of cash, five DBBL guns, four 8mm rifles, two revolvers, one 32 pistols, two country made weapons and 34 grenades in East Godavari and Visakhapatnam districts. These accused were remanded to judicial custody and lodged in Rajamundry Jail. On December 27, 1987, the CPI-ML (PWG) waylaid, kidnapped and held to hostages eight senior Government officials, including the Principal Secretary to the Govt. Of Andhra Pradesh and the Collector of East Godavari District demanding release of eight of its cadres who had been arrested by the police earlier.

The officials were touring the area to review progress in various projects and to meet tribals after attending a seminar organised by the Collector of East Godavari district to felicitate Shri S.R. Sankaranan, Principal Secretary and another official for services rendered in connection with upliftment of tribals. While the officers were proceeding from Pulimetta to Gurthedu, they were surrounded by 12 members (9 male, 3 female) of Sabar and Tandava Dalams led by K. Sudhakar Reddy @ Krishna and Janardan who kidnapped the officials including 1) S.R. Sankaranan, IAS, and Principal Secy. To AP Govt. 2) MVPL Shastri, Collector, East Godavari Distt. 3) T.Vijayakumar, PO. ITDA, 4) Manohar Prasad, Coffee Board, Vizag and ex-PO. Rampachodavaram 5) Subramaniam, IAS, Sub-Collector, Khammam District 6) S. Narshimahara Rao, IAS, Asstt. Collector, Kakinada 7) J. Radha, IAS, Joint Collector, East Godavari District 8) Smt. Puspa Thampi, Sub-Collector, Rajamundry.

After Separating the IAS and non-IAS officials, the extremists demanded the Collector, East Godavari to release the prisoners from judicial custody. When the collector expressed his inability the extremists compelled him to write a letter to the Supdt. of Police, East Godavari putting forward these demands. The letter was carried by Puspa and Radha who were released for this purpose. In addition, Sri Sankaranan briefed the two officers to send word to late Shri Kannabhiran (PUCL and APCLC activist) and Shri Yugandhar (IAS Officer) at

Hyderabad to negotiate for their release. Accordingly Shri Yugandhar and Kannabhiran proceeded to Rajamundry en route to the place of occurrence. In the mean time, the State Government ordered the release of eight prisoners and they were escorted to the area. The extremists, however, sent word through Collector Shri Shastri that no policemen should accompany the prisoners and they should be brought to Gurthedu Tribal School with Shri Yugandhar and Kannabhiran. Accordingly the prisoners were taken in 3 jeeps to Gurthedu and after they were let off, the hostages came to the school in batches on Dec. 29, 1987 after having been detained for 54 hours. The drama ended.

Operational Dimension Due to Use of SPOs

The significance of local police officers in the anti-LWE campaigns have been acknowledged in many countries like Malaya, Philippines and Peru. In many states of India also Special Police Officers added a new dimension to anti-LWE operations. On one hand, Special Police Officers have helped to face the growing security commitments due to intensified Naxalites attacks. Additionally, it has hit at the line of communication, recruitment and intelligence of Naxalites. Knowledge of local intelligence and terrain of SPOs have helped security forces operationally to a great extent.

Operational Lessons with Tactical Bearing

Anti-Naxalite operations have succeeded to some extent in whittling down the Naxalite's fighting potential. Nevertheless, observation and analysis of various operations reveals that many operations suffer from tactical errors, which range from ineffective firing, to low combat capability. On number of occasions, when the opportunity of battle is available to the force their fighting power is so numbed by physical exhaustion that they are unable to translate the opportune moment into bigger success. Sometimes, the security forces conduct operations with reluctance, and some operations are conducted perfunctorily, in a desultory manner. Some local commanders do not possess a tactical understanding of the nuances of operations. It is essential that lessons with tactical bearing have to be mastered as tactical soundness in operations translates into the ability to conduct operations effectively. Victory in combat cannot be achieved without drawing relevant tactical lessons. Some of the tactical lessons are:

- Most of the operations are at section, platoon and company level. Therefore, the tactical performance of junior officers needs to be improved considerably.
- Operational effectiveness of the force can be improved by battle inoculation, tactical exercises without troops, situational training exercises, emergency deployment readiness exercises and other training interventions.
- There is a need for inclusion of subordinates as partners, in thought and action.
- Logistics continues to be an Achilles' heel. It has to be improved and a combat support service has to be created.
- Counter attacks have to be well anticipated.
- Reconnaissance patrols are needed to counter the element of surprise.
- Reconnaissance, rehearsal, and proper debriefing are essential for effective operations.
- Security forces should be aware of and avoid Naxalites' physical traps or human rights traps.
- The ability to deploy and sustain combat forces in interior remote places needs to be augmented. Extensive operational bases have to be created, subject to availability of force.
- The security forces have to pay due regard to security. Local security audit has to be conducted regularly.

Operational Lessons with Strategic Bearing

If tactics is right but strategy is wrong few battles may be won.

Ultimately victory goes to the side, which has adopted a correct strategy. It is essential to learn operational lessons which have a strategic bearing. Some of them are:

- Naxalites are graduating from guerrilla warfare to mobile warfare. Their war preparation, mobilisation of manpower, and resources is of a very high order and their tempo and lethality of operations is increasing. Any hesitation to deploy more force, and the right type of force and resources will be costly.
- Hotspots should be saturated with security force deployment and operational activity.
- Security forces must dominate areas which have an administrative vacuum.
- The operational environment is considerably more difficult than might appear from distance.
- Since Naxalites are determined to use force, there is no other way other than physically defeating them through operations.
- Operations need more punch and staying power on the ground. This can be done by increasing the level of force employed, logistic support and modern equipments.

Conclusion

The above-mentioned stories reveal that incidents have an operational, tactical and strategic impact in combat. Each story represents an attempt to pull together disparate strands which nonetheless have enough in common to be usefully read as one way in which people seek to make sense of the past. Explaining the present helps to envision and enable a future. Such stories are little more than descriptions of day-to-day combat. They allow people to imagine the state of the conflict and could facilitate its transformation. They also help to lay the groundwork to inform, guide, warn and motivate. They inform us about behaviour in combat, and how the security forces should carry out their tasks. Taken together, the stories represent a compendium of everyday combat flashes, and actual actions. They are infused into ground reality and provide people with understanding and vision about what really happened. They also provide critical pieces of the puzzle without which any understanding of incidents is incomplete. They are life experiences and a rich repository of the experiences of combatants. These stories throw a ray of hope and possibilities in dark areas of combat by highlighting the issues and dynamics at play, and can help to determine the range of possibilities in combat. Finally, they serve a heuristic purpose.

The incidents have been condensed to little more than a critical essence to capture a larger meaning and transmit a message. These define a moment that does not end and highlight the combat trend and tempo against LWE which has a possibility of escalation in the near future. Therefore, the urgent need of the day is better and more coordinated and sophisticated operational policies and practices. The hard lessons of operations, if internalised at various levels, will help in reducing operational deficiencies, enhance operational readiness and efficiency, effectiveness and combat power. Lastly, it will not be an exaggeration to say that a proper understanding of the geometry of operations and calculus of combat will improve effective action, maintain operational tempo, generate momentum and, ultimately, yield success.

NOTE

1. Lt. Col. Joshua Potter, USA, Commander Gary Stubblefield, USN (Ret.), and Mark Monday, Ambush (A Professional's Guide to Preparing & Preventing Ambushes. Lancer Publishers & Distributors, Paladin Press, New Delhi, 2011.

8

Police Post Protection in Naxal Infested Areas

The ferocity, frequency and intensity of attacks by the Naxalites on police posts in Andhra Pradesh, Madhya Pradesh, Chhattisgarh, Odisha, Bihar, West Bengal, Jharkhand and Maharashtra has increased by the day. The looting of the district armouries of Nayagarh and Koraput stresses the gravity of the situation. Like other extremist actions the attacks on police posts occur for several reasons, (a) the value sought is overwhelmingly important; (b) the cost of effort is low; and (c) the probability of success is high. The Naxalites not only attack out of any anticipation of reward or out of desperation, but also in response to an opportunity or threat.

Ideological Justification for Attacks on Police Posts

The ideological justification for the attacks on the police was provided by Charu Mazumdar in an article "Avenge the Heroic Martyrs" which appeared in the magazine 'Liberation' of September-December 1970. It was stated that the police in the country have been trained by foreigners, and had always been used as "an instrument for murdering and suppressing the people". He even went to the extent of saying, "these (policemen) are not Indians; they are not of India and called upon the party workers to rouse the most intense hatred for all these cowards, imperialism's running dogs and assassins." Taking the cue from this concept, the present day ideologues of the Naxalites have also made a strategy to attack policemen as well as police stations. Till 2010, the Naxalites have attacked about one hundred police posts, killed more than 500 police personnel besides taking away about 2,000 weapons and a large quantity of ammunition in Orissa, Andhra Pradesh, Madhya Pradesh, Bihar, Chhattisgarh and West Bengal, though more than 80 percent of the attacks have been foiled. The strategy behind attacking police stations is four-fold: (1) demonstrating potency, (2) demoralizing the police force, (3) building Naxalites' armoury, and (4) dominating the area.

The Naxalites propagate that they have to build their armoury by snatching arms from policemen and police posts. They perceive that attacks on the police force and police posts causes demoralisation in the force. Thus, the security force would be preoccupied with defending their posts and would seldom go out on offensive patrolling. Also, because of the attacks on police posts, there would be a tendency to close down vulnerable police stations and police posts in remote areas. Thereby, the influence and dominance of the CPI Maoists will go on expanding in vulnerable areas. By the containment of the security forces in a large number of small posts, the number of aggressive operations that can be launched against the Naxalites is significantly reduced. Consequently, their support line, communications and logistics can be cut off. Lastly, the strategy of demonstrating potency through military initiative against police posts is designed in part to create the impression that Naxalism has momentum and will succeed. In addition to winning adherents for the movement, it boosts and sustains morale within Naxalite's organisations.

If we study the attack on police posts it is revealed that the Maoists do not consider translating their ideological goals into action until the possibility presents itself. The Naxalite attacks are determined by perceptions of incentive and opportunity. Such opportunity can stem from both, the vulnerability of a target and the opening up of opportunities. Once the Naxalites have identified a police post that is cut off or vulnerable, or a police station whose strength is depleted, and staffs are disorganised, then the Naxalites rehearse meticulously and at the earliest available opportunity strike. The strike can take various forms—it could be a sudden lightning attack, a large deliberate attack, or even probing or deceptive attacks. Their attacks are usually well rehearsed and carefully prepared.

In their sudden lightning attacks the Naxalites attempt to neutralize the sentries and give no chance to the remainder personnel to use their arms. If the chance of raising the alarm and warning is so low then the strength of resistance of a police post is almost halved. Generally, attacks occur at night and are launched silently.

Huge Contingent Attack

Whenever possible and whenever the Naxalites think they have superiority of numbers, they will quickly go to the attack. Generally, after completing military training camps, the joint strength of 4 or 5 *dalams* attack a police station. These types of attack are generally noisy ones. They normally encircle the police station from all directions, initially. Then they launch a heavy fire grenade attack accompanied by announcements on a microphone calling for the post to surrender; then they try to capture the police station. They try to overpower the police personnel physically and psychologically.

Deceptive Attack

On several occasions, the Naxalites have used deception and innovation in attacks on police posts. They have used human shields, animal shields, and mobile bunkers to stultify the defence mechanism of police stations. On a few occasions they have used improvised incendiary and smoke bombs and even pesticide guns to spray petrol and set fire to the post while attacking.

Passive Defences

The threat posed to police posts by Naxalites is tremendous. Security of police stations is of paramount importance for the policemen as well as for the Government. Their proper defence is essential to meet any threat. The defence must be so organised that it forcefully prevents the enemy from attaining its physical objectives. This can be done if the following steps are taken:

1. Fortification of police stations:
   (a) Barbed wire fencing of the police station is essential.
   (b) Wherever possible *panjis* may be put.
   (c) Bunkers at ground level and rooftop need to be constructed.
   (d) All post must have a perimeter of mutually supporting bunkers and at least three dominating strong points. All positions should be connected by trenches.
2. Strengthening of police stations:
   (a) The critical minimum strength of a police station must be maintained throughout the year.
   (b) Arms/ammunition of the police station should be adequately supplied, so that the firepower of the police station can be matched to the firepower of the PWG
3. Equipping the police station:
   (a) A good wireless set with scrambler system and fax must be provided so that communication with other units can be maintained.
   (b) Sirens should be provided for sounding alarm.
   (c) Binoculars, periscopes and night vision devices must be provided for sentries.
   (d) Electric generators and other electrical equipment must be provided for lighting.
   (e) Bulletproof jackets and helmets must be provided (at least 3 or 4) to the police stations.

Tactical Offensive Responses

Defence of police stations involves not only passive defensive measures—guarding potential objects of attack or erecting barriers—but a tactically offensive response. In a life and death struggle, tactical offensive responses tend to be instinctive, although a modicum of foresight in visualizing and making provision for certain instantaneous contingencies prior to close combat are possible. Any tactical offensive response has three ingredients: (1) Instant readiness of the force; (2) Immediate action; and (3) Automatic reaction.

Constant Alertness and Instant Readiness of the Force. Instant readiness implies:

- Perimeter vigilance. Having a wired perimeter does not provide safety unless it is under constant observation.
- Effective night observation capability is essential.
- Security arrangements must be known to all personnel within a post.
- Duties within the post must be evenly distributed; and rest also organised.
- Odd-hour security is properly maintained.
- A high all-round standard of discipline is maintained.

Immediate Action. Immediate action drills aim to defeat the enemy by instant and decisive offensive action is the essence of successful defence. Pausing for thought in a killing zone is not a recipe for survival. Immediate action drills consist of:

1. Warning the force.
2. Carrying arms and rushing to defensive positions.
3. Shooting back fast and rapidly.
4. Reloading drill must be done promptly.
5. Use of maximum strength against the enemy's weak points.

Automatic Reaction. The police post attack by the Naxalites is a supremely demanding situation for policemen. They should be able to defend themselves through automatic reaction which has to be drilled into them constantly and thoroughly. Personnel may suffer some loss in the initial burst of enemy fire, but they can turn the tables if they know how to react. They should remember that the enemy is backing on them remaining in the killing zone or running away. By running towards them, the policemen will disconcert them, put them off balance and make it more difficult for them to bring their weapons to bear, particularly automatic weapons. An automatic reaction at the situation of hostages, deception, casualties, injuries, use of fire and smoke bombs must be discussed within the force thread bare, and specific duties must be assigned to each and every police staff, and contingency plans must be prepared.

Contingency Plan. The contingency plan must deal with: (1) Command and control of the situation, (2) Communication, (3) Fire control, (4) First-aid, (5) reinforcement, and (6) Follow-up.

Command and Control. The police station attack is a supremely demanding situation. The in charge of the police station and second in charge and the other ranks must know how to command and control the situation.

Communication. Communication between the force of the said police station under attack and nearby police stations and senior officers is most essential.

Fire Control. The firing should be rapid, but simultaneously economy of expenditure of ammunition should be kept in mind because the attack may come in successive waves.

First-Aid. First-aid of the injured persons is necessary.

Reinforcements. Reinforcements should be so planned that they reach quickly to the affected police station. The reinforcements may approach from all avenues to the police post.

Follow-Up

The Naxalites are expert in making a clean break from any engagement and melting into the jungle. Although they are likely to move mostly on foot, they may use road transport or boats as well. They often use small stay-behind parties of single guns or snipers, possibly protected by mines or booby traps, which will force follow-up forces to deploy and thereby delay their advance, thus allowing the main body of guerrillas to escape. The follow-up must be planned taking into consideration the routes of escape, strength of the guerrillas, their hideouts, etc.

An effective defence can prevent a police post attack. The attackers must be made to feel that they are opposing an irresistible force, which is closing inexorably around them. If the policemen can effectively counter the surprise of Naxalites, through innovation, deception and availability of opportunities, then their attacks can be easily countered. The superiority of the police force in quality achieved through training, the superiority of arms, ammunition and equipment, superiority of tactics will help in deterrence. Finally, when the costs of attack are high and opportunities for violence closed, the chances of any attack on police posts will be reduced.

9

Maniac Mine Blasts

The mine is weapon of choice of Naxalites. It is a low cost device with tremendous psychological impact. Mine warfare has become an integral part of the Naxalites' tactical arsenal in guerrilla zones and theatres. The Naxals are turning the conflict theatres into veritable minefields. Mines are used to facilitate ambushes, impede operations, and act as counter–mobility devices. The objective of using mines is to kill and lower the morale of security force. Mines are also used by the Naxalites to protect their camps and hideouts. Mines are the cheapest option for the Naxals and costliest option for the security forces.

Naxalites are laying landmines in some portion of National Highways – 221, 16, some State Highways and interior roads of Naxal-infested states. In 1986-87, the Naxals learned mine warfare techniques from some renegade LTTE in Bastar and first they blasted the first landmine in 1989. In the 90s, the Naxalites used 2 or 3 mines annually in any theatre. In the millennium decade mine warfare has started on a large scale. Every year more than 200 mines are blasted and about same number are being recovered annually. Widespread use of mines started towards the end of 1990 in Andhra Pradesh and early

2000 in Bastar and Jharkhand. From 2004 onwards the mine blasts per annum has crossed more than 100 in Bastar and recoveries have also increased drastically. In most of the theatres, LWE use a variety of mines. However, extensive uses of mines have been noticed after the formation of the PGA. Now Naxals have also trained the local militia to lay mines and kill security forces.

Naxals use mines and IEDs; IEDs may be defined as an explosive or incendiary device build in an improvised manner, incorporating destructive, lethal, noxious, pyrotechnic or incendiary chemicals. It is intended to destroy, disfigure, distract and otherwise terrorize its victims and create a sense of insecurity among a population. The only limitations on the design and makeup of an IED are the limitations of the builder.

Type of Mines Used by Naxals

Naxalites use mostly home-made mines. Milk can mines are the mines mostly used by Naxals in various guerrilla zones. The tactical use of mines by Naxals has enhanced, so also their demand for mines. Now, they are fabricating mines in their production units which are run by their Central technical committee in deep jungles and in some cities not affected with the Naxal problem. They are using different types of mines e.g. landmines, claymore mines, pressure mines, radio-controlled mines, directional mines and booster of mines. Boosted mines or explosive devices are stacked one on top of the other. Only the device buried deepest from the surface is fired. This reduces the probability of detection and it increases the force of the blast.

Use of Explosives and Other Items in IEDs

A number of explosives and chemicals e.g. ammonium nitrate, potassium chlorate, charcoal, sulphur, and a mixture of aluminium powder and oil are used in mines. An EXPLOSIVE is a mixture or chemical compound, which, when subjected to sufficient heat, shock, or friction, undergoes a sudden chemical change with the liberation of energy and the development of high gas pressure. Explosives are classified as high or low explosives, depending upon the rate at which this reaction takes place. High explosive: Detonate instantaneously—PETN, RDX, C4, Dynamite, Ammonium Nitrate. Low Explosive: Deflagrate slowly-Black Powder, Smokeless Powder; require confinement to be effective. Nitro glycerine ammonia nitrate, gelatines are used in improvised explosive devices (IEDs). The Naxals use about ten tons of explosives per annum. They are also trying local technology to crystallize explosives from fertilizer urea and from insecticides. During the past ten years the Naxals increased their looting/stealing of explosives. They use milk containers, plastic buckets, iron pipes, telephone poles, iron flower pots, pressure cookers, gas cylinders and sometimes specially fabricated iron cabinets. In the incident of the attack against the then Chief Minister of Andhra Pradesh (Alipiri 2003), the Naxals used iron dumb bells weighing five kilograms as pellets which damaged the bullet proof vehicle and injured its occupants. In 2004, Naxals had used directional mines in 2004 in Vizag.

Locations where Naxals Lay Mines

Naxals have shown brutal ingenuity in their mine laying skills. They survey the target and lay mines accordingly. Sometimes, after conducting raids, they mine the place for the reinforcement parties. They have laid mines even beneath dead bodies. They have attached mines with hand pumps; laid mines within school buildings and *panchayat* buildings, beneath bridges, approach road to bridges and on tree tops. In some incidents they have made a hole by drilling at a slant from the side of a road and laid mines leaving no sign on the road. Some arrested Naxals mentioned that, any point where vehicles can be slowed is a suitable place for laying mines. Naxals have laid mines on helipads, foot patrolling tracks, near tree trunks and also in market places. They have also used mines in clusters. In some places they have even used up to one dozen mines and blasted those in one go. The Naxals use V-shaped bamboos or some landmark to align the location of a hidden mine with

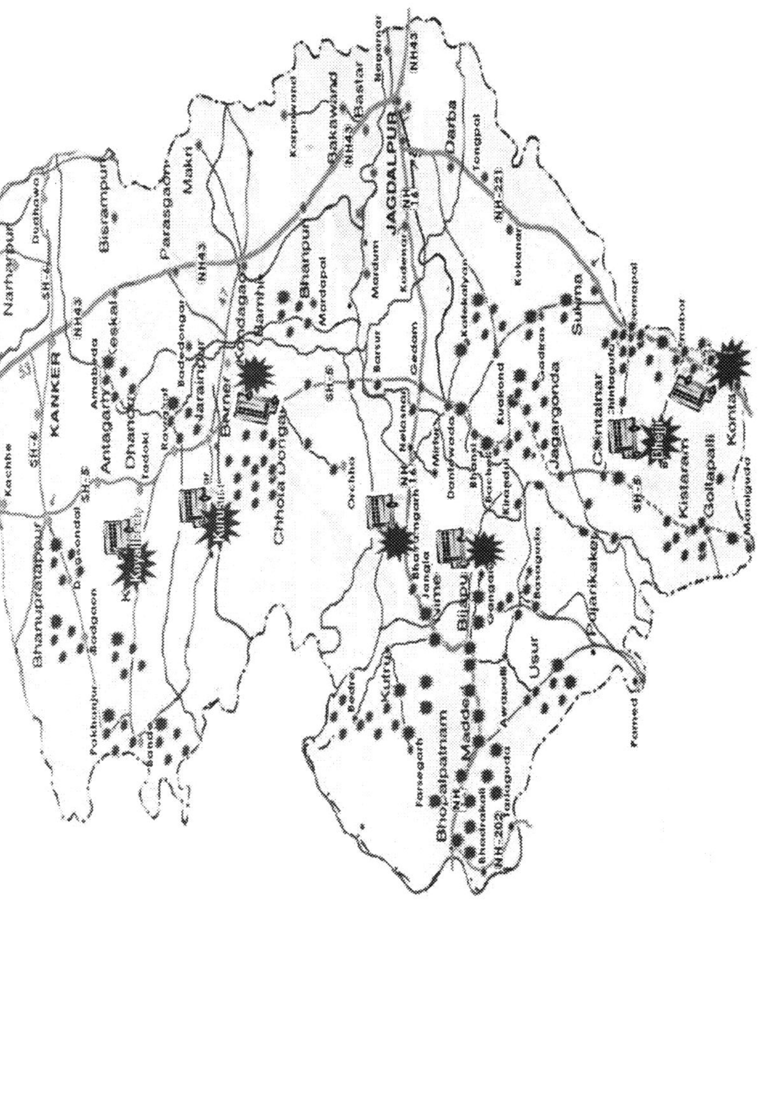

Map 1 : Mines Blast and Recovered

Map 2: Land Mine Blasts 2004 to 2010

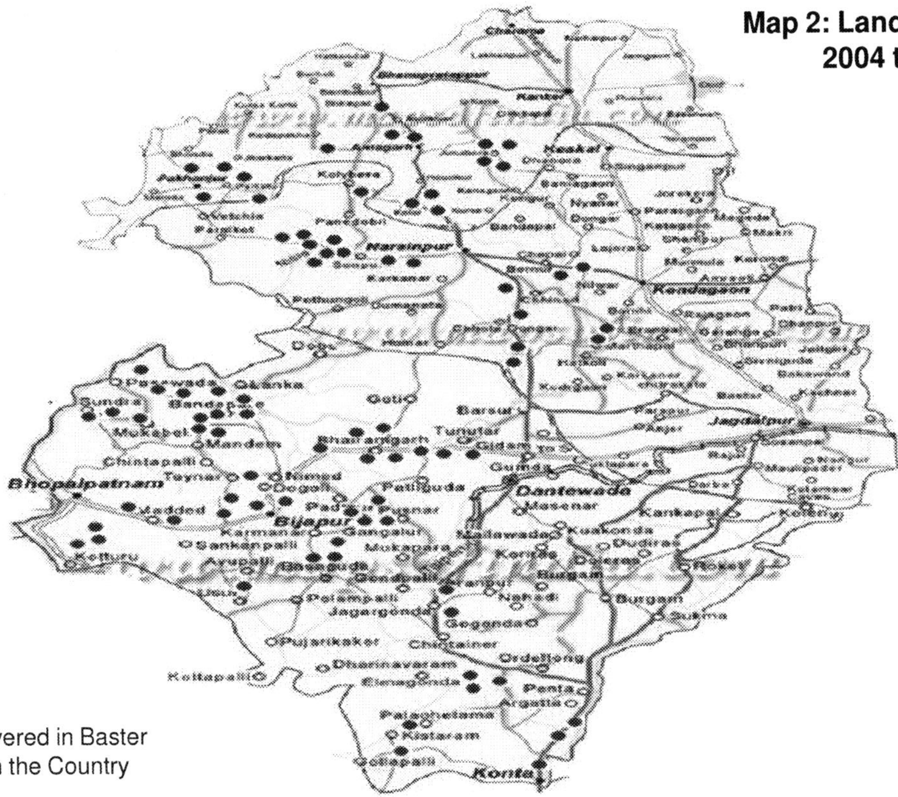

925 Blasts
1007 Mines Recovered in Baster
Highest Number in the Country

a moving vehicle. Naxals use camera flash to detonate mines and in many occasions they have used radio devices to detonate the device. Naxals also use pull and pressure switch, improvised exploder dynamo for detonating IEDs.

Countering Mines

Mines are by far the most hazardous and difficult to clear. Correct identification of the mine is a critical factor in preventing casualties. Neutralisation and disarming drills are needed. Detection and disposal of IED require, trained staff for searching and disposal, trained dogs for searching, and devices for locating them. Dogs have been successfully used to detect mines. Even mongrels, after due training, have successfully located mines on many occasions. Well trained special teams with proper tools kit consisting of Non-linear junction disruptors, rope, pully can conduct de-mining exercises. The security forces every year recovered hundreds of landmines, claymore mines. Sometimes some people use improvised device like log of wood to roll for detonating pressure mines. This device to remove or destroy IED (DIED) is also very useful.

Mine Protected Vehicle

In 1997, during a coordination meeting at Bhubaneshwar, the author showed pictures of Rattel and Buffel (anti-landmine vehicle) to the then Director General of Police, Andhra Pradesh who took up their production with the Indian Ordnance Factory Board. As a result, the ordnance factory at Medak developed the first mine protected vehicle in 1999. Now India is exporting mine protected vehicles to many countries. The vehicle has saved many lives. The Naxals have even used more than hundred kilograms of explosives, at times, to blast mine protected vehicles. The mine protected vehicle had been thrown up to a height of thirty feet, as a result of a mine blast, even then the personnel inside remained alive. However; there is plenty of scope to further improve the vehicle.

Hidden Killers Kill and Maim Civilians

Mines are nuisance and hidden killers. They have killed and maimed many innocent civilians. They are indiscriminate weapons harming combatants and civilians alike. Anti-personnel mines pose the greatest long term risk to humans and animals since they are typically designed to be triggered by any movement or pressure of only a few kilograms. Anti-personnel mines are littered by the Naxals on main roads, footpaths and near water pumps. Civilian deaths and injuries due to landmines in Bastar, Bihar, and Jharkhand have increased over the years.

Conclusion

Placing minefields without marking and recording them for later removal is a war crime under the Protocol of the Convention of certain conventional weapons, which is an annexure to the Geneva Convention. Two urgent things are required (1) create public opinion against this atrocious act of laying mines and causing murder of innocent public and (2) improving solutions. To-days' counter IED solutions will be unworkable tomorrow. Therefore, continuous up gradation of detection systems and detection technology is required.

10

Intensity and Impact Analysis of Left-Wing Extremism

Left Wing Extremist (LWE) activities are the outcome of neglect. Neglect of a politico-administrative system can consist of the failure to understand the socio-economic and political limitations and aspirations relevant in any area, the failure to scrutinize the activities of organised bands and the non-functioning of the local administration. Such neglect can be the fault of policymakers and decision-makers owing to calculated ambiguity, lack of understanding or lack of information and distance from the centre of power. Both Government and society of a country have to pay the price for such neglect and the nation has to bear the brunt as a result. The growing menace of left-wing extremism in Central India had surprised the decision-makers. Unexpected-uprisings by any extremist group overpower law-enforcement agencies, state governments are shocked, local administration is crippled and the public is put under duress to support the insurgents or extremists. With the growth of underground organisations and their activity, their sphere of influence increases and thereby undermines the influence, authority and legitimacy of law-enforcement agencies and the administration, virtually causing the collapse of state power. Ignoring ground realities feeds delusions that can lead to short-term catastrophe and long term defeat. Evil comes in many guises. Unfortunately, at the early stage of infestation nobody recognizes the problem and by the late stage the problem becomes incurable.

The above situation of sudden manifestation and virulent infestation of insurgency automatically raises some classic questions:

1. Was there any early warning of LWE?
2. What are the present dimensions of LWE?
3. How effective are government counter-measures?
4. How effective are the security forces?
5. Which areas need governmental attention?

These pertinent questions can only be answered by analysis. Analysis of LWE is tedious, difficult and complicated but analysis of these questions highlights two important underlying concepts: (1) the early warning system; and (2) measuring the effectiveness of government counter-measures.

Early Warning

The early warning system should not be a case of 'crying wolf' but it must be objective: it must be based on ground reality. Early warning system is essential to signal the onset of LWE in any area. On the basis of their signals the security system of any government will be able to assess a new or developing threat to achieve an accurate perspective on the problem. As a result the government may not have to wait for the problem to worsen and it can anticipate difficulties and initiate pre-emptive and preventive measures.

Measuring the Effectiveness of Counter-measures

Measuring the effectiveness of counter-measures is essential because the onset of insurgency starts a protracted conflict in which, by its very nature, the trend is very difficult to discern. Even a non-fighting security force can pretend that they are fighting and a non-performing administration pretends they are administering. So there is a need to achieve a framework for measuring the involvement of administration. On the basis of evaluating the effectiveness of counter-measures the amount of ground any government is losing or gaining can be determining. This will help the government to evolve an appropriate response by utilizing its resources and capabilities to the best advantage.

Monitoring

The signalling of early warning and evaluation of the counter-measures can only be done by monitoring. This is a process by which the socioeconomic and politico-administrative conditions of target areas are analysed in terms of their conflict propensity and it can be either remote or engaged. Engaged monitoring has precedence over remote monitoring because it can project the exact ground developments. Proper monitoring can reveal and explain the phenomena and in order to analyse these a framework is required which consists of two broad concepts:

1. Impact analysis; and
2. Intensity analysis.

Impact analysis has two models: (1) impact of the activities of extremists; and (2) impact of activity of the government/administration. By applying a number of different variables, these models can show the areas of onset and intensification of conflict. They are also used to measure the transition from collapsed administration to establishing governmental control. The variables used are the plausible parameters, which indicate different phenomena of LWE. They are duly vetted and properly selected by examining their contextual significance with reference to insurgency and have been given particular weightage according to their relative strength and relative capability for influencing LWE positively or negatively.

Conceptual Problems

The models have two underlying conceptual problems: (1) accuracy and appropriateness of the weightage given to different variables; and (2) sufficiency of the variables used in the models. In order to overcome both these conceptual problems, two steps were taken:

(1) The views of about 200 IPS and some IAS officers with regard to the accuracy of the weighting of different variables were considered and then the weightings of different variables fixed. A questionnaire was circulated among the officers where they were asked to indicate the weighting to be given to each variable and to indicate whether any variables in the list should be either kept or discarded. Thus their views regarding the appropriateness of the variable were also taken into consideration and some variables included accordingly.

(2) The variables were selected from study of the types of LWE/insurgent activity and security force activity that occurred in 1998 and 1999 in Jane's insurgency magazine.[1] The types of incidents occurring frequently and those resulting in either aggravating insurgency situations or ameliorating them particularly were taken into consideration.

The models need to be applied initially to a police station. After computing for police stations and finding the level of intensity and impact of insurgency in their vicinity, the level of intensity for the district, state and other areas can then be calculated. The equations for impact analysis and intensity analysis are put up separately for each model.

Impact Analysis

Impact analysis consists of two models:

(1) Impact of the activity of LWE; and
(2) Impact of the activity of administration.

The sum of the weightings of all the variables for each model of impact analysis is 100 but the weightings of any variable will be counted the same irrespective of the number of its occurrences in any particular area. The actual level of impact of insurgent activity or the activity of administration in any area depends on the occurrence of different variables in that particular area. It is the sum of the weightings of these different variables that indicates the actual level, whether it is low, medium, high or extremely high.

Now the models will be discussed separately and serially. First of all the impact of insurgent activity will be discussed. Insurgents initially have to mobilise the people and prepare their base. Only after mobilising people and organising themselves can they be offensive. Insurgents initially commit illegal but seemingly innocuous activities which are not immediately recognised by the administration but are actual harbingers of difficult times.

Impact of LWE Activity

The impact of insurgent activity is reflected in six broad activities: (1) mass mobilisation, (2) recruitment of cadres, (3) controlling the public, (4) collection of funds, (5) paralysing administration, and (6) conducting parallel government. After gaining public support through exploiting the accumulated social tensions, the insurgents start the economy of extortion and politics of collusion that ultimately lead to social paralysis and administrative breakdown.

The tactics followed by insurgents to mobilise the masses are multifarious. Generally, they seek a following by attending public meetings, *bandh* (closure of schools, shops, public offices, etc., through intimidation) and anti-government allies, as well as by non-celebration of national festivals and oll boycotts. They also try to recruit dropouts from schools nd colleges, persons displaced by any governmental projects nd other vulnerable sections of society. Collection of funds s done by extortion from contractors, government servants, raders, transporters and industrialists. Extremists then start iphoning public money from local government bodies and lifferent departments through intimidation and also levy llegal taxes on the rural public and rural markets. Sometimes he insurgents collect money through the smuggling of ontraband goods.

Support from the press, providing a flow of information o insurgent groups, further helps to improve their tranglehold over the public. After achieving all these, LWE gradually try to eclipse the administration by infiltrating lifferent offices at the local level through persuasion or terror. Those who do not yield face their wrath. As a result, mass ibsenteeism or exodus of government servants occurs. It further precipitates the issue by showing the inability of the idministration to conduct developmental activities in the interior or local areas. When the administration becomes paralysed, the insurgents start a parallel government by conducting *praja* courts (kangaroo courts conducted by insurgents in front of a crowd), illegal taxation and many other similar activities. They control the public through both intelligence and terror and their dictates, such as no activity after late night, create a fear-psychosis among the public. Activities such as the forcible grabbing of land and its redistribution through the *praja* courts terrify the public into mute acceptance.

These scenarios of LWE onset can be portrayed through the model in Figure 1. After quantifying the impact of LWE activity by placing it in the following grade, the real level of impact of LWE can be graded accordingly:

Figure 1: Impact of LWE Activity

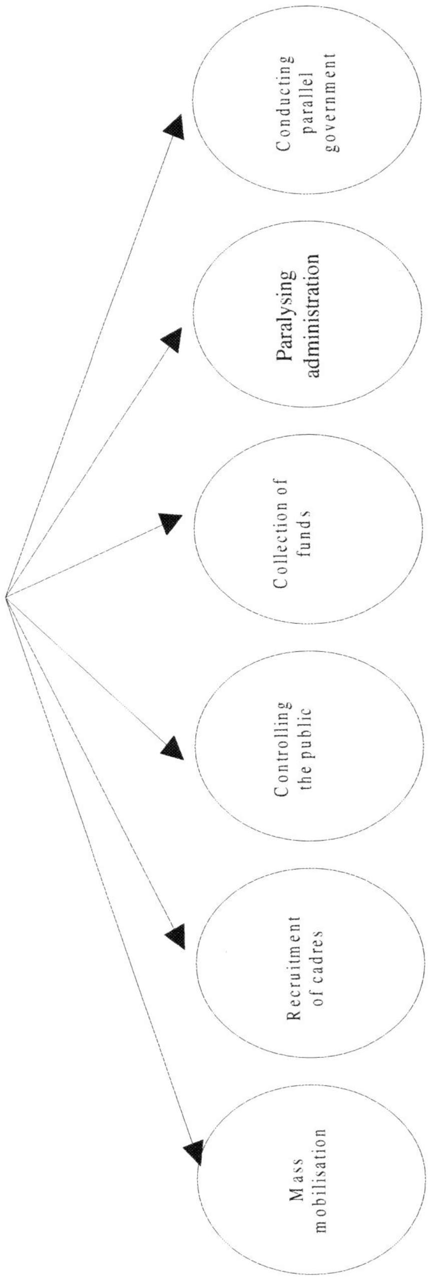

Activity	Score
Non celebration of national festivals	10
Poll boycott	10
Inability of administration to conduct developmental activities	10
Exodus of government servants, mass unwillingness, resulting in mass absenteeism	10
Infiltration into government services	10
Recruitment into insurgent groups	7
No activity after late light	6
Siphoning of public money	5
Extortion	5
Contraband smuggling	5
Praja courts	5
Forcible grabbing of land and its redistribution	5
Siphoning of public money	4
Support from press	4
Anti-govt rallies; public meetings; *bandhs*	4
	100

Note: For the purpose of impact analysis the weightings will be counted the same irrespective of the number of occurrences of the particular variables in any particular area. (PS = police station)

Impact of insurgency in PS area = Sum of the weighting of all variables that occurred in any PS area

$$\text{Impact of insurgency in any district} = \frac{\text{Sum of the impact of all affected PSs}}{\text{No. of PSs in any district}}$$

$$\text{Impact of insurgency in any state} = \frac{\text{Sum of the impact of all affected districts}}{\text{No. of districts in any state}}$$

Low grade	=	25
Medium grade	=	25 to 50
High grade	=	50 to 75
Extremely high grade	=	75 to 100

Impact of Administration

The insurgents subvert by out-administering the area. The impact of insurgent activities described above reveals the area and degree of out-administration. So, to combat insurgents, it is the first and foremost duty of the government to restore local administration in the affected areas (see Figure 2). The influence the government lost by default has to be regained by serious effort.

Celebration of national festivals and the arrangement of free and fair elections will exhibit the image of functional administration. Ensuring proper utilisation of public money at local government and department levels will prove that administration has been restored. Proper management of forest produce, solving land disputes, solving water scarcity and electricity problems in rural districts, establishing health camps and streamlining the functioning of schools and hostels, as well as constructing interior roads, will bring village development, directly and indirectly. These efforts to develop the villages and rural areas will help regain public support for the government.

LWE generally take advantage of the inaccessibility and remoteness of rural areas to set up their bases and then spread to other places. So construction of roads and bridges and maintenance of good communications can reduce the spread of insurgency in any area. If the environment of political unrest, social turmoil and economic justice is taken care of then insurgency will lose much of its breeding ground. Providing health facilities and efficient public distribution systems, streamlining the administration of schools, solving land disputes and the problems of displaced persons of any governmental projects specifically will all help to achieve this end.

Lastly, LWE has to be countered through propaganda for this is one area to which it is susceptible. The banning of LWE gives a big jolt, as has been proved in the case of the PWG (People's War Group) in Andhra Pradesh and other places.

Public awareness schemes, public grievance redressal camps, publicity about surrender and rehabilitation and of appeals to family members to join the mainstream are all techniques through which the weakness of the insurgents can be exposed and the strong points of the government propagated. This will help in gaining public support.

Figure 2: Impact of Administration

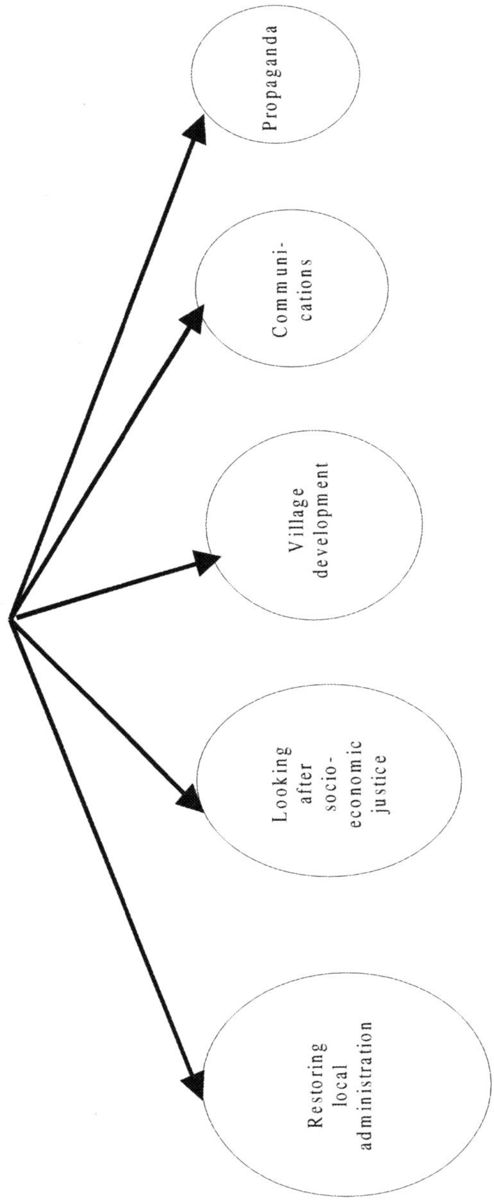

Activity	Score
Conducting free and fair elections/celebration of national festivals peacefully	10
Ensuring proper utilisation of money at local govt. dept level	10
Defusing developmental booby traps	10
Construction of new roads/bridges and maintenance of old roads/bridges	10
Efficient PDS system in interior districts	10
Proper management of forest produce	5
Rehabilitation of victims of insurgents	5
Solving land disputes	3
Ensuring fair wage	3
Solving the water scarcity/electricity problem in interior locations	3
Streamlining the functioning of schools and hostels.	3
Health camps in interior locations	3
Banning of insurgents	10
Publicity of wrong doings of insurgents	3
Public awareness schemes of achievements of govt. and benefits of different schemes	3
Public grievances redressal camps	3
Publicity of surrender and rehabilitation	3
Public appeals from family members to join the mainstream.	3
	100

Without the above the war against the insurgents cannot be won. All the above aspects demonstrate that the administration can achieve a strong impact through performance and publicity to win hearts and minds.

All the variables except 'Defusing developmental booby traps' are self-explanatory. The variable developmental booby trap denotes the fact that any huge developmental project, whether hydroelectricity or national park, displaces poor people. The disadvantaged people are wooed by the LWE to join its bandwagon.

By applying the same simple equation of summing up the weightage of the variables that occurred in any area, the level of impact of administration in any PS area can be calculated and by computing the average of the affected police stations the level in any district can be determined. Again the level of impact of administration in any state can be shown by applying the same equation of impact of insurgent activity.

Intensity Analysis

Intensity analysis consists of two models: (1) intensity of insurgent activity (see Figure 3); and (2) intensity of security forces activity (see Figure 4). These two models are slightly different from the models of impact analysis in that, whereas the sum of the weightings of all the variables is 100, the actual weightings of any PS area are calculated by finding the weighting of each variable.

Figure 3: Intensity of LWE Activity

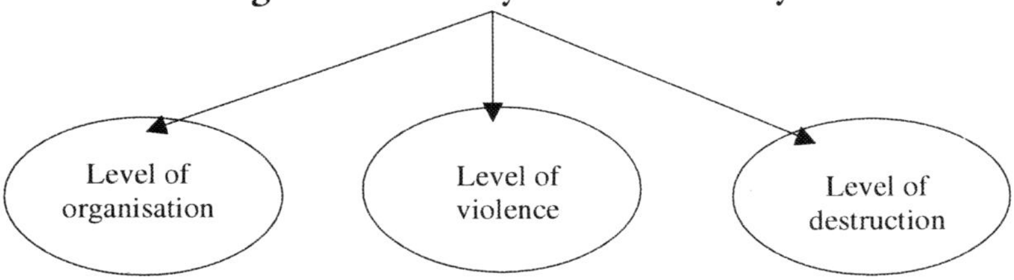

Intensity analysis **LWE/Naxalite activities in any PS area**	**Weighting**
Suicidal squad attacks	12
Car bomb attacks/rocket fire	12
Public massacre	12
Number of *dalam* gangs/bands	10
Attack on PS/SF posts/govt. installations	10
Use of landmines/ambush/grenade attacks and bombs	6
Killing of SF/political leaders/informers	6
Organising military camps	5
Kidnapping of govt. officials/public	5
Wounding of SF/govt. staff/public	4
Snatching of weapons from SF/police/public	4
Looting of banks/treasuries/markets	4
Snatching wireless sets	4
Encounters/exchange of fire	3
Destruction of public property	3
	100

Figure 4: Impact of Security Forces Activity

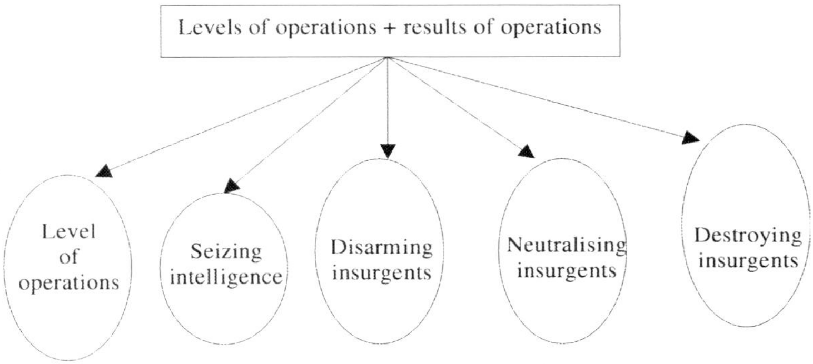

Intensity analysis of SF activity Police/SF activity in any PS area	Weighting
Raid on insurgent HQ/rear of insurgent HQ	15
Insurgents killed	10
Raid on insurgent training camps	8
Important documents seized	8
Ambush	7
Arms ammunitions seized	6
Explosives recovered	6
Insurgents apprehended	5
Arrest of supplier and harbourer	5
Insurgents surrendered	5
Dumps recovered	5
Sting/CAT operations	4
Encounters	4
Nullifying insurgent attack	4
Area domination	4
Mopping up operations	4
	100

After a consideration of their positions, if any, are being made, the intensity of insurgent activity is then dependent on three factors:

(1) The level of organisation of insurgents. This may include the formation of armed squads and organisation of military training camps in any area for the insurgents.

(2) The level of violence of LWE. This denotes the pattern of violence, which may be directed against security forces, public, government officials and police informers; for example it may be directed at the capture of weapons and wireless sets or collection of money. The methods of perpetrating crime, such as car bomb attacks or rocket fire, also reveal the magnitude of the violence.

(3) The level of destruction. This applies to destruction of both public and private property.

The intensity of insurgent activity is calculated by the following mathematical formulae:

Weighting of each variable = Weighting of each variable × No. of incidents of concerned variable

Intensity of LWE in PS area = Sum total of the weightings of all variables in any PS area

$$\text{Intensity of LWE activity in any district} = \frac{\text{Sum total of weightings of all affected police stations}}{\text{Total No. of PS in any district}}$$

$$\text{Intensity of LWE activity in any state} = \frac{\text{Sum total of weightings of all affected districts}}{\text{Total No. of districts in any state}}$$

Government uses security forces to counter insurgency in any area. As more forces are deployed, huge resources are utilised to modernize the force. But often, the security forces indulge in tokenism or pseudo-fighting. Since fighting insurgency is a very difficult and risky task, most of the commanders believe in temporizing, in other words, the commanders and security forces become more tenure-oriented and mark time. Most of the time they do not engage with the insurgents and as a result the insurgents grow in strength and attack the security forces, inflicting serious casualties on them. So there is a need to find out whether the security forces are really fighting the insurgents or not, which can be achieved by using the model of intensity of security forces activity. This can be gauged from the level of operations conducted by the security forces and the results of those operations accrued by the security forces.

The level of operations constitutes both offensive and defensive operations. These may take the form of raids on the rear of insurgent headquarters, ambushes, raids on training camps, sting operations, CAT operations, encounters, mopping-up operations, area domination and nullifying LWE. The results of these operations conducted by the security forces include collection of intelligence, disarming insurgents, neutralizing insurgents, destroying their supply lines and destroying the LWE themselves.

By using the values of variables in the following mathematical equations, the impact of any security forces activity of any area can be quantified.

$$\text{Weighting of each variable} = \text{Weighting of particular variables} \times \text{No. of incidences of concerned variable}$$

$$\text{Impact of LWE in PS area} = \text{Sum of the weightings of all variables that occurred in any PS area}$$

$$\text{Impact of LWE in any district} = \frac{\text{Sum of the impact of all affected police stations}}{\text{Total No. of PS in any district}}$$

$$\text{Impact of LWE in any state} = \frac{\text{Sum of the impact of all affected districts}}{\text{Total No. of districts in any state}}$$

After quantifying the impact of security forces activity, the levels of SF activity can be graded as low (30), medium (30 to 60), high (60 to 100), and extremely high (above 100), as per the weightings of the area.

Again, this performance can also be mapped. The mapping of performance will highlight the regions where the security forces need to strengthen intensity of activity and the regions where the security forces have dominated the ground. Besides getting the overall picture about the activities of the whole SF deployed in any area, it can help in calculating the performance of different units deployed in any area by applying the same mathematical formula.

Weightage of each variable = Weightage of particular variables × No. of incidences

Intensity of activity of any particular SF unit: Sum total of all variables performed by SF unit concerned.

After finding out the performance of each unit, the performance of different units can be compared. The present performance of individual units can also be compared with past performance. In some areas security forces drawn from different organisations operate and this helps in calculating the performance of different forces objectively.

Different Hypotheses

These models of impact and analysis have validated the following hypotheses:

(1) Subversion of any area by LWE occurs more by out-administering the area.

(2) By calculating the impact of LWE in any area early symptoms of the onset of insurgency can be diagnosed. Incipient conflict and latent threats can be revealed.

(3) $$\frac{\text{Intensity of insurgent activity}}{\text{Intensity of SF activity}} > 1$$

The above equation reveals the upper hand of insurgents. It speaks eloquently about the dominance of LWE in any area.

$$\frac{\text{Intensity of LWE activity}}{\text{Intensity of SF activity}} < 1$$

This situation marks the trend for SF gaining ground.

(4) Impact of LWE activity + Intensity of LWE activity = Total scenario of LWE.

These hypotheses are testable. The level of LWE and the level of government counter-measures can be quantified by using this framework. If the data of any area is fed into the model then the impact and intensity analysis with regard to insurgency and with regard to counter-measures can be done reliably. So this framework of analysis makes good theoretical and methodological sense.

Conclusion

This framework of intensity and impact analysis highlights some important conclusions:

- The framework provides a system for timely evaluation and systematic analysis of LWE. It helps in the description of reality and as a basis for ready prescription of concrete political and administrative initiatives. These models caution the incumbent regime to defend itself with vigour, determination and skill.
- This model will help the government in gaining knowledge about what transpires early in an LWE. Because of the focus on incipient conflict and latent threats, the government can shed apathy and complacency, and move quickly to improve and extend its own administrative capability. As a result, the states can easily manage the causes and consequences of violence.
- The administration in LWE-infested areas is mostly paralysed, the degree of paralysis varying from area to area. In order to hide non-functioning, the administration pretends to administer. By using the model of impact of insurgent activity one can find the area that is out-administered.
- By using the model of impact of the activity of administration one can find the area that has been regained by the administration. It can also prove the effectiveness of counter-measures.
- The intensity of LWE activity reveals the pattern of violence they perpetrate. It reveals not only their tactics and targets but also their theatre of operations. These

can be graphically presented by adding them to area maps to help the security forces commanders plan their strategies and tactics accordingly.

- In a crisis scenario the government puts in many security organisations to fight insurgency. Since development audits of security forces and performance evaluation of the different units vis-à-vis the insurgency are not taking place rigorously, most of the units slip into inaction, with a tendency of marking tenure or showing tokenism. By applying the model of intensity of the activity of security forces, the proper performance evaluation of different units of different security organisations can be conducted. Pseudo-fighting, tokenism and inaction can be exposed; the forces can be properly deployed and utilised.
- Impact of the activity of administration and the intensity of the activities of security forces are complementary. Only the joint application of coercion, development and propaganda can counter LWE. Both the impact of administration activity and intensity of the security forces activities can fight LWE effectively.

In summary, the impact and intensity analyses can provide very good empirical evaluations. They can shed the greatest light on the initial onset and subsequent escalation of LWE, as well as the LWE propensity of any area and it makes credible and informative analyses. This model can possibly estimate government counter-measures. It can measure the administrative attentiveness and resilience of the administration and regime endurance. All these evaluations are highly illuminating for policy makers, so that the analysis also has interesting policy ramifications. This framework has the added advantage that it is easy to use and can be applied to any area; the interpretive procedures have the potential to generate conclusions, which can be useful for any tactics, planning any strategy or formulating any policy by the decision makers.

NOTE

1. Jane's Insurgency 1998, and 99.

11

A Model Action Plan for Maoist-Infested Regions

Action requires a plan; an action plan needs scenario planning. Scenario planning with conceptual elegance is essential for fighting left-wing extremism. Scenario planning and agenda setting shape the salient substance of action planning. The action plan is basically an agenda setter for system building, security building and force building. Therefore, a good action plan needs to be formulated with the objective of developing a system to fight the Maoist threat, contain it and ultimately eradicate its pernicious effects. With these objectives in mind, the anticipated and felt needs of the area, the police force and other branches of administration have to be conceptualised, strategized and encapsulated in the form of a Model Action Plan. The issue of proportion and imagination with regard to the overall system's requirements must be taken into consideration while shaping the action plan. The Model Action Plan has three broad aspects: (1) Policy; (2) Operations; and (3) Organisation.

Policy

The Maoists control the area they have infiltrated by violence and propaganda, using the administrative organisation that they set up in opposition to local government in the area. In interior areas they have thus destroyed the indigenous administrative and democratic fabric. To marginalise the Maoists and defeat their terrorist campaign and restore civic administration, a large-scale policy of redemption has to be carefully chalked out. Such a policy must have a correct and appropriate subset of policies. If the policies are correct then no amount of tactical errors will damage the ability to fight the battle successfully. If the policies are wrong, however, then, in spite of huge tactical advantages, it will still be defeated. In the context of the Maoist problem it can be said that in 90s many states did not have various policies of surrender, rehabilitation etc; as a result the induced setbacks had hampered anti-extremist operations to a large extent. Later on many States developed those policies. For the purpose of action planning the policies can be broadly divided into two categories:

1. Policies related to the police department and other security forces with direct bearing on the Maoist problem;
2. Policies related to other departments of government, as well as the police, with indirect but major bearing on the Maoist problem.

Policies related to the police department and other security forces with direct bearing on the Maoist problem. These address the effects of infiltration on security and provisions for dealing with the terrorists:

- Surrender/rehabilitation
- Response to problems such as Maoist kidnappings
- Incentives
- Propaganda
- Security
- Infiltration of Maoists into government departments

- Provision of magisterial powers to sub-divisional police officers (SDPOs)

Policies related to other departments of government and police with indirect but major bearing on the Maoist problem. These address the effects of infiltration on security and provisions for dealing with the terrorists:

- Vigilance action
- Transfer policy
- Village development
- Smooth running of schools, hostels and Balak Ashrams (forest area schools)
- Unemployment
- Road construction
- Social welfare
- Health
- Encroachment of government land
- Model village
- Clustering of government buildings
- Town planning in Maoist-infested area
- Public distribution system (PDS)
- Forest produce
- Monitor and review
- Restoration of civic administration.

The appropriate policies on all the above issues help in rejuvenating the systems. In many states some of these policies already exist; but in the states where the policies on above issues are not available should formulate policies immediately. These policies, thus, have to be closely tailored to the process of countering extremist activities in order to strengthen the local administration against them. Appropriate policies will enable a number of well-coordinated and well-synchronised actions on a number of fronts to redeem the situation.

Operations

Combat power comes from having a sound operational plan.

Well-laid out operational plans are required if the momentum of operations is to be achieved and maintained. Such a plan must have offensive and defensive components. The defensive component will comprise security arrangements for police stations, district police (DRP) lines, battalion HQs and district headquarters and sub-divisional headquarters, while the offensive component must have "clear and hold" and "search and smash" policies. Operational security must have prime importance while plans are being formulated.

The operational plan must take account of the complete tactical environment and situation. These will provide pictures of the extremists, terrain, topography and ground situation, and give an estimate of the situation, the scope and complexity of the problem. The operational plan must have a crystal-clear concept of the operation from start to finish. The brief skeleton of the operational plan has the following elements:

Objective of Operations. The outcome of any campaign hinges on the identification and maintenance of the objectives of the operation. The objectives therefore must be clearly defined, decisive and attainable.

Force Requirement. Area characteristics, task and enemy strength have a great bearing on the strength of force required in any area. The principle that "a good attack plan calls for gathering a strong force" should be closely followed while projecting force requirements for any operation.

Reconnaissance. Physical, photographic and aerial reconnaissance of the area of operations must be done as these are necessary to pinpoint strategic advantages and disadvantages for deploying forces as well as to monitor the movements of the terrorist forces and their proximity to resources and populations.

Deployment. The ability to deploy and sustain combat forces intelligently is absolutely crucial for effective battle. Proper deployment of forces in the right number, at strategic places, will increase the ability to take immediate advantage of whatever unforeseen operational opportunities arise.

Combat Support Service. Conducting operations against left-wing extremism implies waging a protracted war. In such a war operational forces require a number of support services for the essential replenishment of rations, water, arms, ammunition, batteries and petrol and oil (POL). Other important support services include medical aid, causality evacuation, post-mortem facilities and, crucially, transportation, communication, bomb disposal and intelligence collection.

Assault Plan. No plan ever survives an engagement intact but nevertheless the meticulous preparation of an assault plan gives security forces an edge over the enemy. Therefore, it must incorporate all the minute details of operation, including the different types of operations to be performed in any given area with the different stages clearly set out, and it must be both area-specific and task-specific.

De-induction plan. After achieving the objective the extra forces that were mobilised must be de-inducted. The de-induction plan must have a security element.

While discussing the elementary characteristics of operational plan here it is worthwhile to quote Mao's guidelines which are mentioned below:

> "A Commander's correct disposition stems from his correct decisions, his correct decisions stem from his judgements, and his correct judgements stem from a thorough and necessary reconnaissance and from pondering on and piecing together the data of various kinds gathered through reconnaissance. He applies all possible and necessary methods of reconnaissance, and ponders on the information gathered about the enemy's situation, discarding the dross and selecting the essential, eliminating the false and retaining the true, proceeding from one thing to another and from the outside to the inside: then, he takes the conditions on

his own side into account, and make a comparative study of both sides and their interrelations, thereby forming his judgements, making up his mind and working out his plans. Such is the complete process of knowing a situation which a military man goes through before he formulates a strategic plan, a campaign plan or a battle plan. But instead of doing this, a careless military man bases his military plans on his own wishful thinking, and hence his plans are fanciful and do not correspond with reality. A rash military man relaying solely upon enthusiasm is bound to be tricked by the enemy, or lured on by some superficial or partial aspect of the enemy's situation, or swayed by irresponsible suggestions from subordinates that are not based on real knowledge or deep insight, and so he runs his head against a brick wall, because he does not know or does not want to know that every military plan must be based on the necessary reconnaissance and on careful consideration of the enemy's situation, his own situation, and their interrelations.

The process of knowing a situation goes on not only before the formulation of a military plan but also after. In carrying out the plan from the moment it is put into effect to the end of the operation, there is another process of knowing the situation, namely, the process of practice. In the course of the process, it is necessary to examine anew whether the plan worked out in the preceding process corresponds with reality. If it does not, or does not fully, correspond with reality, then in the light of our new knowledge, it becomes necessary to form new judgements, make new decisions and change the original plan so as to meet the new decisions situation. The plan is partially changed completely. A rash man who does not understand the need for such alterations or is unwilling to make then, but who acts blindly, will inevitably run his head against a brick wall."[1]

Organisation

Operations cannot be sustained without sound organisation. Therefore, organisational planning has to be done beforehand to ensure that the organisation will equip itself as expected when finally its forces face the onslaught of Maoist infiltrators. Organisational planning consists of the following elements: (1) institutional; (2) manpower; (3) infrastructure; and (4) resources.

Institutional Planning. Institutional remedies should be formulated to confront the depredations of left-wing extremism because the Maoists have formed a network of organisations dedicated to extending their sphere of influence. Institutional reorganisation and rejuvenation of security forces have to be carried out to counter this growing network of labyrinthine, secret and divisive organisations through which left wing violence breaks down the institutional framework. There is an urgent need for institutions to be created which will form the framework for a system to fight the Maoist threat.

Intelligence Units. More intelligence and a selective force can together defeat the guerrillas. It is essential for a dedicated full fledged unit to be set up for collecting and collating intelligence. The unit must have well-trained personnel and the equipment to deal with "humint" and"techint".

Government Railway Police Units. Some of the important railway stations do not have government railway police (GRP) attached to them even though Maoist extremists use these major stations for transit purposes. It is vital that the government establish GRP stations at these key points on the railway network to discourage such usage by terrorist forces and weaken their mobility.

Commando Units. A coherent specialised fighting force of jungle fighters has to be raised to take the war to the Maoists on their own ground because it has been proved that hunter-killer teams gain much success against them. Crack counter-extremist units thus must be maintained in a high state of readiness to counter the terrorist threats.

Training Units. A jungle warfare training institute for the police is required to invest them with a new set of operational and survival techniques. A 'train hard and fight easy' dictum is the grassroots doctrine of counter-insurgency operations and jungle craft training is essential to fighting successfully. A well-equipped, properly manned, training institute with correctly designed curricula will train officers in tactics for countering guerrilla warfare waged by the Maoists.

Full-time Supervisory Officers for Operations. Each district must appoint a Deputy Superintendent of Police (Operations) for better management of anti-Maoist operations. It is vital for ensuring that operations are fully effective and continuous at all times of the year because, for most of the time, the SP of the district is kept busy with VIP duty and law and order problems, and he has to devote most of his time to dealing with conventional crime. A separate, dedicated officer is required for anti-Maoist operations because this is a very demanding task consisting of many sub-tasks, for example manpower planning, logistics, intelligence, communications and coordination with other forces, and intelligence collection. Again, in highly infiltrated areas a Deputy Inspector General must be assigned the task of overall operational management. These two posts definitely fulfil the wide range of operational responsibilities in the region.

More Compact Police Subdivisions. For ensuring policing, each subdivision should be compact. The range of control of each SDPO must be three to four police stations. Besides administrative work, much mandatory investigation work has to be done by the Deputy SP. The SDPOs must be entrusted with magisterial powers to maintain peace and enforce good behaviour among notorious characters.

Legal Units. Legal units have to be created at police headquarter level to deal with any court cases arising from security forces counter measures.

Establishment of New Police Stations. The roots of left wing extremism lie in the lack of effective state presence across large swathes of forested areas of the country. A number of police stations must therefore be established at strategic places.

The jurisdiction of each police station must extend in densely Maoist-affected areas to approximately 100 square kilometres in highly infiltrated areas; to 300 square kilometres in mildly infiltrated areas; and to a minimum of 400 square kilometres elsewhere. Today, in extremely infiltrated areas the jurisdiction of some police stations currently exceeds 500 square kilometres and in other areas each police station has a jurisdiction of more than 1,000 square kilometres.

Establishment of Cultural Troupes. Chetna Natya Mandli, the cultural wing of the Maoist' organisation, conducts mass propaganda in rural areas through dance and song. To counter this Maoist propaganda, security forces should have cultural troops recruited from among local people who, with police escort, can go to different villages where they will perform special cultural programmes designed to woo the masses.

Establishment of Police Medical Units in all the Districts. Medical services at some of the Maoist-infiltrated areas are very poor. Those policemen deployed in interior areas who are injured and sick are thus deprived of timely medical help. It is vital therefore for police medical units to be established.

Manpower Planning

The anti-Maoist operation is manpower-intensive. Many people with a wide range of different skills are required for conducting different tasks. Besides the range of duties, available space and the total strength of the Maoist forces have a great bearing on the size of manpower of any police force.

Most of the police stations have far less strength; even that of the DRP lines is inadequate. The police station is the basic unit necessary to fight anti-Maoist operations effectively. So the strength of the stations has to be increased to such a level that the station can both defend itself and launch small anti-extremist operations. Some of the highly Maoist infiltrated police stations have a police ratio of only 1-2-8 (sub-inspector, head constables and constables) which cannot withstand a Maoist attack. The police outposts in Maoist infested areas need to be upgraded to police stations and at a few strategic places temporary bases for security forces also have to be established. The strength of DRP lines of all the districts of the Maoist-infested region have to be upgraded.

In the recent past a few cases of infiltration of Maoists into the police force has been noticed. So this important aspect of manpower planning should not be lost sight of. A proper mixture of local people and outsiders has to be maintained and proper security vetting has to be carried out on a regular basis.

Extremist activities are generally the work of young men. The old and physically unfit men of the constabulary are no match for the young irregulars. So there should be some mechanism and policy to induct young blood into the police force in specifically Maoist-infested areas.

Infrastructure

Developing the infrastructure of an area is a high return investment. A well considered security infrastructure is the first line of defence as the infrastructure position that is precarious constrains the operational environment of the security forces. The security force without proper infrastructure is at risk exposing itself to LWE attacks and thus it devastates the morale of the security forces. The survivability of the security force depends to a large extent on the strength of building, fencing and *morchas* (sentry posts). The following infrastructure must therefore be developed in infested regions.

- Police station building
- Staff quarters and supervisory officers quarters
- Police hospitals
- Police school
- Firing range in each district
- Operations briefing room/sand model room at district and range HQs
- New police stations
- Barracks for force

- Fencing of police stations outposts, DRP lines
- Proper *morchas*/trenches
- Solar lighting of all police stations and all the DRP lines
- Provision of adequate toilets at police station level
- Counter insurgency training centre
- Obstacle course
- Construction of strategic roads.

Police hospitals, police schools, firing ranges, operations briefing room, sand model room and obstacle course must be developed in all district headquarters. Fencing of police station, DRP lines, with concertina fencing for a quarterguard and vulnerable police stations must be done. Proper tower *morchas* and underground *morchas*, trenches at police stations and DRP lines must be constructed to fortify these buildings so that these defences can absorb the huge attacks of Maoists. Strategic roads with police security must be built to facilitate development and control of the area.

Resources

Maoists are regularly upgrading their arms and ammunition so the police must look after their own equipment. Resources play a vital role in fighting efficiency, which depends entirely on both logistics and resources. The resources that are required can be divided under the following heads:

- Communication
- Surveillance
- Arms/ammunition
- Mules/vehicles/helicopters for transportation
- Equipment for photography
- Computer equipment
- Equipment for training purpose
- Recreational facilities
- Navigational systems
- Resources for medical and sanitation purpose
- Protective equipment
- Miscellaneous.

Communication. Every police station must have telephones and high-frequency links. In some of the stations which do not have a telephone, connection has to be via long-range cordless phones. The parties going out on operations have to carry satellite phones.

Surveillance. Police stations and police parties must have binoculars, night-vision devices, a hand-held thermal imaging system and stealth cameras.

Arms/ammunition. The police force must have firepower superior to that of the Maoists. They must have AK-47 assault rifles, MP 5 submachine guns, INSAS light machine guns and assault rifles (Indian small arms system), 2 inch/51 mm mortars, and AGLs (automatic grenade launchers). Old ammunition must be used only in training exercises and new ammunition during operations. Sometimes the Maoists have used a human shield strategy in an attack and this creates a dilemma for the police using maximum force. In these scenarios the police have to use non-lethal weapons, therefore the police party must have tracers, stun grenades, pepper-spray pellet guns and laser dazzlers.

Mules/vehicles/helicopters for transportation. Mobilisation of the force is the main problem when conducting operations. The police force must have means of transport, appropriate to various situations that range in type from helicopters to mules. Helicopters have extensive use in anti-Maoist operations and have also been used for reconnaissance, force deployment and casualty evacuation purposes. The police must have muffled motorcycles, anti-landmine vehicles and de-mining vehicles. Anti-landmine vehicles currently are very useful in mined areas in operations.

Computers. All the SDPOs must be provided with computers, scanners and laser printers. All the SPs must have scanners and laser printers. All the districts must be provided with LCD projectors and laptop computers.

Photography. Digital cameras must be supplied to each

police station for investigative, intelligence and training purposes.

Dog Squads. Each police subdivision must have dog squads.

Training. Equipment must be procured for a mechanical firing range. Low-cost gadgets used for moving targets will be of much use to inculcate firing capabilities among the forces. Other low-cost training gadgets must also be procured.

Recreational Facilities. Games facilities have to be supplied to each police station so that the policemen get adequate recreation. Volleyball, basketball, weight-lifting and chess material may be supplied to each police station while DRP lines must be provided with a good gymnasium. Each Maoist-affected police station must be provided with a television.

Navigational Aids. Topographical map sheets and digitised maps must be procured for the force. Global positioning systems should also be provided.

Resource for Medical Sanitation purposes. Medical mobile operation theatres with all the facilities for an emergency operation system must be provided in all police districts so that the mobile operation theatre can be put very close to the scene of encounters to save the lives of people injured during the conflict. All police stations must be supplied with a first-aid kit and water-purifying tablets and all must have adequate toilets and water facilities. All the posts must be supplied with Syntex tanks and water filters.

Protective. Bullet-proof vests and helmets must be supplied to every police force that actively participates in anti-Maoist operations.

Miscellaneous. Vulnerable police stations and DRP lines must have a CCTV system and alarm system. Explosive detectors must be procured for de-mining purposes.

The acquisition of resources, development of manpower, institutions and infrastructure must follow the rule of immediacy or urgency and rule of criticality. According to the rule of immediacy the total needs may be classified as vital, essential and desirable. Vital needs must be fulfilled immediately and then the essential and desirable needs have to be dealt with. The rule of criticality suggests that critical minimum resources, infrastructures, resources and institutions must be decided for every area and the need fulfilled urgently, otherwise it will jeopardise the internal security of the whole country.

Conclusion

Planning to tackle the Maoist threat should be improved. The consequences of fundamental planning omissions become great obstacles to action. The habit of undertaking everything with insufficient means, flawed policies or lack of policies and the tendency not to recognise the ground realities of field proves fatal for the internal security of the country. The Model Action plan has delineated the problem correctly and prioritised the issues appropriately. It has captured the essence of the anti-Maoist action plan but any plan is only as good as its execution. Now the decision makers have to apply policy reasoning to make proper institutional arrangements, mobilise adequate resources, strengthen manpower, conduct rigorous operations and achieve the strategic objective of containing and eradicating Maoists from their regions.

NOTE

1. Mao Tse-Tung On War, Natraj Publishers, Dehradun (2008) pp 13-14

   Strategic plan is a long term plan basically should be for 3 to 5 years. Operational plan is related with operations by using existing resources.

   Tactical plans deals with responses to situations.

12

Strategy and Tactics on Trial in the Conflict Against Left Wing Extremists

Introduction

Left Wing Extremism (LWE) presents a serious internal security challenge to India that needs a careful and coordinated policy response from both the security and the development front. For the CPI (Maoists) (Communist Party of India), the main outfit propagating LWE, the plan and execution of this style of people's war against the state is like Churchillian 'riddle wrapped in a mystery inside an enigma'. At one level, the LWE can be described as a 'democratic revolution through tactical offensives with tactical speed in the protracted people's war of strategic defensive.' At another, it can be simply castigated as terrorism disguising itself as 'class struggle' and 'social justice'. Any riddle, mystery or enigma cannot be understood or solved without finding the missing links or the keys. The keys are counter-strategy and tactics and these have evolved from the challenges presented by LWE. While some counter-responses have worked well, others have failed and, in fact, compounded the problem.

Before developing any comprehensive counter-approaches it is important to understand the riddle, mystery and enigma of the LWE strategy and tactics.

Strategy and tactics are overused words, and poorly understood concepts. The words seem honorific and attractive, but most of the time they are used ambiguously. Strategy originates from the Greek word '*strategos*' meaning a general. Tactics comes from the Greek word '*takitas*', meaning a foot soldier. Together, both words have marched a long journey of more than two millennia. Strategy and tactics, as concepts, are used by multiple disciplines, often loosely. It is critical to understand their meaning, mechanism and dynamics.

Why Do We Need Strategy. Strategy involves the big picture i.e. the overall plan of how the campaign will achieve its organisational goals and objective. Tactics deals with the nuts and bolts of operations. It mainly concentrates on people and their actions. The task of tactics is to determine the ways and means, the forms and methods of fighting that are most appropriate to the concrete situation at a given moment. Therefore, tactics varies according to the situation, the time and the terrain. There are some timeless tactics of guerrilla warfare derived by using the principles of assessment, adaptation, deception, timing, and assessment of a ground situation. The enemy also plays a major role in devising correct tactics. Leverage, deception, timing, pace are important components which make any tactics successful. The proper permutation and combination of possibilities can produce innumerable successful tactics. Any error can cause tactics to fail.

Strategy and tactics guide purpose and action. Strategy is the analytical thought for commitment of resources to action and assessment of threat. The essence of strategy is to match strengths and distinctive competence with terrain in such a way that one's own organisation enjoys a competitive advantage over rivals competing for the same terrain.

Strategy is a conscious, deliberate process; an intensive implementation system, the art of ensuring future success. Strategy defines the organisation and provides people the aim of the organisation. Strategy sets direction.[1] Strategy provides an organisation with a long-term view and hence the ability to take risks or do things which do not make sense in the short run. Strategy focuses on effort and promotes coordination of activity. It provides consistency and reduces ambiguity. Strategy basically represents a fundamental congruence between external environment and internal capacity.

Strategy and tactics deal with multi dimension facets of conflict—people, society, economics, intelligence, technology, adversary, politics, security organisation, etc. They are mainly the reflection of geographic, economic and political considerations and are important offensive/defensive devices. Fighting any conflict needs a combination of strategy and tactics, and for winning both are essential. The force which knows tactics beats one that doesn't. On the other hand a successful strategy achieves victory before battle.

Strategy/Tactics Contrast

Strategy and tactics intertwine in their usefulness but they are not synonymous. They are interdependent and can be interchangeably used e.g. violence and propaganda can be both tactics and strategy. Sometimes, the same concept can ascend from tactics to become strategy, e.g., destroying the only link to a camp. Strategy stops at the border of the combat zone and tactics begins on contact with the opponent. 'Contact is a word which, perhaps better than any other, indicates the dividing line between tactics and strategy.'

The distinctions between strategy and tactics are encapsulated on next page.

Strategy	Tactics
Strategy is a great resource	Tactics is a deadly weapon
Vision is strategy	Execution is tactics
Strategy is an idea	Tactics is an action
People view strategy as a thinking process	People view tactics as a doing process
Strategy focuses on jungle not on trees[2]	Tactics is a point of reference, or points of reference
Strategies define the overall character mission and direction of the organisation	Tactics deal with action events, propaganda events, and communication events
Strategy is a dynamic flexible process Strategy provides the road map	Tactics is more action based Tactics is generally a single-use plan
Strategy is about shaping the future while managing the present	Tactics depends on ground, response and the situation
Strategy is the theory of the use of combat for the object of the war[2]	Tactics is the theory of the use of military forces in combat
The best strategy is to be always strong[3]	The best tactics is to be always agile and alert
Strategy is the study of the laws of a war situation as a whole[4] Strategy is holistic	Tactics deals with a partial situation
Strategy is doing the right thing	Tactics is doing things right
Strategy is firm and steadfast, does not change much	Tactics is always in need of adjustment
Strategy is exacting, demanding and unforgiving; small mistakes can spoil the entire plan	Tactics can be extemporaneous or premeditated

The above facets deal with the nature, features, and functions of both concepts. Strategy uses a broad spectrum of tactics. Tactics are part of strategy, subordinate to it and serving it. Strategy involves absolute economy of efforts and a high degree of flexibility which necessitates constant adjustment of tactics. Right strategy puts less pressure on executing tactics perfectly.

Catalogue of Strategic and Tactical Errors in Handling LWE

Strategy wins war and tactics wins battles. This aphorism highlights the weight of respective errors. An ardent study of history reveals numerous tactical/strategic errors. Mao pointed out five strategic errors of the Japanese during the Chinese revolution (i) piecemeal reinforcement, (ii) absence of main direction of attack, (iii) lack of strategic coordination, (iv) failure to grasp opportunity, and (v) encirclement of large but annihilation of small numbers. These strategic errors continue in the present day fight against the Naxalites, to some extent. Mao attributed piecemeal reinforcement to two factors (i) underestimation of enemy strength, and (ii) shortage of troops. The Naxalites have also mentioned in their Polit Bureau document of 2009 that they should exploit any situation arising because of shortage of troops. Clearly, strategic errors can be devastating. But a confused or wrong strategy can be as lethal as blind grenade.

Flunk Strategies

- Strategy of bluff
- Strategy of avoidance
- Strategy of delay
- Strategy of bragging
- Strategy of dealing with only one part
- Strategy of hands-off

Some States in dealing with Naxal situation often find their efforts not resulting in desired outcomes. Efforts means little if the strategy is misplaced. As a result of incorrect strategy, they move operationally, in an incremental and invisible manner away from where they are supposed to go. Strategies of dealing with only one part, bragging, delay, bluff, and putting things under the carpet are flunk strategies used by decision makers of some states. They only compound the problem and provide strategic benefit to the opponents. They are strategic miscalculations of the highest order. As one-time tactics, bluff, avoidance or putting under carpet can help temporarily. But, in the long run, pseudo/wrong/confused strategies become counterproductive. Strategy, correctly formulated, shapes tactics. But, "tactics uninformed by strategy, or misinformed by incorrect strategy, is like a car without a steering wheel: It may get somewhere, but probably not where its driver wants it to go."[5]

Tactical Errors

LWE tactics on a spectrum of violence and destruction has caused strategic concern. Not understanding many timeless tactics of guerrilla warfare, e.g., "luring a force into a trap" is a grave tactical error of the highest order committed by security forces. If the security force does not cope with the tactics of the other side then they simply get involved in shadow boxing. There is every possibility that the security force contacts and the other party smashes. Therefore, the force that knows tactics beats that one that doesn't. This impact of tactical errors can be summarised in Sun Tzu's wisdom:

> "When the tactics are wrong and the strategy is wrong, the war will be quickly lost.
>
> When the tactics are right but the strategy is wrong, battles may be won, but the war will be lost.
>
> When the tactics are wrong, but the strategy is right, battles may be lost, but the war will be won."[6]

Mainframe of LWE Strategy

Over a period of more than three decades, Naxalites have

developed their strategies with the objective to disorganise and confuse by politics and defeat by force. They have formulated their grand strategy of protracted war, and their military strategy of armed struggle with the creation of guerrilla bases; and their political strategy of using the democratic contradictions of the Indian polity to their advantage. Most of the strategies have been borrowed from Mao and Giap. They are using the timeless Chinese tactics of "use few to defeat many and use many to crush few", "misleading the security force and catching him unawares", "tactics of concentration to conduct raids and dispersion to protect oneself and politically organise masses", "tactics of fighting no battle unprepared." They are also using the Vietnamese tactics of guerrilla warfare and mobile warfare and even the slogan of Dien Bien Phu 'dare to win and dare to fight.' Many political strategies have emerged during various stages of their movement.

Various Polit Bureaus and central committee meetings of Naxalites have formulated various strategies. In 1995, the All India Special Conference of CPI (ML) Peoples War Group decided on adopting some strategies of the then PWG, e.g., joint action committee for democratic rights, while discussing merger with party unity. The 9th Congress of PW, in 2001, chalked out many strategies e.g., formation of a peoples guerrilla army, regional bureaus, central publishing bureau, sub-committee on political education, sub-committee on *mahila* movement etc. The Central committee meeting of 2004 provisionally decided to convert the PGA to PLGA, which is the main document of strategy and tactics of revolution adopted by the CPI Maoists. The 4th PB meeting of April 2006 formulated the main strategy to fight *Salwa Judum*, start international websites and internationalise issues. The CPI (Maoist) 9th Congress, in 2007, formulated few specific strategies, e.g., transform prisons into political universities, turning PLGA to PLA, guerrilla war into mobile war, support to nationality struggles, dalit struggles, SEZ and displacement struggles etc. Besides the above strategies formulated through resolutions, the CPI Maoists in their literature of strategy and tactics of the Indian Revolution, have formulated many subtle deliberate military and political strategies over the years. These are:

Fact File of CPI (Maoist) Strategy

- Grand Strategy of Protracted War[7]
- Strategy of Exploiting Democratic Contradictions of Indian Polity[8]
- Strategy of Negation of Democratic Politics
- Strategy of Internationalising Issues
- Strategy of Propaganda and Misinformation
- Strategy of Smothering People's Resistance Through Coercion
- Strategy of Isolating Security Forces
- Strategy of Opening Many Fronts Through Underground and Over Ground Organisations
- Strategy of Security of Layers
- Strategy of Social Investigation[9]
- Strategy of Creating Guerrilla Bases[10]
- Strategy of Honeycomb Network of Different Organisations in Guerrilla Zones and Guerrilla Bases
- Strategy of Mobilisation of Public
- Strategy of Urban Movement
- Strategy of Converting Mass Struggle to Armed Struggle[11]
- Strategy of Self Criticism

The strategies of LWE are deep and complex. An analysis of the above strategies makes it crystal clear that State power is the LWE's strategic goal. Tactically, this is being sought through local guerrilla operations that challenge government control of specific areas. LWE try to achieve their strategic goal by the astute application of many strategies and tactics. They have formed a Strategic United Front (SUF), with various underground organisations, which implements military strategies. Besides the SUF, the Politbureau and the Central Committee of the CPI Maoists play key roles in spelling out various political and military strategies. By creating guerrilla bases and by the use of the tactics of guerrilla warfare and mobile warfare the Naxalites execute their military strategy. Through their activities like Tactical Counter Offensive Campaigns (short raids) they spread the area of Red influence and try to achieve their military goal. By networking with other extremist outfits of the North East and Kashmir, the Naxalites try to implement their military strategies. They use the strategy of seizing rural areas to isolate the urban areas and create an urban Maoist movement. They start with creating mass struggles in various areas and then convert these mass struggles into an armed struggle, which is their main strategy. Here, the Naxalites exploit the issues of displacement, SEZ, formation of new States, etc. They begin by establishing revolutionary base areas in the countryside where the enemy is relatively weak and then aim to gradually encircle and capture the cities which are the bastions of enemy forces. They follow the strategy of expansion of base areas and expansion of troops.

Along with a military strategy, they have crafted effective political strategies which have three major goals (i) unity between the CPI Maoist party and cadre, (ii) party, PLGA and people, (iii) disunity between people and security forces. They try to create a mass struggle through propaganda, agitation and action. Then they try to convert the mass struggle into an armed struggle, as in Lalgarh. Through their clever political strategy they use the Revolutionary United Front to save their guerrillas from the security forces.[12] The Naxalites have formed a Tactical United Front (TUF) under a subcommittee on mass organisation (SUCOMO). The TUF includes the Revolutionary Democratic Front (RDF), the People's Democratic Front of India (PDFI), and the committee against violence on women (CAVOW), the committee for the release of political prisoners (CRPP).[13] The TUF plays a pivotal role in the implementation of the political strategies. Political activities are considered more important than military activities and fighting less important than propaganda. Political strategies complement military strategies with the main objective of New Democratic Revolution.

Do the decision makers appreciate the danger that the above strategies of the LWE constitute for Indian democracy and the economy? Do they understand its ramifications? Many understand their strategy and have formulated many options. But now it is high time for the regime to formulate a counter strategy to fight and forestall LWE.

Formulation of Strategies and Counter Strategies by Government

The best strategies are subtle. However, there are a number of timeless counter strategies of a general type which can be used for fighting the Naxal menace. Ramon Magsaysay successfully used the grand strategy of making the system efficient and the other strategies of civic action, intelligence, and counter operations. Templar successfully used the strategy of guerrilla warfare training, counter guerrilla operations, support of local people and local village defence committees. President LB Johnson of the US attributed the Vietnamese ordeal to the strategy of delay in putting more forces in Vietnam. From a study of the above strategies and also the situation of Peru, China, Malaysia we may filter the following few fundamental strategies:

- Strategy of capacity building.
- Strategy of early prevention.
- Strategy of denying LWE time and space.
- Strategy of isolating LWE.
- Strategy of Intelligence.
- Strategy of redressing grievances of affected areas.
- Strategy of perception management.
- Strategy of reconstruction of administration.
- Strategy of merging security and development.
- Strategy of public cooperation.
- Strategy of using strict law.
- Strategy of civic action.
- Strategy of application of all elements of national power.

The above fundamental strategies remain the same for all times and all situations. But they need fine-tuning and there is also a need for formulation of many specific strategies. It cannot be accomplished without answering Clausewitzian and other questions:

1) What is the nature of conflict?
2) What is our aim?
3) How well do we do it?
4) What is the time frame?
5) What resources and means will we employ in doing it?
   a) Where have we been?
   b) Where are we now?
   c) Where do we want to go?
   d) Where should we go?
   e) Where can we go?
   f) Where shall we go?

Answers to these pertinent questions help in getting a correct assessment of the situation and requirement and in return, help in developing sub-strategies and ultimately in formulating the correct strategy and set the strategic response. In sum, the lessons in strategy are as follows: grasp the realities of the situation; determine the objectives(s), use one's strength against enemy weaknesses while negating the reverse; seize and hold the initiative; and be flexible. The art of formulating the strategies relies on the ability to discover what is most appropriate to a particular context and to abandon policy approaches when it is evident that they will not yield the results being pursued.

There are a few steps to develop strategy: 1. systematic analysis of information, 2. critical appreciation to assess threats and opportunities, and 3. search for options. There is a very fine line between setting strategy and micro-managing combat. A meaningful strategy can not evolve without understanding the strategy of the enemy.

Calibration of Strategy

Calibration of strategy is like playing strategy game; it is monitoring of LWE strategy and the ground situation and then reviewing and updating our own strategy. The first principle is to recognise the strategic pattern, and understand the adversary's strategic pattern. It is only then that an emerging strategic scenario can be developed. In an organization, low levels of discrepancy or divergence between goals and achievements are likely to be interpreted first as a failure of execution not as a failure of strategy. Unless a major crisis hits people do not review or update or formulate correct strategy.

Strategy calibration needs both strategic foresight and insight; an ability to perceive, analyse and make sense of complex strategic situations as they develop, and to be ready to take advantage of them. Strategy is based on foresight, on anticipation, the chess master's ability to see many moves ahead, where his lesser opponent sees only a few. But foresight is only as good as an ability to understand and map out an environment and anticipate its evolution. The search for genuinely strategic options should be broad and wide. Sources include the logical possibilities present in the actual situation, successful past strategies, individual ingenuity in office and biases or preconceived notions people advocate or endorse. Any tactical defeat can force a party to change its strategy. Strategy needs constant tactical adjustment.

Strategy Implementation

Strategy which remains hanging in the operation room is of little worth. Strategies most often fail because they are not executed well. The most brilliant strategy is only as good as its execution. According to Sun Tzu there are three strategic principles—commitment, observation and preparation which play a pivotal role in the formulation and implementation of strategy.

- Commitment is the first strategic principle; it sets the stage for victory. One has to put the organisation into a situation where the people have no choice but to commit to organisation goals.

- Observation is the second strategic principle. Watching closely and critical attention provides raw data about what is really happening; rapid, profitable adaptation feeds on facts about ground reality.
- Preparation is the third strategic principle. Effective execution on a tactical level that is at the point in time when opportunity presents itself depends on preparation done before the moment of action arrives. Preparation includes developing organisational structure, streamlining processes, positioning resources, encouraging flexibility and training personnel. Therefore, the government side has to generate appropriate, prudent and affordable measures for effective preparedness.

The first rule in strategy is of painstaking attention to the needs and wants on the ground. Nevertheless, priorities are numerous simply because everything has to be done from the beginning. However, a strategic approach requires what is urgent.

Structure and Resources Constrain Strategies

Another important fact is that our strategy and operations are constrained by resources and organisations. Any brilliant strategy of the government depends more on the organisation and the team for its execution. If the organisation and team is unresponsive, uncreative and the team has hidden agendas then the strategy has no meaning. If there is no proper organisation then the strategy cannot be implemented. As an example, it is surprising that even in an internal war we do not have a proper engineering unit to assist the security forces to reconstruct damaged roads and bridges. In remote areas anti-LWE operations are terribly constrained by natural barriers.

Structure and resources must fit the strategy. Structure is the way activity is organised and managed. It is the structure of the security force—the chain of command and the relationship of the parts to the whole—that gives strategic significance to the force. In keeping with the requirements, new institutions like special intelligence units, commando units, and remote area development agency must be organised to face strategic situations.

The execution of strategy depends mostly on the strength and capability of the government organisation. It must be streamlined and the work force should be duly motivated. To create realism in strategy one must link it to the people process. The right people should be placed in difficult posts. The people process is more important than either the strategy or operations process as it is they who can operationalise the strategy. The people process evaluates individuals accurately and in depth. Putting wrong people to execute key parts of strategy causes failure to the entire strategy; this is very common. Linking people, strategy and operations is imperative.

The organisation has to be constructed piece by piece and the strategy has to be worked out step by step and tested. Along with organisation, the material resources for action have to be assembled bit by bit. One does not only have to mobilise resources, but also make the best use of available resources. Appropriate technology should be designed to help as force multipliers. Therefore, one must develop effective institutions, put right people at key places, mobilise resources and reinforce what is working to turn great strategies into great performances.

Strategy-Tactics-Operations Link

Strategy, tactics and operations are interlinked concepts; though they are fundamentally different in nature, scope and ramifications. Sometimes the operational commander, without a proper understanding of the significance and ramifications of a particular issue takes strategic decisions which turn out disastrously, for example, opening new posts in a far-flung combat zone, thereby frittering away all the reserve troops. This can create major problems at the operational level. Similarly, some commanders who are busy with tactical issues, and indulge in back-seat driving, create functional problems at the tactical level. Occasional mentoring and reverse mentoring on particular issues has relevance, but continuous level jumping invites bungling and subsequent ordeals.

Strategic centralisation along with tactical autonomy is required. The manner of the overall posture, both offensive and defensive, the defining of the broad line of operational issues related to morale, training, intelligence, public relations, coordination with other troops creation of posts, etc., should be dealt with at the strategic level.

The domains of strategy, tactics and operations interact. The strategy domain deals with the goal, while tactics deal with skill, while operational aspects are concerned with implementation. Operations determine where and when to fight, tactics dictate how to conduct the fight and strategy whether to fight or not. At every level of operations, strategy is indeed war on a map. Operations are the discipline of realising strategy in the context of the background of infrastructure, systems, resources and processes using the vocabulary of tactics. Operations convert strategy and tactics into reality through appropriate deliberative, reactive and opportunistic planning, scheduling, allocation of resources and risk management in the fog of action. If strategy, tactics and operations are disjointed then the net result will be negative.

Operational issues should be linked to strategic goals and synchronise strategy with tactics. The overall strategic performance will be meagre if tactical or operational virtuosity is contradictory. Strategic performance is related to, but does not result from military performance at the operational or tactical level of war.

Piece of Advice

Protracted conflict needs enduring advice regarding the factors which count. The concepts of strategy, tactics, resources, manpower, law, perception, management, civic action have a tremendous impact on conflict. The studies of conflict situations of various countries point out that effective military strategy/tactics in tandem with good political strategy can ensure success.

- Sun Tzu has written that people are able to see the tactics, but not the strategy behind any success. Therefore, fighting the Naxal strategy and foiling their tactics is the most important and the prime task for the decision-makers.
- Timeless strategies necessitate capacity building, early prevention, isolating LWE, intelligence, denying LWE time and space, perception management, redressing grievances of people in affected areas, reconstruction of the administration, public cooperation, using laws effectively. These issues should be immediately chalked out by each affected state taking into consideration the areas affected.
- A strategy formulator must have strategic insight, foresight and commitment, so that he can genuinely search for strategic options and formulate a correct menu of strategies.
- Structure and resources must fit strategy. If there is any discrepancy in either structure or resources, then it must be addressed immediately. Mobilising resources and developing human resources are essential.
- Sound political strategy should be developed to counter the numerous political strategies of LWE, specially related to SEZ, displacement, as well as the *dalit* and *adivasi* struggle.
- Strategy of security and development should move in tandem to be effective.
- As pointed out by Mao, the LWE exploit the situation of piecemeal reinforcement. Therefore, the right type of force, in sufficient number, has to be developed both for offensive and defensive operations.
- There should be two sets of strategy; one for extremely infested areas and the other for mildly infested areas. Mildly infested areas need SSB type of troops which

can deal simultaneously with security, civic action and perception management.

- Extremely affected areas need hunter-killer teams of elite troops, like the Greyhounds, for offensive operations and separate troops for security operations.
- Operations should synchronise tactics with strategy.
- Operations with tactical acuity and strategic clarity only will bring success.
- Unless the right people are placed at important positions, operational efficiency will not emerge. Strategy cannot be executed unless people processes are corrected.

Conclusion

LWE cannot be underestimated. Being equipped with both home grown as well as borrowed strategies and tactics from Peru, China, Vietnam, and Nepal, they pose a serious threat. LWE aspires to cause strategic paralysis of the decision makers. The real challenge lies in developing correct and specific strategies with unity of purpose. It is high time for the decision makers to fight the strategies and tactics of LWE rather than merely fighting the effective of LWE. With prudent strategic and brilliant tactics it is possible to counter the strategies and tactics of LWE; it can better be achieved by strategic planning, strategic coordination of forces and resources. Unfortunately, leadership in some of the states affected by LWE has not shown the right inclination to deal with the issue. In fact, some security force leaders think of the LWE problem from a tactical framework rather than from a strategic viewpoint. To counter the growing menace of LWE a significant change in attitude, approach and orientation of the political, administrative and police machinery at various levels is necessary. It is for this reason that many tactical and operational aspects of counter-measures against LWE have no strategic foundations.

NOTES

1. *Strategy Safari*, p. 15.
2. Carl von Clausewitz; *On War*, p. 141. The supreme, the most far-reaching act of judgement that the statesman and Commander have to make is to establish... the kind of war on which they are embarking: neither mistaking it for, nor trying to turn it into, something that is alien to its nature.
3. Ibid. p. 175.
4. Mao-Tse Tung *On War*, p. 13. Naxals follow Mao's strategy, tactics meticulously. As done by Mao, they preferred protracted war because they think by exploiting the situation, they can transform their own troops from weak to strong and over the period by exploiting the short comings of the regime they can weaken the security force.
5. *Fiasco: The American Military Adventure in Iraq*, p. 184.
6. *Art of War* by Sun Tzu translated by James Clavell, p. 6. Besides Mao, Naxals study the book Art of War Most of the senior Naxal Commanders keep a copy of Art of War. The Chapters of attack, defence, and use of terrain give insight into real combat.
7. *Strategy and Tactics of Indian Revolution*, pp. 10 and 31. The provisional CPI Maoist Central Committee approved and published this document along with other documents of party constitution etc. This document is a cloning of Mao's document, it provides a total roadmap to the Naxalites to achieve their objective. Based on this document Naxal during various Polit Bureau meetings. Central Committee or CMC meetings formulate specific strategies.
8. Ibid., p. 17.
9. Ibid., p. 58.
10. Ibid., pp. 10, 50, 51.
11. Ibid., pp. 112, 114, 119.
12. Strategy and Tactics of Indian Revolution. p. 80.
13. P.V. Ramana; Maoists Tactical United Front and Urban Movement, p. 4.

13

What Needs to be Done?

"How best to save Indian democracy from the depredations and annihilations of Naxalism; and wage war against extremism" is the greater cause of concern. Naxals are increasingly waging savage battles against Indian democracy; they posed serious threat to Indian/India's democracy, to the nation, and to all its institutions. They are continuing with most violent and destructive episodes. Naxals are progressively increasing spheres of influence and sphere of activity. The CPI Maoists have spread to more than 212 districts in the country and continuously new areas of vulnerabilities are emerging. They have presence in about 27% area of the entire country, and entrenched in about 4 per cent of the forested remote areas of the country. Along with the growing organisational network the outfit has continuously sharpened its teeth by adding new weapons and mine technology to its arsenals. The run over of Koraput (2004 Feb.), Madhuvani (2005 July), Nayagarh (2008) Tarmetla (2010), the use of Rocket launchers in A.P. and Chhattisgarh, reveal the level of militarisation and sophistication of the outfit. The ever spread of Naxalism, the merger of MCC and PW, the military gradualism, vituperative propaganda, ever expanding organisation, their networking with other terrorist outfits within the country and outside the country, the generation of black money worth crores of rupees, the infiltration of naxalites into many segments of society, the formation of intelligence unit, the "People's security service" by the naxalites, their international networking through CCOMPOSA and RIM, all point out that the storm is gaining more force, and the red fire will cause inferno in some parts of the country. The trend shows continued high level extremism for the foreseeable future. One should dispel the fatuous hope that naxal problem will be solved automatically.

Naxals Unleashed Nation Destroying Process

Naxals are predators upon the system, and the frontal organisations of naxals are parasites of the system; in the last analysis they are great threat to the system. Following the Marxist tenet of withering away of the State, Naxals are making efforts to destroy the Indian democratic nation from within the system as well by attack from outside of the system. Naxalities draw up comprehensive strategic plan by area selection, cadre deployment, ideological, political, organisational, military preparation, concentration of leadership and coordination. Seriousness of the problem can be conceptualized in a variety of ways. Security declines and security commitments have enhanced drastically. Danger though imminent seems less apparent. Naxals along with the labyrinthine frontal organisations have unleashed sinister nation destroying process. Naxals following the principle of judo hit at system's weaknesses and use the strength of the system against the system. Naxals actions are intended to dislocate the state structure. They are destroying infrastructures like, schools, Hostels, Hospital, Panchayat building, roads, bridges. Naxals have seriously damaged forest management, PDS, health services, banking system in remote areas. Forcible land occupation and redistribution has affected agricultural activities. They are destroying democratic institutions like Panchayati Raj through violence. Naxal violence and revolutionary politics have tremendous adverse effect on agriculture and industrialisation process in infested areas. It has huge negative effect on the economic growth of the country. Naxals are not only destroying the infrastructures, causing murder and mayhem of innocent people, but also they are making efforts through their sub-national theory to balkanize Indian nation. Naxals are waging system demolishing and nation destroying war. Due to LWE conflict what shambles state of nation is becoming!

Proposed Course of Action to Nix Naxalism

The Nation should nix Naxalism. The Nation cannot passively wait, progressively hemmed in and ultimately get overwhelmed by naxals. Countering naxalism has become beyond any doubt the top national security problem. All-out-efforts must be made for counter measures. Crises have an unfortunate way of taking revenge on those who fail to make use of them at the right time. Doing nothing and side-stepping the problem could become the most dangerous option of all. If the threat remains unrecognised or if the preventive measures implemented in response to a recognised threat are inadequate, the probability of additional attacks, losses, and casualties increase manifold. In order to avoid inexorable aggravation of crisis, now, it is high time to seek the remedies, and respond rapidly and decisively against the menace. Some of the states of India have waged the war against this menace for many years, and achieved many successes. But, the menace has not been completely eradicated, the repertoire of collective action marked inability to rout the menace. In spite of the efforts and sacrifices of the security force, the strength and spread have increased in new areas which imply that the fight against Naxalism needs further intensification. Complexity and messiness of the problem suggest that there is no one step solution to the problem.

Warn of its impending and quickening developments the regime should take stock of what has been achieved and what needs to be done and intensify correct efforts to uproot it. Attempt to address one part of a problem without treating it holistically can make things worse. The resolution of conflict requires initial understanding and de-escalation initiatives. The obduracy of Naxalite problem has obtruded the choice of option for countering it at systemic, political, policy, strategic, tactical, and operational level.

More than that, to beat naxalites means to fight not in the sharp black and white of formal combat, but in a gray, fuzzy obscurity where politics affects tactics and influence strategy and where rule of law has to confront serious challenge from rule of terror and rule of politics. So the anti-naxalite operation is a total war, its political psychological, socio-economic aspect must be given proper consideration and a solution to it must be sought according to systematic, long term planning. There are no easy answers and cures for such a complex phenomenon. Comprehensive initiative to improve, rejuvenate the system is required. The first priority is to re-examine ground reality in depth and find out solutions, priorities, and necessities.

There is no magic formula or silver bullet to solve naxal problem. However, regular evaluation of various systems and sub-systems, processes and situation of the nation like educational system, criminal justice system, industrialisation process, should be correctly evaluated and efforts should be made to improve by replicating success and changing which is not working. The search for genuine notions should be broad and wide. Problem appraisal and solution identification is important. It includes logical possibilities present in the actual situation, successful past options, individual ingenuity in office, possible hopeful notions of successful practitioners' advocate or endorse. Multi-causal phenomena require a system wide response. Algebra of agenda for conflict resolution should include notions which can make the system work efficiently. The decision makers should evaluate the challenge and evolve the system.

Improve the Entire System through Vigorous Nation Building Process

Prevention of nation destroying process and preemption of nation building process is indispensable today. An appreciation of the complexity of the issues is required. The ultimate goal of nation building is to develop and protect all the resources and various systems of the country. Any system which works for few decades develops snags and becomes weak; it becomes susceptible to attack of any virus, bacteria. The system needs strengthening. Go-to-the-basic is the dictum to improve the system. The system should preserve its basic values, basic structures. The basic function and role of institutions must be refreshed. Nuts and bolts of the system should be re-evaluated and the systems should be made more reliable. Retro-fitting into the system and streamlining of the system is also required. It must be done after recognizing the short comings of the system by making continuous assessment of the system. The system has to make a commitment to manage the causes not just consequences of violence and unrest. The system should provide a continuum of strategies, tools, capabilities, strong law, and institutions for dealing with today's complex and asymmetrical challenges.

The nation destroying process needs to be curbed and nation building process should be given momentum. In 1967 to 70 the system was unprepared to face such violent upsurge, willy-nilly it subdued the threat in 1972. In the second decade of 21st century the system has to prepare further to finish the menace; the system should be empowered, enabled and energised. Clear underestimation of the phenomena causes inability of the system to provide adequate timely solution to the problem which can be costly. If the system is ignoring ground reality, wake up late to the occasion it will bring short term defeats and long-term disasters. The system should act with vigour, determination, resoluteness, decisiveness, and skill to defend itself politically and militarily. Naxal problem is a multi-causal phenomenon which requires a system wide response. There is a general tendency that in any system, any problem any where causes some problem every where.

The system has to make a commitment to manage the causes not just consequences of violence and unrest. The basic broad causes are (1) militarisation of the society and creation of wrong strong man who hijack the society, and challenge the state, (2) unemployment (3) less priority on developing human resources (4) lopsided priorities, (5) slow mobilisation (6) slow and less than optimum functioning of the system. Many of the systems are functioning with 30 to 40 percent of outcomes. The systems should be overhauled and improved to yield more than 60 to 70 percent outcomes. Again, the key thing in any counter extremism is the efficiency of the system. The Government side and force are up against an invisible, spirited, uninhibited organisation whose decision making is due to its nature fast and therefore, the Government side must be double efficient and capable than the naxalites. The absolute and immediate necessity is to demonstrate urgency, focus and attention to safeguard against the heightened risk of naxalism. Somebody may disagree to the rating of 30 to 40 per cent efficiency of the system. In that case let it be called 'X' and the desired performance of the system should be '2X'.

Entropy of the system is responsible for slowing down the system. The concept of entropy says two things (1) the energy is still there but it is not available for doing work or improving the system and (2) the disorderliness of the system can be reduced by pressure. The disorderliness of the system is at the root cause of slow progress of the system. If anybody deeply analyses these causes he will find that there are many lacuna with various systems and processes e.g. educational system, security system, budgetary system, developmental system. Problem appraisal and solution identification is important. Streamlining of the system is required; it should be an on going process. Nation's sensitivity to incidents is very high, and nation's sensitivity to requirements of various systems should be enhanced. Few of the requirements of various systems are narrated. However, this is not exhaustive.

Improve Educational System

All the top leaders of LWE of Vietnam, India, Nepal-Giap, Kondapalli; Ganapati, Prachanda, Charu Majumdar-all were teachers for sometime. Even in the first phase of Naxalism the educational system of India was blamed for malfunctioning of socio-political, economic system. Therefore, at the out set the seeds of discontent should be destroyed from the education system. Educational system needs much reform, but here only four important points are raised:

(1) We have agricultural universities but no agricultural schools. As a result none of the needy students get any orientation of agriculture. After becoming literate, crores of rural boys feel it below dignity to work on their own field. India is predominantly an agricultural country; more than 50 percent of population is dependent on agriculture. There is urgent need to start agricultural schools with rural technology.

(2) Admissions in to ITI should not have any compulsory educational qualification of matric; so that large number of interested boys can get vocational qualification.

(3) Bal ashrams in remote naxal affected areas face serious problems from naxalites. Naxals take away their meals and sometime take away the boys and girls. The Bal ashrams should be located at those places where security can be easily provided.

(4) Central and Navodaya schools, ITI, science colleges should be opened in the district headquarters and at bigger sub divisional headquarters of Naxal affected districts so that the local people get plenty of opportunity for education and the government officials do not feel constrained to work in those areas.

Improve the Security System

It is a fact that India which is a heterogeneous society, which has thousand times more socio-economic problems has many times less budget for police, and security system. People think that if they spend more on security what will happen to development? This mindset has to be changed for following reasons. Annual losses due to security incidents, law and order incidents run to trillions. This can be prevented by increasing emphasis on homeland security. India being the largest functional democracy and growing power, its enemies have tried many times to foment disturbance in India; and now terrorists and extremists have acquired mega kill capabilities. Again, security is the foundation upon which only development can grow, otherwise the development will collapse. People should remember a single crime can create havoc in the country. The economic tangible losses due to 26/11, 9/11 cost many trillion dollars. Security is the basis of peace and development. Peace and development needs protection. Without proper security system development will not be sustainable. Therefore adequate budget should be allocated for security. More grants to develop force structure is required so that security framework of many states can be properly developed.

Many times naxals have broken jails and escaped. In their documents they have mentioned that they are using some jails as some kind of their schools for indoctrination of other jail in-mates. Therefore, there is need for high security exclusive jails for extremists and terrorists.

In the recent past attacks on Rail way has marked some increase. Rail way, affected National high ways and vital installations should be protected by deploying required amount of troops. Rail way commando battalions and state industrial forces should be raised in affected states to look after the problem.

Law is the most effective anti-dote for all such subversive and divisive activities. Empirical evidence shows that after being released from jail naxals are again joining the outfit. So, there is a need for some special strong law to deal with such type of extremism. First phase of naxlism was crushed by MISA, DIR, and Prevention of Violence Act. In the first phase more than 17000 (Seventeen thousands) naxalites were arrested in West Bengal. TADA, POTA, had tremendous impact in curbing terrorism in Punjab.

Budgetary System

- Budget is the central instrument for the formulation, coordination and monitoring of policy. The budgetary allocation of resources is the first concrete decision for fighting any problem. Well structured and executed budget can help in fighting naxal menace to great extent.

- Budget session should start from 31st May, so that open seasons of March, April, and May can be utilised for effective budget spending.

Prevention of Corruption

Without fighting greed based corruption vigorously, 25 per cent battle against naxalism cannot be won. Naxalites are siphoning off huge amount of developmental funds. Serious vigilance action against the misappropriation of public money must be taken. Intelligence and vigilance are I.V. fluids for system's health. Strong campaign against greed based corruption should be taken.

Some public service commissions of some states are unable to recruit every year. Even some of the recruitment processes are sub judice. Some of the recruitment processes of class three and four employees in some States are cancelled due to wrong practices. Any public servant recruited through corrupt practice will definitely indulge into corrupt practices. Therefore, the recruitment processes of all departments should be streamlined in such a manner that there can be no scope for corruption.

National Resources including Forest Land should be Protected

People have strong notion that land distribution and land reform will solve Naxal problem. Operation Bargha-land reforms was conducted in West Bengal by Chief Minister Late Shri Jyoti Basu from 1977-86. But by 2005 Naxalism again resurged in West Bengal and by 2010 it became a major problem. Land issue is exploited by Naxals to generate loyalty and support base. Land issue is raised by naxalites to gain political power. In some areas naxals have distributed even forest land to their supporters. When naxals fight for land they fight not exactly for land but for political power. Therefore, all the national resources must be duly protected. Forest land encroachment by Naxal supporters should not be allowed; otherwise, after two decades there will be no forest in India which will cause severe drought in many parts of the country.

In-Accessibility Neutralisation and Social Service Optimisation

In-accessibility neutralisation and social service optimisation are two most important issues which have tremendous impact on preventing naxal menace. Inaccessibility of the area is one of the reasons of underdevelopment of the area. The Socio-economic problems of the areas which provide the breeding ground of discontent must be addressed. The naxalites exploited these discontents and spread its tentacles. In order to garner public support and hide their heinous activities the Maoist units perform petty developmental activities. Long standing problems of development dating back to several decades still remained critical issues of concern in remote areas. Efforts should be made to marginalise the extremists' agenda with regard to the general population. Solving multitude of local problems will help de-escalation of conflict. The vigorous implementation of Government schemes viz. land reform, Public distribution system, educational program, redressal of grievances will prevent public from falling prey to the machination of the LWE. Therefore, vigorous developmental administration in the area will definitely ameliorate the situation. Social and material damage produced by violence should be repaired by reconstruction and reintegration. Communities in remote areas are desperate for security and basic services.

Role of Political Will and National Will

The naxalites imbroglio scenario may be plainly portrayed as the clash between political will of the democracy and revolutionary will of naxalites. Naxalites have the political agenda of marginalizing the political system and in their scheme of things will has far reaching significance. They try to destroy the political will and endurance of the nation by protracted war which consists of guerrilla warfare and political warfare. There are lessons that war can be won militarily and lose politically. Therefore, there is need to focus political attention on the problem and more attention on solutions to the problem. Maintaining the political will to fight the menace and end the conflict is required. Sophisticated political, psychological application of instruments of national power can not take place without invoking the political will of the state. The immanent political will stirs and urges everything into action. Discovering or creating the political will is necessary for prevention and resolution of conflict. Political will is essential for addressing the divisive political issues exploited by naxalites and also for addressing the political dilemmas being faced in the process by the regime. Political will can also be generated and maintained by administrative skill. Questions of decisions and choices of action arise with will. Will acts as a great factor in combat, as a force and as force multiplier. The will has to be rightful, reasonable, and resourceful. It should be the Iron will of Mahatma Gandhi, Sardar Patel, Indira Gandhi and Lincoln. The political will should create the National will. The failure to invoke national will was one of the major strategic failures of Americans in the Vietnam War. Loss of political initiative will inevitably involve a loss of military initiative.

Deliberation, Decision, Action

Naxals depend more on the weaknesses and contradictions of the democratic system. Moreover conflict resolution and building peace require knowing and addressing the causes of conflict which can be achieved through proper deliberation. Therefore, focused deliberation, fast and hard decisions and timely accurate actions are indispensable to fight naxals' protracted war. Focus on problem, problem magnifies, it seems very big insurmountable. Focus on solution though difficult seems achievable. Half steps, miss-steps won't solve problem; full-fledged action is required. Decisions should be taken after thorough deliberations and decisions should be implemented by vigorous action on the ground. Action is the goal. Action, reflection and reassessment and new action are also necessary. Actions should flow to the real priorities first. In extremist situation the men of action should have some say in deliberation. Men of action can only speak about ground requirements, doable tasks and make deliberations fruitful. Timeliness of decisions becomes essential for generating tempo of action. The moment of deliberation must be moment of decision and next should be the moment of action.

Recognise, Prioritise, Mobilise

Solution to the problem cannot be sought and achieved unless the problem is recognised. Disease and problem kept hidden, comeback in a serious manner. There is a tendency to hide and deny the existence of extremist/terrorist problem, till violent incidents take place. Generally, naxalites indulge in violent activities when they are totally entrenched in any area. Much before violence, they survey the area and establish their foothold in the area. Priority should be given to identify naxals' presence and over ground activities and act early to prevent conflict. The overall problem has been recognised at various levels. However, its various ramifications need to be understood correctly at different levels. Ambiguity in recognition of the problem, anomalous priorities, and poor mobilisation invites doom for war fighting efforts. In a climate of vacillation and ambiguity it is difficult to resolve differences of opinion over appropriate actions to determine priorities, or to address contrasting view of purpose. In an unpredictable environment of limited resources conflicting priorities have tremendous adverse effects. There are many demands on resources, many worthwhile causes, and many voices prescribing action. People can disagree over priorities; can dispute over the appropriate course of action. It has required a sense of priorities of choosing which evil to deal with first. Geography has also a great bearing on priority. Decision makers have to set right the priorities, build the force, and develop the system. Most glaring deficiency is in the mobilisation system. A rational policy is that achieves maximum special, organisational gain. Greater alignment between priorities and capabilities are required. Successfully fighting any extremism depends on the ability to mobilize resources. Sensible priority setting, economics before politics, and nation before personal and group is required. Hope and lessons come from proper combinations of priorities, mobilisations and programs.

Coherent and Efficient Policy Approach

Conflict situations aggravate due to major policy errors. 'Get the policy right' is the most important counter measure of any extremist affected country. A policy is a guide to thinking. Rational policy is the most important factor of Clausewitz's trinity of non-rational force (violent emotion, chance and rational policy).[1] Policy attributes and political imperatives should align. Policy cycles cause public and governmental attention to ebb and flow dramatically. Some of the tried anti-dacoity policy to an extremist situation had failed miserably in the past. Properly thought-out policies with regard to security, development and administration are required. Development policy is a matter of both contestable political choices and sharp economic analysis. Policy questions should not be treated in lackadaisical manner. In many cases ready solutions or policies are neither available nor anticipated. Situations are not properly understood and confusion exists about course of action. Perspective, theory, good practices and successful initiatives can guide policy. Better policies can be formulated from current theoretical postulates deduced from ground realities. Policy responses in different domains will help.

Expert (who has worked on the ground successfully or has expert knowledge) contribution to policy formulation should be increased. Ecological impact, economic efficiency, security impact, operational practicality should guide policy. When the radar of ship commits error of mere one degree instead of reaching correct destination of suppose Mumbai, it may reach Cochin. Similarly, in the present situation people suffer for some wrong policies of the past. Pernicious impact of any policy is felt after a decade or more. With comparative perspective policies should be identified and evaluated, if needed alternate policies should be adopted. Theoretical, methodological and empirical analysis should be utilised. Ecologically, socially, economically appropriate policy should be adopted. Peace, justice and sustainability should be the motto of public policy. The times call for thinking deeply and afresh and for creating new policies to fight, forestall, and eradicate the menace. The policies with regard to Naxal problem as pronounced by Government of India is mentioned below:

Policy to Deal with the Naxalite Menace

The Government has a clearly defined policy to combat the challenge posed by the naxalite menace. This policy comprises the following components:

I. The Government will deal sternly with the naxalites indulging in violence.

II. Keeping in view that naxalism is not merely a law and order problem, the policy of the Govt., is to address this menace simultaneously on political, security, development and public perception management fronts in a holistic manner.

III. Naxalism being an inter-state problem, the states will adopt a collective approach and pursue a coordinated response to counter it.

IV. The states will need to further improve police response and pursue effective and sustained police action against naxalites and their infrastructure individually and jointly.

V. There will be no peace dialogue by the affected states with the naxal groups unless the latter agree to give up violence and arms.

VI. Political parties must strengthen their cadre base in naxal affected areas so that the potential youth there can be weaned away from the path of naxal ideology.

VII. The states from where naxal activity/influence, and not naxal violence, is reported should have a different approach with special focus and accelerated socio-economic development of the backward areas and regular interaction with NGOs, intelligentsia, civil liberties groups etc. to minimize overground support for the naxalite ideology and activity.

VIII. Efforts will continue to be made to promote voluntary local resistance groups against naxalites but in a manner that the villagers are provided adequate security cover and the area is effectively dominated by the security forces.

IX. Mass media should be extensively used to highlight the futility of naxal ideology and violence and loss of life and property caused by it and developmental schemes of the Government in the affected areas so as to restore people's faith and confidence in the Government machinery.

X. The states should announce a suitable transfer policy for the naxal affected districts. Willing, committed and competent officers will need to be posted with a stable tenure in the naxal affected districts. These officers will also need to be given greater delegation and flexibility to deliver better and step up Government presence and above all improve governance in these areas.

XI. The Government of Andhra Pradesh has an effective surrender and rehabilitation policy for naxalites and has produced good results over the years. The other states should adopt a similar policy.

XII. The State Governments will need to accord a higher priority in their annual plans to ensure faster socio-economic development of the naxal affected areas. The focus areas should be to distribute land to the landless poor as part of the speedy implementation of land reforms, ensure development of physical infrastructure like roads, communication, power etc. and provide employment opportunities to the youth in these areas.

XIII. Another related issue is that development activities are not undertaken in some of the naxalite affected areas mainly due to extortion, threat or fear from the naxalite cadres. In these areas, even contractors are not coming forward to take up developmental work. Adequate security and other measures would need to be taken to facilitate uninterrupted developmental activities in the naxal affected areas.

XIV. The Central Government will continue to supplement the efforts and resources of the affected states on both security and development fronts and brings about greater coordination between the states to successfully tackle the problem.[2]

Again, Govt. of India's policy has been published in November 2007 on Naxalism, is mentioned below:

Policy Approach of the Government to Deal with Naxalism-I

- Government remains committed to deal strongly with naxalites indulging in crime and violence.
- The overall objective being to uphold the law of the land, provide security of life and property and provide a secure environment for development and economic growth, Government's approach is to deal with naxalite activities in a holistic manner, in the arenas of the security, development, administration and public perception management.
- Considering the inter-State ramifications of naxalite activities, the need for inter-State coordination and cooperation is self-evident, both in terms of uniformity in approach and in terms of ground-level joint police action, with the intent to enforce the law of the land and to deal with naxalite crime and violence in accordance with the law established.
- The States should further improve the police responses and pursue effective and sustained police action against naxalites, individually and jointly.
- There should be no peace dialogue by the States with naxalite groups unless they give up crime, violence and arms.

- The States should formulate and implement effective surrender and rehabilitation policies for naxalites who shun crime, violence and arms. Mass media should be extensively used to highlight the futility of naxal ideology and violence and loss of the life and property caused by it in the affected areas.

Policy and Approach of the Government to Deal with Naxalism-II

- States are being assisted in, and requested for, steps as are important in dealing with naxalite activities, that is:
  - ➢ Essentials for effective policing, like:
    - ✓ providing secure police station buildings, trained personnel, basic amenities for the personnel deployed and specialised equipment, weaponry and vehicles at the police station level;
    - ✓ strengthening of the State intelligence set-ups, for enhancing capabilities for collecting, sharing and using actionable intelligence;
    - ✓ optimal utilisation of existing training capacity and creation of additional training capacity;
    - ✓ raising specialised units/task forces, trained in counter-insurgency and jungle-warfare, for anti-naxalite operations;
    - ✓ expeditious filling up of the vacancies in the State police forces;
    - ✓ improvement in the police-population ratio, in consonance with law and order requirements;
    - ✓ adequate provisions for equipment, weaponry, mobility, communication, training, police buildings and housing and forensic science in the State police budget;
    - ✓ expeditious investigation and prosecution of naxalite crimes.

Policy and Approach of the Government to Deal with Naxalism-III

- All-round development of affected areas, with qualitative implementation of Central and State development schemes, and with fair deal to deprived segments.
- Other aspects relevant to naxalism, such as:
  - Fair and firm revenue (land) administration, with attention on elements like proper maintenance of land records, expeditious recording of mutations and fair disposal of land disputes, without undue delay.
  - Appropriate mechanisms for grievance redressal, public contact and public awareness, for creating an overall positive environment and confidence of the people in the State administrative machinery.
  - The Central Government will continue to supplement the efforts and resources of the affected States on both the security and the development fronts and to bring about greater coordination between the States for effectively dealing with the problem.[3]

Strategic Acuity and Tactical Agility

Naxalites jolly well understand 'Strategy wins war'.[4] They have formulated grand strategy of protracted war and a dozen of assorted political and military strategies to achieve their game plan. Without coherent, correct, and counter strategies the incumbent regime cannot win the internal war which is more intellectual in nature. Inadequacy of counter extremism as strategy has to be made good. Vagueness at the top transforms into confusion and lethargy at the bottom. Therefore, strategic clarity is required. Every strategy of guerrilla war is a geo-strategy. However, correct evaluation of the situations and Naxalites capabilities can help to formulate correct strategy. Strategy should meet four critical tests (i) empirical (ii) logical integrity (ii) Common sense (iv) practical utility. Strategy correctly formulated shapes tactics. Properly executed tactics wins battle. Tactical errors have caused tremendous loss of security forces who are engaged in anti-naxal operations. Improvement of command in combat and various trainings can reduce tactical errors. More than tactical errors, errors in strategic estimates can cause devastations.

Naxals treat security force and the regime from strategic point of view as paper tigers and from tactical point of view as real tigers. Therefore, the decision makers have to take sufficient care to formulate and calibrate strategy and the force on ground should execute sound tactics. However, in pursuit of strategic objectives one should not neglect tactical truths. Lastly the quote of anonymous General is worth mentioning "you may not be interested in strategy, but the strategy is interested in you." It implies the S.F. and administration must counter the strategy of Naxalites by understanding different dimensions of strategy pertaining to people, politics, preparation for combat and execution of combat.

Action Plan at Local, State, and National Level

Naxals perpetrate offensive actions, propaganda and political agitation to destroy Government institutions, security force infrastructures and to simultaneously win over masses. In order to counter Naxalites' offensives, the regime, the security force the administration have to conduct various actions at various levels. But unfortunately the planning to tackle the Maoist threat in many infested areas is woefully bad. The consequences of fundamental planning omissions become great obstacles to action. Therefore, action needs action planning.[5] The action plan is basically agenda setter; it sets the agenda for the purpose of system building, peace building, security building and force building. Touchstone of real resolve is the implementation of action plan. Action plan for block level, state level, and national level peace building of highly affected areas should be prepared and implemented. Security building of police station, district and state level should be prepared and implemented. Force building at state central level should be prepared taking into consideration the operational capacity requirement. Action plan at all level should be built developed, and implemented in time bound manner and also refined periodically. There should be periodic review of action plan preferably half-yearly.

Security Domination and Administration out Reach in Isolated Physical Space which Encourages Extremism

The most fundamental need of counter-extremism is the presence of security force and administration at remote and conflict prone areas. As free trade zone encourage trade, so also free guerrilla zone where administration is absent, encourages naxals to develop their outfit there and wage guerrilla warfare. All grounds are not suitable for extremism; Naxalites initially select difficult hilly terrain where presence of security force and administration is nil or minimum as their area of operations. Gradually they fan to other areas from these so called safe heavens. Putatively ungoverned space acts as the breeding ground of extremists. They use these areas as bases, hideouts, training centers and as well launching pads. Most of the infrastructures of the naxalites are located in these areas. The administration and security should gradually regain control of these areas; they should not let naxalites retain support areas or sanctuaries.

In hilly remote areas the criteria for establishing various administrative units on the basis of population should be replaced by the criteria of area. These hilly areas are sparsely populated; there occurs the tyranny of distance. Many times a poor man from a remote village in order to get some govt. work or P.D.S. benefit has to move more than 30 K.Ms and half the distance he walks. It becomes even unmanageable for the officials to reach many areas of their jurisdictions.

Preventive Deployment of Security and Administrative Forces in Mildly Affected Areas and Newly Targeted Areas

Naxalites believe in the principle that the more scattered their forces and activities the security force will find it very difficult to handle. The resources of security force will fritter away while handling the problem in far off scattered places. In most of the far off new places naxalites are moving unopposed because of deficit security in those areas. States should identify mildly infested naxal areas and newly naxal targeted areas; states should prepare plan, mobilize resources fast. Then the state should make preventive deployment of security and administrative resources in these areas to prevent the spread of naxalism. Again as such prevention is easier than elimination, and eradicating naxalism in mildly affected newer areas is fast achievable. Here, one should remember that whichever party holds the ground first and controls the public that party will march in that area. Therefore, March of Naxalism has to be scotched from new areas and back rolled from mildly affected areas.

Counter Institutional framework to Combat Naxal Machine

Naxalites have created a combat machine that is conducting guerrilla warfare vigorously. They have created a complex organisation with an ability to plan strategically, tactically and operate precisely, effectively. Naxalites as predators are destroying institutions by wanton destruction and savage violence in highly infested areas; and as parasites, as termites they are destroying some institutions from within. Problems that require stronger and lasting solutions are often not susceptible to quick fixes. Strong institutional remedies are required. A long term counter Naxalism framework has to be created. Efforts should be made to develop institutions which enable effective operations. There is a need to develop think-and-do-tank in all the states to counter naxal menace.

Violent conflicts break down the institutional framework. Naxalites are not only breaking jails but also they are using jails as the breeding centre to create more cadres from other jail mates. Jails are being used by them to serve criminal-subversive design. Jails as well as the entire criminal justice system need rejuvenations. Intelligence/vigilance institutions need further strengthening and streamlining so that they can operate to achieve the economic strangulation of the outfit. Special commando units in each affected states must be created to fight the effectives. Remote area development agencies need to focus more on the development of the remote areas.

Information operations

Naxals use lies, half-truths, bluffs, intrigues to frame wrong perception among public. They also manipulate facts to serve strategic interest. In combat, perception is everything. Left wing conflict has been rightly considered as armed propaganda. Naxals fight with bullets and bullshits; they fight with guns and slogans. A good slogan beats a good solution. Naxalites through misinformation, propaganda create many artificial problems and then transform those to real one. Naxalites through information manipulation transform many smaller problems to bigger one. Extremist is like a professional magician who tricks the audience by turning a false image into a perceived reality.[6] Information operations are the key elements in anti-naxal operations. Information is a strategic resource vital to internal security.[7] In information warfare strategic, tactical, operational warfare merge.[8] Naxalites use perception management to influence the attitude, objective reasoning of local people as well as intelligentsia. Through their cultural troops- Chetana natya mandali, Jana natya mandali and their regular meetings at village level they try to conduct propaganda. The Maoists through cultural troupes, literature, pamphlets, meetings, propagate their ideology of class war. Sometimes they hire some intellectuals to make propaganda for them. They flood internet with pro-naxal articles to influence the public.

They tried to pursue their aim through the power of gun and through political propaganda. The regime needs to do counter propaganda at local, provincial and national level; its objective should be to highlight the wrong doings of the Naxalites and the positive aspect of Government schemes and works. Serious counter propaganda through electronics media, cultural troupes, through all India Radio must be made vigorously. The misdeeds of naxalites, the reward on the naxalites, and the good schemes of govt. must be publicised seriously. The administration should build and preserve public opinion support and also act to influence the attitudes and behaviour of local populations. They should communicate messages which reflect ideas and actions for containing conflict and maintaining peace and order. The security force and administration have to use more brains and fewer bullets.

Development and Security in Tandem

Naxalites try to isolate security and subsequently try to destroy both development and security in affected areas. In remote areas there are inputs which reveal that naxalites hijack developmental schemes. Therefore, there is a need for application of development and security in tandem. Development without security is untenable and security without development is unsustainable. Conflicts add extra urgency for development. Development and security are much more inclusive, organic and transparent. Development is dependent on security and vice versa.

Communities in remote areas are desperate for security and basic services. The Government agencies must make efforts to marginalise the extremists' agenda with regard to the general population; because grievances are seeds of extremism. They should co-opt naxals' objectives so that naxals don't get any cause to gather crowd under any banner for conducting mass struggle. Solving multitude of local problems will help de-escalation of conflict. Moreover agrarian reform, greater rural economic opportunity, and a credible system of justice can ensure that the salutary effects of a counter naxalites campaign will be permanent. Nations that have contended successfully with left wing extremism have taught that the role of force is secondary to that of coordinated political, social and economic development. Conflict can be resolved by entrenching security and by cleaning developmental malaise and by bringing all round development of the area and affected people.

Public Resistance against Naxalites and Public Participation in Development and Security

The ultimate action to eradicate the menace lies with the public. If the public start disowning the naxalites, then naxals can be easily eliminated. Initially, confidence building measures have to be taken by showing the Government's intention of dealing naxalites with heavy hand. Sound rehabilitation policy has to be launched; people's efforts to resist the naxalites must be institutionalised through village defence societies. Public resistance must be protected. Public is the fulcrum of Left wing extremism. Public can tilt the balance of power to any side. Naxalites are afraid of Salwa Juddum, Sendra & similar public resistance movement.

It is pertinent to mention about success of people's resistance in Peru against Sendero Luminoso as mentioned by Robin Kirk in the famous book 'The Shining Path':

> "The Shining Path was finally defeated not by the army and its blind blows, but the police and the people themselves, who rebelled against the rebels and made the countryside, Mao's launch pad of revolt, hostile to them. What it lost is all too clear in these pages: a chance, perhaps fragile and doomed from the outset, at a more equitable society. For all of its admittedly laudable ideals-justice for the disenfranchised, bread for the hungry, respect for the downtrodden-the Shining Path sowed only misery for Peruvians". [11]

Public resistance becomes a dynamic social struggle against revolutionary utopia. Public resistance movement can be a contested space which contains significant potential for development, peace and scope for conflict resolution. Development and democratic reconstruction can take place. Public support and participation can improve response of administration and Government. Public participation can give a new spin to development and security. It can develop the area, isolate the naxalites socially, politically and as well defeat them physically. It can secure and serve the population better and there by rendering LWE futile. However, support from the population is mostly conditional. If people get adequate security then public support becomes easily available.

Macro Level Complacency and Micro Level Inadequacy

India is a huge country with huge military power and paramilitary forces. Sometimes, this sense of complacency impedes solution to local problems. In due course of time the local problem mutates to regional problem and then to national problem. Non-availability of adequate resources at the micro level creates a hopeless situation. Continuous failures to make the means actually available at the ground correspond with the failure to pursue the end. Enhancing local capacity is very much required. Small tools and resources become inadequate to solve big problems. Extremists are concentrated in remote areas; they out number security force and administrative agencies there. This is the ubiquitous source of vulnerability of security force and administration in few guerrilla zones and guerrilla base areas. These areas need to be saturated with good quality administrative/security forces and other resources. The lack of infrastructure at these places further aggravates situations. These issues need to be addressed. The regime has to equip and empower suitably local levels to robustly challenge Naxalism.

Need Good Leaders at All Critical Levels and Places

In Guerrilla war the premium is on leadership. Only men of courage, tactics and great skill can make the system work. Effective leadership is every thing; leaders are critical resource. Leadership style is the external manifestations of internal principle. If a leader is reckless, he will waste resources, if short tempered he can be provoked to act rash. If he is egoist he can be deceived by flattery. If he is self centered he will hesitate to take decisions at critical moment. Putting effective people into positions of authority is absolutely necessary to create an orgnisation that can successfully execute adaptive strategies during competitive engagements. Commitment and character of the leader set the stage for eventual victory. It is the war of companies, platoons and sections. Platoon/ section leaders are the linchpin of operational effectiveness. Good section platoon leaders may save the situation and poor leaders can ruin the force and situation. During peace time, good leaders at the top level can manage, but during crisis and conflict good leaders are needed at all levels. Good leaders at cutting edge level with special initiative, endurance, understanding and enthusiasm can accomplish mission. To lead means devise correct methods of work. Leaders should learn to play piano means active coordination and firm grip.

Success comes from well-trained leaders who are educated for judgment and able to adapt to evolving requirement and apply critical reasoning and creative thinking to respond to complete ambiguous situations. Problem-solvers who understand the complexities of the operational environment and possess the adaptability to rise to ambiguity and rapidly changing situations with critical reasoning are required at critical places. The leaders-cum- officers must deal with a world of 24/7 information and public scrutiny, cope with perpetual ambiguity and uncertainty, and adjust to ever-changing goals. In a life and death situation the only way to deal is to use reasoned, patient and empathetic style. Local level officers must be trained to anticipate and take the initiative to adapt and innovate without the need to check back for instructions and directions. Following Mao's tactics Naxals have started leadership programs for their cadres. Now it is high time that sufficient care by decision maker should be taken to develop leaders at all levels. Success comes from well-trained leaders who are educated for judgment and able to adapt to evolving requirements and apply critical reasoning and creative thinking to respond to complex ambiguous situations. The leaders should be problem-solvers who understand the complexities of the operational environment and possess the adaptability to react to ambiguity and rapidly changing situations with critical reasoning. Leaders make things happen. They face reality and mobilize appropriate response. They encourage doing the same. They determine directions of the organisations from where they are to where the organisation needs to go. Leadership is professional commitment. Leaders work to achieve objective. Good leaders perform proficiently. Leaders determine success.

Leaders with verve, energy, courage, sincerity, humanity, discipline, commitment and credibility can deliver the results.

Special Forces to Fight Special Problem

Effective counter Naxal operations need radical changes in organisations of regular battalions, combat tactics, skill, equipments. The main requirements for the troops on the ground are capability to stay longer period in the jungle, team cohesiveness, and capability for night operations, good communication and rapid deployment. This has been achieved by Grey Hound and up to much extent by other similar special and elite forces. Therefore, Special Forces are highly required in the changing context and character of present LWE situation. Special Forces provide a perspective on the application of force in an intensified conflict. With the intensification of conflict many long range operations with highly ambitious nature becomes imperative. Special Forces are versatile, agile and suited for operating against irregulars for their discreet action and jungle craft capability. Since much of guerrilla confidence is built upon the security of a sanctuary, the operation of a hunter-killer team in those areas have tremendous impact on guerrilla operation. Therefore, the creation and utilisation of the special task force can completely shift LWE operation from defence to offence. Special Forces use special equipments and weapons and have special impact. Developing Special Forces and elite troops is the most important requirement. Special Forces cannot survive in isolation but with symbiotic relationship of conventional paramilitary, military and police force. Special Forces can survive with less expenditure and high result. They are more mobile and offensive troops. Special Forces act as force multipliers. The institutional influence of elite, Special Forces need to be created through special motivation, training and equipment so that it will have tremendous demoralizing impact on the irregulars. Special Forces and elite forces are the most useful and usable troops against extremists.

Effective Management of Combat of various Phases and Piling on Pressure

One important aspect of resolving Naxalites challenge is defeating the military power of the Naxalites. Naxalites are continuously upgrading their weaponry, tactics and command structure. Maoists gain fresh momentum after every successful ambush. But, with every successful operations of security force, naxalites also suffer double setback due to loss of their manpower and weaponry. Small successes create positive momentum that is then carried forward and reinforced. The security force should maintain momentum amid intermittent setbacks and difficulties. Security force should make efforts progressively to regain more naxal stronghold areas and consolidate those areas. Therefore, in order to defeat Naxalites the states must continuously upgrade their security forces, and security framework. The states should build their forces extensively, develop correct force structure. Force level should be enhanced. There should be strategic reserve at national and state level to meet contingency and to fight the evasive and mobile war of naxalites. Security force should acquire more strength to fight. Security forces have to play hard, play together, and play smart. Force maintenance should be done through proper training, rotation, motivation of force. Naxalites are developing various commands of their military forces. Therefore, due precaution should be taken to develop proper command of various forces. The above efforts of management of combat and micro-management of combat should be done systematically to obviate command errors. Naxals for smooth management of combat follow Mao's strategic defensive,equilibrium, and offensive stage; similarly S.F. should also divide the entire combat into various phases to achieve better management of combat.

Management of Combat in Three Phases

Combat against naxalites like chess consists of basically three phases viz.:- (1) opening game (2) middle game and (3) end game; the phases are in consecutive order. But, unlike chess nobody in combat can straight jump to middle game or end game without undergoing through opening game, unless the opponent completely bungles. Opening game basically deals with the preparation of force, defences. However, preparation of force and defences remain as permanent feature. Combat is a dynamic and ever pursuing phenomenon. The effective pursuit of opening game yields better result in middle game and the professional management of first two games can result in early end game. Experience shows that opening game is difficult because everything has to start from scratch; middle game is very brutal because both the contenders fight for their existence; and the end game is magical. Some of the states are in opening game and some are in middle game phase; naxalites in few places are in middle game phase and in many places in opening phase. The problem has infectious tendency; the States where it has been noticed should start immediately opening game. Prevention at the early stage is much easier and less costly. Opening game preordains development of combat power and efficiency, reduction of vulnerability of force, and improvement in understanding of combat. However, the above requirement is applicable in all three phases of the combat.

Combat Power and Vulnerability of Force

The anti-naxalite operation will yield result only if there is sufficient increase in the combat power of the State. The regime needs adequate combat power to engage the naxals in effective combat. Combat power needs to be generated adequately to pursue combat vigorously. Excessive combat power of extremists will definitely create more problems for the regime. Combat power is the joint function of resisting power (defences), striking power (offensive forces and resources), integrating, staying and finding power (intelligence). Resisting power is the defensive power of the regime; it includes all the troops, structures, and devices for security and protection of vital installation and important personalities. Striking power is the sum total of troops, and equipments for conducting offensive operations. Integrating power includes the capability to rehabilitate the ex- combatants; the power to take the ex-combatants into the mainstream. Staying power includes logistics and capability of force to remain in battlefield. It can be put into a mathematical formula:

Combat power = (Resisting + Striking + finding + staying + integrating) power – vulnerability of the force

Vulnerability of the force is a very important concept; it impinges on the outcome of battle. Many times combatants study the habit of the force and exploit the situation. Terrain, distance, force fatigue and visibility of force have tremendous adverse impact on the outcome of combat. However many people have peculiar views of combat; people think small victory may lead to big failure so they plead for more inaction. People think inaccurately that small failures may lead to big failures, or small victory; small victory also may lead to big victory; but they are not sure. Without conducting proper study trend of combat can not be predicted. Therefore, it can be said that vulnerability of force can help in finding the direction of combat and also mould the outcome of combat. Sometimes the force fatigue plays major role in any battle; force fatigue induces tremendous errors in battle. Similarly, visibility, terrain, distance have adverse impact on combat. The prediction of correct trend of combat can be achieved from the correct study of the vulnerability of the force. Vulnerability of the force can be computed by subtracting habit of the force, difficult terrain, distance of area of operations, force fatigue and visibility of force from the total sum of command, control, coordination, communication, intelligence, training, and technology. This also can be put into a mathematical equation as mentioned below:

Vulnerability of the force = (command + control + coordination + communication + intelligence + Training + technology – habit-terrain-distance-force fatigue-visibility of force)

Fundamental Wrong Understanding of Nuances of Combat Leads to Serious Errors

From the sublime to ridiculous is but a single step; so also in combat, narrow margin exists between victory and defeat, life and death. If the forces are faster by few seconds they can remain alive in the battle ground and snatch victory from the jaws of death. The cause of error may be slight, but the impact can be enormous and it may lead to loss of lot of impetus. Effective management of combat presupposes nuanced understanding of various operations. Counter Naxal operations consist of offensive, defensive and stability operations conducted along multiple lines of operations.

Counter Naxal operations are least doctrinally clarified. A galaxy of issues and influences converge on it. Many times counter guerrilla operations are filled with command errors, political errors, and errors of personal incompetence, technical inadequacy and plain misfortune. There are plenty of errors in judgments at all levels due to lack of understanding of conflict, defence and offense and their inter-relationship, own force and enemy, rules of engagement, situational awareness, local superiority, unity of efforts, economy of forces, unity of purposes, perseverance in the time of setbacks, importance of mobility, terrain, training, rapid deployment, mobile reserve, circumspection, celerity, crisis response training, mission essential task, maladroit monitoring, mental preparation of troops, appropriate number, equipment and technology mix, force structure, logistics, logical lines of operations, combat support service, strategy, tactics, operations in exterior line and interior line, tactical attacks in a war of strategic defence, tactical speed in a war strategically protracted[12] and fighting intelligently. Greatest danger is also from over simplification and impatience.

As a result of wrong understanding of combat, operations become desultory. Some people think no operations no problem, small operations small problem, big operations big problem. Some advocate only offence, deprecate defence and claim that before breakfast they will finish the problem. Much about defence is misunderstood by people because it is not what it seems and what people project in the name of defence. Some considers naxals like bears, hornet of honey bee will not harm if they are not disturbed. Some people rely only on mass rather than on mobility. Art of operations consist well reasoned circumspect defence followed by rapid audacious raids and attack. The errors recur; conflict aggravates with mistakes. It results in operations with reluctance and hesitation. Reckless and careless operations are outcome of wrong understanding. Mistakes happen but unforced errors should not take place.

Command, Control, Coordination, Communication, Intelligence, Training, and Technology need Improvement

Conducting a successful counterinsurgency campaign requires a flexible, adaptive force led by agile, well informed people; this can be possible only by developing proper C4IT2. C4IT2 are very important conceptual tools with the commanders to launch effective combat. Each individual concept has tremendous impact on combat. Some Commanders conduct operations for years without understanding nuances of operations. Of course operations have to be learnt through operations. But, learning should be correct and faster; people should be open to learning. Many smart people don't like to learn. In some areas some forces are deployed in the battle zone for more than a decade in violation of battle roaster. The commanders should develop ability to deploy and sustain combat forces in an extended crisis; they should create mutually supported posts so that force multiplication can take place.

Plan and execution of combat depends upon understanding of Command and Control. Quality of command and control decide system performance and mission effectiveness by establishing intent (the goal), determining roles, responsibilities and relationships, rules and constraints, monitoring and assessing the situation and progress. Integral to command and control are the allocation of existing resources and the search for additional resources. Command and control also implies guide, conduct, supervise or direct. Command and control occur concurrently with real time guidance or direction. The basis of C2 is authority. Official authority—the position of the commander, personal authority—the equation, reputation, skill, character of the commander play major role in real time supervision, guidance and direction. A good Commander consider close up view, over all view, enemy commander's view while deciding unity of effort. Agility is the most important attribute of command and control approach. The Commander should have agility which means he should have the ability to rapidly change his orientations in response to the happenings in the external world. Disorientation of command can lead to panic, chaos and the breakdown of control thereby causing low morale and breaking of team spirit which may cause the force to sink deeper into defensive and deadlocked positions.

Command is the nerve center of any security force. Commands must be task organised. Function oriented command system is logistics. Output oriented command is operational. Both the command should be properly managed and there is a need for unified command to look after the entire combat. As per Clausewitz the best system of command is to have a genius on charge first in general and then at the decisive point.

The integrity of command structure of security force including police must be maintained. It should be seen in correct perspective. The commander's job is to be a sentinel for his unit. A unit of security force does well only when the commander performs well; he supervises the unit properly. One of the most important responsibilities of senior commander is to assess a given situation and set the strategic response. Unless the commander make correct sense of operational situation he cannot define correct strategies for action. It is expected of command to take firm and immediate decision. Command should form correct team and activate team commitment. Commander should understand various factors of combat and even remain aware of it. Commander should develop new creative approaches to operational problems e.g. maneuverability, survivability, and capacities.

The main target of naxalites like any other combatants target more the mind of the commander than the body of the soldiers. Therefore, the command in combat has to be improved. Rudimentary command structures which have been ruined in many forces should be re-developed. Commanders have to be tested and tempered in fighting. The commanders should have troop leading capability. There is problem of deployment. Some commanders view that core area should be tackled first, others think periphery should be taken first. Naxal problem is like a poisonous snake it has poison in its tail and teeth. If one hits the tail it will retaliate through its teeth; if its head is attacked by security force then tail will attack security force. Therefore the Commander has to decide the correct line of attack. Freedom of decision and fullest operational initiative to commanders in the field is the need of the day. Judgment and intuition are basis of command. The commander has to develop guidance and operational procedures.

Sometimes the Commanders act recklessly, thoughtlessly, and in the process endanger the lives of their subordinates. Thoughtlessness should not be considered as, bravery. Vagueness at the Commander level turns into confusion and lethargy at bottom. If the command is vague and half hearted by the time it reaches the field it will be meaningless. If people work unsupervised, then they will revert to their natural selfishness, they will see in command what they want to see, and their behaviour will promote their own interest.

Each commander asks his field men to tune to his frequency, but most important is the commander should himself tune to the ground reality. A commander who temporizes has reduced chance of making error; but, at the same time he fails to take initiative which results in weakened confidence among its troops. It causes the will to fight of SF falter. It has been noticed during decade long combat that the lower echelons of command are perpetrating higher percentage of mistakes. Some commands have fatal propensity for taking bad advice. Divided and crippled command cannot give result. Constantly micromanaging in the background upsets command who is busy fighting hard engagements. Some commanders kill initiative of the junior commanders by centralizing all authorities. Teams do not win games and battle by good moves, but lose by bad moves. It is the responsibility of the commander to take good moves and avoid bad moves. A distant journey tests the strength of a horse and a guerrilla war tests the strength of the commanders. The guidelines for commander can be summed up from Mao's quote which is mentioned below:

> "swimming in the ocean of war, the commander not only must not flounder but must make sure of reaching the opposite shore with measured strokes. The laws of directing war constitute the art of swimming in the ocean of war".

Coordination

Professionally the security force at all levels should be more serious, more keen, more skilled and more coordinated than the Indian cricket team. Then only they can withstand the naxal offensives and also defeat the naxals. Coordination has to be achieved through cooperation. Team building is essential for accomplishing missions. Casualties are a part of war; instead of blame-game SF should conduct error analysis and error rectification. Joint training, rehearsal, dining and games can also achieve more coordination. Coordination is an ongoing process. Some coordination problem remains when many agencies work together in achieving any mission. But, sometimes some media magnifies it.

Communication

Communication is the essence of command. Communication capabilities are indispensable for operational security. This is one vital sector where many improvements are desired. Secured and real time communication is the crux of the problem. Equipments for secured communication and equipments for easy communication from remotest places are required. Infallible communication is never a reality. Therefore, considering imperfect communication as natural the commanders must organize alternative system of communication.

Naxals are using variety of means of communications from drum to digital system. Sometimes through I-com sets they listen to the communications of security force. They are also destroying communication towers in remote areas.

Intelligence

Anti-guerrilla war is an intelligence war. Operational 'eyes and ears' capability is inevitable in the combat situation. To beat the LWE on the ground, the first essential is knowledge about enemy, people, terrain, own force and operational environment. Basic intelligence about naxal organisation and operations and regular, accurate and timely intelligence about position are required. Knowledge about naxal, his methods, strength, weaknesses, tactics and techniques are required. Knowledge of the own force their capability and vulnerability also must be studied properly.

One of the roles of intelligence is to generate mindset, awareness and preparedness by collection and dissemination of information and high level of discourse about LWE and tactical response to it. Most important aspect of anti-naxalite operation is intelligence. All the affected states must develop full fledged special intelligence unit to deal with this problem. In Malaya the most important aspect which helped anti-insurgency operation was the creation of intelligence training centre for not only the intelligence operatives, but also all cutting edge level officers and men of security force and other branches were trained to collect intelligence.

> A highly efficient Intelligence (Special Branch) Training School was established for the first time in Malaya. Not only did it train Special Branch personnel; it provided short courses for some executive officers of the Army, "General Duties" Police Officers, and certain civil departments of Government.

> Templer told Harry Miller, a journalist for the straits Times, "The Emergency will be won by our intelligence system-our Special Branch". Special Branch did not begin to obtain

effective intelligence in the Chinese villages of Malaya until police posts in those villages had themselves been made secure. This must be the first step to any real progress in counterinsurgency. It worked awfully well. Successful intelligence is largely cumulative and is the first step to any real progress in counterinsurgency.[13]

There is a great need to create a big training institute for cutting edge officers of the security officers to enable them to transform even each S.F. man into intelligence collector. Most of the ground level intelligence can only be collected from the ground which the pure intelligence operatives cannot procure. Again intelligence lead to operations and operations also leads to tremendous generation of intelligence. If the operational man does not have knack for intelligence then many gold mines of intelligence will get buried in the ground. The post combat interview of force yields tremendous inputs. The S.F. should learn two basic analysis: (1) analysis of naxal actions, (2) net work analysis. Study of Naxalites' network without valuable background into the nature and functions of networks is unhelpful at best and at worst misleading. To be successful the SF must continuously evaluate and prioritise his organisation and allocation of intelligence resources. The most important way to fight naxals is with a better organised, better equipped and quicker intelligence system. Dynamic conflict environment necessitates agile, effective intelligence system.

Train Hard and Fight Easy

Human performance improvement for all type of personnel is essential. However, it is more important for the members of security force. The members of security force should learn basics of endurance, firing and field craft. They should learn correct weapon keeping, carrying and using habit. The security force should learn to be strong in attack, assault and pursue; they should be quick in advance, assault, clear the battlefield and withdraw. They should have the skills of weapon firing, mine defusing, grenade throwing and armed combat, first aid. They should be first in observation, discipline, and initiative.

Their defences against traps, surprise, fire, spies, and accidents should be excellent. They should learn how to survive in the battle field and win in combat. Adapting training to address emerging in-theatre tactics is required. Security force has to work in teams; therefore they should be trained as teams. Better training can be imparted through good trainers which are becoming rare species in police and paramilitary forces; it should be consciously developed and properly motivated. Most of the police forces have no knowledge about guerrilla warfare. So, proper training for the police force about guerrilla warfare must be imparted and proper guerrilla warfare training facilities developed. "*Fight the guerrilla like a guerrilla*." This seems to have made a good quote, but not a good commitment. Only through training, motivation this can be achieved. Training should be in touch with actual combat. SF need following periodic training inputs on following concepts:-ambush and counter ambush, force protection, mine awareness, fire coordination, situational awareness, night operation, recce patrol, scout, field signal, maneuvers, combat leadership training. Naxals with their military instructors' team have started some training of leadership development programme, ambush and other field craft inputs. Another interesting feature is that in some highly infested naxal areas the local boys play ambush game regularly. Since these areas are forest areas there is nothing new that the boys take interest in ambushing; ambushing and hunting have many similar actions.

The security forces have to imbibe a new set of operational and survival skills and they need to be properly motivated. Body and mind of the troops must be trained to face the shocks and rigours of combat. Good training is imperative in the active preparation for combat. Training should be in touch with actual combat. However, the best tactics of S.F. can be negated by failure to teach the troops the problems, hopes and fears of the local population. The troops must be taught the principles of force or physical action. Every use of force must have justifiable reason. It must not be an act of revenge. The action must be designed to prevent guerrilla activity or illegal acts.

Use of Technology as Force Multipliers

Irregular wars are extended walking tours. Security force is forced to march large distances regularly with huge loads in full scale march order kit of First world war. Jungles work as black holes for security force. Even if the force level is raised yet it seems inadequate in vast area. Their major problem also lies not only in how to fight the enemy but also how to exist in the field, and in difficult terrain. The security force at times bivouac in the open, they suffer many deprivations. Here tools and technology can work as force multiplier. Taking inspiration **from Archimedes' statement 'you give me tool I can lift the** earth ,' it can be said that give appropriate technologies and tools to security force they can solve the extremist problem. Air support, bullet proof jackets and sentry posts, good combat kit, water purifier, night visions, anti-mine equipments, exoskeleton uniform mobile medical units, sensors, radars etc. which can be customised according to ground needs. In the national level some organisations should conduct research and development task to develop tools and technologies which can work as force multipliers. These can serve as intrinsic and extrinsic force multiplier. The force multipliers can reduce fear of battle more than that the fear of fatigue and considerably improve combat effectiveness.

Combat Efficiency

Combat is hunger, malaria, dysentery, blister foot, heat, injuries and one has to be there to know what it is. Accidents, errors, indiscretions and gross waste of combat effort saps combat efficiency. Combat efficiency is the key to operational effectiveness. Thousands of troops may be deployed, but, if its operational effectiveness is zero or negative then it serves no purpose. As a result combat becomes fragmentary and subsidiary. One has to factor the issues which help troops in snatching victory against overwhelming odds, and find out the issues which contribute to fiascoes. "Why-operations-fail" deserves discussion. Failed operations are combinations of errors and omissions; reckless, careless and disorganised operations are due to poor battle drills, poor troop leading capability of the tactical and operational commanders. Suitably led, motivated and trained force can fight well. Rewarding personnel for good work boosts the morale and rewarding wrong persons for ostraneous reasons demoralises personnel. Out-of-turn promotions have worked as great motivation for the force. Bravery inspired by devotion to duty should be duly recognised. Small victories boost morale and at the same time big losses demoralises troops. Nonetheless, de-motivating and demoralizing factors are huge. Human rights trap, landmine trap, sniper, malaria, jaundice, poor facilities in the camp demoralise the troops.

Morale and health factors had corrosive effect on performance. Efficient casualty evacuation by chopper boosts morale. The sense of purposelessness depresses morale. More than combat, fatigue brings fear among the troops. SF gain in moral force through physical training; drilled, grilled and disciplined men fight well. The need for rest and building up energy is required for improving the strength and stamina of the force. Morale is the willingness and ability to give one's best in difficult and trying circumstances. Training can raise the technical and tactical level of the security force. The better the soldiers are trained, the higher is their morale.

Defensive measures can mute the negative consequences of tactical surprise. Operational art and tactical flexibility are prerequisites of counter guerrilla operations. Flexible standard operating procedure capable of adjusting to varying degrees of threat must be set forth. SF should generate appropriate, prudent and affordable measures for effective preparedness. Naxalites exploit the weaknesses of security, when they find the force prepared then they do not raid, drop the idea and go back. Un-organised operations and poor security are the natural results of a failure of supervision and discipline of force. There is a need for better, more coordinated, sophisticated operational policies and practices. Improvisation is the natural order of warfare. Matchless harmony of execution through understanding and practice is required for accomplishing combat missions.

Root and branch reconstruction of security force is essential. Many battalions of armed police have more than thirty percent of vacancies, chain of command is broken, age of more than 25 per cent is above than fifty years; definitely all these shows that the combat efficiency of those battalions will be low.

Conflict creates breeding ground for errors; the tensions of combat also add to errors. The psychology can be used to improve combat effectiveness; study of situational awareness. Spirituality related to death defying attitude, control of alcoholism, attention to detail can help in developing better combat psychology for troops which will add to its effectiveness. The spirit of one for all and all for one should be imbibed in to the force. The troops should react instinctively and instantaneously to dangerous encounters. Discipline is essential for combat efficiency. Boldness and circumspection create enabling environment. Combat means using weapon, saving self, and hitting enemy. The troops should understand that the fight begins with each individual member of security force. Combat behaviour management is essential. Some of the force which has the habit to fight from a distance and hide on the shadows should change their habits.

On the march when the troops are careless then they are easily surprised. Observing enemy has more significance. The party who can see first will hit first, those who hit first can win the battle. Combative temperament of the force needs to be developed.

Therefore, rigorous performance evaluation of the troops is required. Periodical review of operational outcomes must be done to assess the productivity of troops. Performance should also be analysed more on the basis of misses than on the basis of saves. Operational setbacks also should be threadbare analysed in closed door to prevent recurrence. Patience and caution are the first and most important rules for a successful operation and for the prevention of unnecessary casualties.

Span of success coincide with operational priorities. Sustained operations by right type of troops can yield success.

Agility accrues operational success. Agility stems from decentralised initiative. The troops grip on gun, ground, grenade and population will help in accomplishing the mission. Security forces have to be organised, trained, equipped and motivated for the conflict. The rotten shots have to be improved; in gun battle only 15 to 20 per cent fire. The capability to work in buddy and team has to be imbibed into the force. Consolidated defence, pre-operation appreciation of logistic, ground and enemy position helps in improving combat efficiency. People underestimate the power of will, skill and tenacity in combat. Morale, motivation and combat technique plays major role in improving combat efficiency.

Locate, Isolate, and Eradicate

Locate, isolate, and eradicate, these three activities sum up entire anti-guerrilla operations. These three words sound very simple, but these words are highly loaded. In a study of LWE of Vietnam and Philippines to locate gangs of LWE in jungle it was revealed that it took 600 hours of patrolling of SF to locate once a gang and out of about 10 contacts one became successful. Find out location of evasive, masked naxals and their infrastructures, hideouts, base area or areas is a difficult task. It requires tremendous amount of efforts, careful study of organisational matrix, terrain studies, photographic and physical reconnaissance, and possibly infiltration of the movement. Naxals are highly mobile, therefore locating should be done in day to day basis. Isolation involves separation of naxals from their sources of information, food, funds, resources, supply of ammunitions and explosives. Naxals should be isolated from intelligence, recruits, and finally from supportive population. Isolating the outfit from their mass base is required. Serious endeavours should be made to break naxals' connection with civilian population and establish Government authority and social order. The most important anti-naxal measure is about depriving Naxals, of supplies, information and recruits. This can not be achieved without physically dominating the ground and without performing the first task of locating the Naxals.

Eradicate the problem by fighting well and fighting with principle. People should remember that a wily maoist rarely provides a massed target; and since the extremists create layers of defences the security force have to break layers one by one. However, the SF have to pursue the extremists relentlessly, deny them the ability to train, deliberate, plan and conduct operations. Token performance by SF must be shunned. The present ground realities of combat against Naxalites require nothing less than a thorough and comprehensive initiative of troops. Sustained reactive and proactive operations as per the need of the ground should be conducted by imaginative, intelligent and bold leaders. One should not be disappointed if the first wave of attack does not reap the desired benefits. Waves of operations need to be conducted. Eradication presupposes reliable information and demands extreme operational flexibility and a high degree of mobility. It will be well to remember that these activities are not rigidly compartmental. Hostile will resides with the conspirators and combatants; the hostile will of naxals should be broken by law. Efforts of SF in stead of becoming little more than an elaborate means of buying time should be focused on making determined advance. The operations should aim to encircle and finish Naxal by preventing re-supply of resources to them and by preventing escape, and re-infestation of cleared areas. The SF should move fast, strike hard and finish rapidly winning the combat. The security force must act with plan, unity of efforts, purpose, and thereby seize the strategic initiative. Strategic initiative can be achieved by securing the security posts and line of communication and by rendering the bases of naxalites insecure. Proper force building efforts and area developing efforts must be made. Strategic opportunities must be exploited by arranging intensive intelligence and extensive operations. The developmental, political, and security forces must grasp the realities of the situation, determine the objectives, and seize the initiative, use nation's strength against the problem. Ultimately with synchronised development and domination the naxalites can be eliminated.

Suggestions

- Budget session should start from 31st May, so that open seasons of March, April, and May can be utilised for effective budget spending.
- There is urgent need to introduce agricultural schools with rural technology to solve unemployment by orienting large number of rural masses towards efficient agricultural system and rural technology.
- Admissions in to ITI should not have any compulsory educational qualification of matric; so that large number of interested boys can get vocational qualification.
- The Bal Ashrams in naxal affected districts should be located at those places where security can be easily provided.
- Infrastructure deficit Naxal affected district headquarters and bigger sub-divisional headquarters should be provided with sufficient infrastructures and resources for running Central schools, Hospitals, science colleges so that the local people get plenty of opportunity for education and the government officials do not feel constrained to work in those areas. There should be sufficient housing for the staff.
- Strong campaign against greed based corruption should be taken. Town planning of new districts and sub-divisions should so be planned that security becomes a built-in feature.
- Any public servant recruited through corrupt practice will definitely indulge into corrupt practices. In all States the recruitment processes of all departments should be streamlined in such a manner that there can be no scope for corruption.
- Budget for Homeland security should be increased. Hundred percent central grants should be given for developing forces in states.
- Keeping in mind jail breaks by Naxals and terrorists, high security exclusive jails for extremists and terrorists should be created.

- Strong anti-terror law as recommended by Administrative Reforms Commission may be enacted.
- Efficient Regional forensic labs with cyber forensic, explosive, ballistic experts, brain mapping, and lie detector facilities must be created to help investigation of complicated extremist crimes by examining evidences against those crimes.
- Forest produce and other locally available products should be so utilised that more employment generation can take place in affected areas.
- Development of forested areas is not sustainable because pattern of human settlement is not sustainable. People living in hunting gathering stage cannot be developed by more pumping of funds. The settlements of human beings in forested areas need to be changed to cluster system to make development viable and protected.
- Administrative reach and security presence has to be ensured in those isolated areas with hilly jungle terrain which are being used by Naxalites as their base areas and hideouts.
- Proper action plan at all levels should be formulated, implemented and every half-yearly progress should be reviewed. Every year action plan should be re-drawn to make it more realistic.
- Decision makers need to frame correct strategies and fight the strategies of Naxalites; and simultaneously tactical errors which are the biggest factor of defeat and losses of forces should be rectified.
- Naxals' revolutionary politics of revolutionary united front should be countered by democratic forces. The regime should formulate correct strategies to counter the divisive, dangerous politics of RUF. As a result, reduction of political space of Naxalites will automatically reduce depth of Naxalites.
- Public participation in development and security is the major anti-dote against Naxalism. Therefore, any public resistance against Naxalism should be supported by Government.

- In due course of time the mild Naxal local problem mutates to serious regional problem, and subsequently to national problem. Therefore, micro level inadequacy of structure, funds, tools, manpower, and infrastructure should be addressed at the earliest.
- In mildly affected areas troops with skills for dealing with security, civic action and psy-ops should be deployed for containing the menace.
- In Guerrilla war the premium is on leadership. Only men of courage, tactics and great skill can make the system work. Now it is high time that sufficient care should be taken to put good leaders at the cutting edge of each organisations.
- Extraordinary problems need extraordinary resources. Sun Tzu correctly said victory needs overwhelming force. In order to make current interventions and initiatives more effective, operational capacity requirement should be realistic.
- Special Forces and elite forces like Grey Hound in sufficient number should be created in affected states to fight Naxalites' people's liberation Guerrilla Army.
- In extremely Naxalites infested areas development is the solution, security is the precondition and in mildly affected areas development is the precondition and security is the solution. Security and development must be applied in tandem to resolve Naxalite conflict.
- March of Naxalism has to be scotched from reaching new areas. Prevention is easier than elimination. States should identify mildly infested Naxal areas and newly targeted naxal areas; and then the states should make preventive deployment of security administrative and development resources in these areas to prevent the growth of Naxalism.
- Appropriate technologies and tools as force multipliers have tremendous significance in war against Naxalites. Research and development wing should work continuously to develop appropriate low cost technology.
- Force level should be increased, force structure should be improved and pressure should be piled on to recover the

lost ground and to defeat the military powers of naxalites. Well trained and equipped Special Forces need to be created in all the affected states to fight the problem.

- Malaya benefited in counter insurgency operations by establishing national level intelligence school for training personnel. Similarly regional intelligence training schools should be created for training concerned troops and personnel for collection of intelligence.
- According to Sun Tzu, people are able to see the tactics, but not the strategy behind any success. Therefore, fighting the Naxal strategy and foiling their tactics is most important. Formulating the correct strategy is vital.
- Structure and resources must fit the strategy. If there is any discrepancy, the issue must be addressed immediately. Mobilising resources and developing human resource is critical. Many important organisations like the commando units, intelligence units and engineering units must be developed for combat as well as for combat support service.

Prognosis

The naxalites have a grand strategy of destroying our political system and Government from outside and as well from inside the system. Pace and intensity of guerrilla activity has multiplied. Fighting against naxalism is at a varied pace. In some areas the tempo of operations against naxals is high; in some area it is low. In few areas naxals have received major jolts from security force. At the same time, in few pockets it is gradually eroding the effectiveness of Government institutions locally. Resilience of security and administration to left wing extremism in some areas are reducing day by day. Therefore, there is no possibility that the conflict will end soon. It is the start line, still a marathon to run. The SF have to fight the LWE first to a stand still and then to marginalise their agenda with regard population. There are no easy cures for such a complex phenomenon. An appreciation of the complexity of the issues is required. Lack of issue perspective is perhaps a more plausible explanation for fundamental errors in analyzing, understanding and applying to the phenomena which should be corrected. Correct perspective is required to act in present and plan for future. Even some of the intellectuals are not able to see the hidden traps laid by the Naxalites; they are either lost sight of local, national and galactic perspectives vis-à-vis the naxalites or they are intentionally meandering about the issues pertaining to left wing extremism.

Naxalism has metamorphosed from tragedy of local common people to the tragedy of the Indian democracy. It poses threat to public order and political order. Security situation is grim if not bleak. Without security everything else grinds to a halt. Attacks on Railway, bank, jails explosives magazines have increased and in near future the security of there installations will further increase as happened in Peru, Vietnam and Nepal. The security commitments will increase manifold. With the intensification of anti-naxal operations Naxals will become more desperate in months ahead and will try to hit soft targets. When the base areas of Naxalites would be threatened then they will redouble their harassing attacks elsewhere to scatter the forces and reduce the pressure. It is not the matter of brave or afraid, but a matter of safety of the lives of human beings that security and all round defences for various targets should be organised. The targets face possible eventualities from all directions and there must be security defence measures for all directions. Here, one should remember that the best defence is good defence; and good defence is all round defences. Barring some areas, large chunk of areas are not in crisis zone, but in between cusp and crisis. Apocalyptic image of the challenge is not correct for all the areas; but if the problem is not countered effectively then it has the potentialities to snowball.

Conclusion

The Naxalite problem has taken the country in a disastrous direction. Naxals through subversive, sinister process are causing social dissension, economic disruption, political chaos and armed movement. Naxal problem has evolved, expanded and mutated into an ever wider threat. We have to reshape the perspective and strategies. Now the strategic realities must be realised, the inadequacies of manpower, resources must be rectified; a thoughtful security infrastructure and all round development must be planned and implemented. Some states faced some reverses in the opening phases, but one should remember words of Che Guevara that extremists cannot win against democracy.

Time is the biggest factor in the fight against naxalites. The delay and loss of time at all the levels must be curtailed. If the regime can manage to prepare in time, it can withstand naxal offensive. The SF and administration should organise space in such a manner that it could be made to yield time and organise time efficiently so that it could yield will. The resultant will of the SF, administration will strengthen the National will to fight extremism. The fast beat the slow not the big beat the small. If the regime hopes to escape the chaos and loss and save democratic polity, it needs to act fast to tackle the Naxalites. Here it is pertinent to remember the words of Professor Huntington:

> "Guerrilla warfare is decisive only where the anti-guerrilla side puts a low value on defeating the guerrillas and does not commit its full resources to the struggle."[14]

Same words also have been echoed by Professor Walter Laqueur:

> "Guerrilla war is decisive only when the anti-guerrilla side is prevented for military or political reasons from committing its full resources to the struggle."[15]

Whether and how this challenge can be overcome is now more topical than ever. It is high time to resolve differences of opinion over appropriate actions. Clash of social, political, economic, and cultural objectives and situations conspire against unity of efforts. People should remember that if the security force fails today tomorrow there won't be any politics; and when the security forces fail, so did the hopes of people of the area. The situation is grim, but one should remember that through desperate actions Naxals are digging their own grave. India is undergoing cataclysmic armed rebellion due to the violence of the Maoists. Disturbances forecast that fighting would be bitter and spasmodic. Reflection and reassessment of trend and tendency of the problem and counter measures reveal that holistic approach with speed and accuracy can turn the table. The regime should co-opt naxals' objectives and combat their operations. Lastly everybody should remember that the unity, integrity of the country and national security is supreme issue, no other issues are more important than national security. Therefore, ultimately the regime must make serious efforts at all levels to destroy the will and hope of naxalites to save the democracy. A tiger uses his full strength to kill a rabbit, so also a nation should use his maximum strength to kill the menace. Naxals are targeting Indian democracy, Indian democracy should target Naxals. The Nation has possibly arrived at a definitive stage where it needs to crush the revolutionary adventures and ambitions of the naxalites.

NOTES

1. Clausewitz, Carl von, *On War*, p. 24.
2. Status Paper on The Naxal Problem, Ministry of Home Affairs, Internal Security Division 31-10-2006.
3. Status Paper on Naxalism as on November 30, 2007, Ministry of Home Affairs, Govt. of India.
4. Nayak Giridhari, Strategy Analysis Vol. 34, No. 4 July 2010.
5. Nayak Giridhari, U.K. Police Journal Vol. 78, 2005, A Model Action Plan for the Maoist-Infested Region, Vathek Publication, p. 229.
6. Hoffman B. and McCormick G.H., July-Aug 2004, Terrorism signaling and suicide attack Conflict terrorism, Vol. 27 No. 4, p.268
7. Ed. David G.J. Jr. and McKeldn III T.R., 2009, Ideas as Weapons Influence and Perception in Modern Warfare, Pentagon Press New Delhi, p. 29.
8. Ibid.
9. Naxalites document Polit Bureau report of 2006.
10. Naxalites document, DKSZC Report.
11. Gorriti Gustav and translated by Robin Kirk, 1999, 'The Shining Path'—A History of the Millenarian War in Peru, University of

North Carolina Press, p. XIV. Once upon a time The Shining Path of Peru was almost sweeping Peru; victory was very close to the reach of its hand. But the people's resistance and intelligence operations turned the table. However, CPN Maoists of Nepal followed Shining Path to some extent.

12. Mao Tse-Tung, *On War*, Natraj Publishers, Dehradun (2008), p. 23. Naxalites launch war of attrition by following Maoist strategy of protracted war in which war of quick decision has much significance. The Naxalites discover the weak points of security force, and then they use the terrain, PLGA and militia to annihilate the security force.
13. Laqueur Walter, 2009 Guerrilla Warfare, New Brunswick, New Jersey, p. 392. Laqueur Walter has quoted Huntington's assertion that guerrilla warfare prospers till the regime is not fully prepared to fight. In his study Laqueur makes it clear in his study that after 60s most of the Guerrilla Warfare in the world failed. Some of the guerrilla warfare which had link with the independence of that country only succeeded.
14. Ibid.
15. John A. Nagal (2005) Learning to Eat Soup with a Knife, The University of Chicago Press, Chicago and London.

ANNEXURES

ANNEXURE I

Report of Central Committee CPI (ML), 1970

CPI(M-L) Call: Guidelines of Naxal Secret Plan

People's Revolution for the Liberation of North-East India – Through the Barrel of the Gun:

We are Determined to WIPE out Congress – Zamindar – Feudal Bourgeoisie Gangsterism in a few Years

Our plan includes also Nagaland, Bhutan, Nefa, Sikkim and Darjeeling

In continuance of our recent conference somewhere in Bhutan - Goalpara border jungle hideout between the Central Revolutionary Polit Bureau Comrades of CPI (ML) Committees of Assam, Bihar, UP, West Bengal and East Pakistan the Central Committee decided the following guideline for our Plan of People's uprising in the States of North-East India including Bhutan, NEFA, Sikkim and Darjeeling. Separate guideline has been issued for our Pakistan corrades. This sort of guideline is especially meant for the trained cadres, in the execution of our armed uprisings for the down-trodden Indian workers, students and peasants liberation under the never-failing inspiration and thoughts of our great Chairman Mao-Tse-Tung.

Chairman Mao says that India, Nepal, Bhutan, Sikkim and Nefa are his five fingers which needed immediate liberation through the barrel of the gun. Besides, Laos, Cambodia, Vietnam, Thailand, Malaysia, Philippines, Burma, Indonesia,

Singapore, Australia, New Zealand, Pakistan, Burma, Indonesia, the Afro-Asian countries will certainly be Liberated from the age-old bourgeoisie-feudal domination and will march hand-in-hand towards prosperity by modeling themselves after Communist China. Everything China adopted to achieve all round prosperity through establishing the people's own administration may surely be applied by our brave comrades – controlled people's guerrillas in their respective countries' mass struggle through the power of the barrel of the gun.

Every bit of cooperation and coordination between our comrades and those of China, Pakistan, Burma and other South-East Asian countries must be maintained in all circumstances. One of the advantages in the case of the ruling parties whether in India, Pakistan, Bhutan or Nepal is the feudal rulers have a very slender and uncertain relationship with the people and the peasants and workers out of unemployment, hunger, dirt and disease have become desperate against the tyrannical rule. One advantage in the case of . . . . .

III. The Central or more important units should situate in some convenient place or congested residential areas, such as, Kathmandu, Bhatgaon, Lalitpur, Birganj, Nepalganj, Raxaual, Bhairawa, Raithat, Biratnagar, Jhapan and Bhadrapur in Nepal, Chamarchi, Phuntsholing, Paro, Thimpu, Tasigang, Zong, Lorhi, Singhi Zongr Lingsi Zong in Bhutan, Goalpara, Dhubri, Tejpur, Rangiya, Bomdilla, Shillong, Silchar, Kohima, Manipur, NEFA and Nagaland, Dalsingpara, Hashimara, Siliguri, Jalpaiguri, Cooch Behar, Dinajpur, Malda, Balurghat, Murshidabad, Khejurighat, Farakka, Rampurhat, Bolpur, Purulia, Kalna, Durgapur, Midnaporo, Hooghly, Howrah, Bandel, Chinsurah, Scrampror, Santipur, Krishnanagar, Arambagh, Kalyani, Barrackporo, Baraset, Basirhat, Belghoria, Dun Dun, Baranagar, Cossipore, Patipukar Belgatchia, Narkeldanga, Ultadanga, Beliaghata, Calcutta, 24-Parganas and Sundarban in West Bengal and all the important towns and places in UP, Bihar and Orissa.

It would be much better for security reasons if such residences were surrounded by trees and bushes, gardens or tanks. Dress and tastes of the Naxalite comrades in residence there should be of strict conformity with those of ladies and gentlemen of the locality. In most cases the leading figures of these central units should not go out very often to move about among the ordinary workers. Obviously they should maintain liaison with Comrades in Nepal, Bhutan, UP, Bihar, Orissa, West Bengal, Assam, Pakistan and rest of North East India and also with Chinese comrades in Pakistan and Nepal.

(IV) Many should be presented to municipal police station people or staff of border check-posts, village or district panchayats or administrative offices and detective departments in order to bribe those willing to supply important or vital informations. Some arrangements may be made by our comrades with members of the local law courts, government treasuries and secretariat in every district and those of rival political parties and social or religious organisations and establishments such as temples, churches, monasteries, gurudwaras, libraries, schools, hostels, and hospitals, cultural and sport clubs.

(V) Every unit must have its safety device, usually at its doorway. In case of any emergency, the device would exhibit a special warning signal to be notices by our party comrades only. The 'Visitor' on perceiving the signal would shy away or pretend to have found the wrong house. In case of our comrades operating in India-Nepal or India-Bhutan border areas should procure the services of innocent looking Nepalses and Bhutanese, train them properly and plant them as sentries with rosary or prayer wheel in hand and 'Om Mahi Padma Hocmi' or such other 'Mantras' in their lips.

(VII) Since bachelors usually arouse suspicious when they go for renting a house or houses, the system of "Lodging units" or mess should be introduced. This would require as female cadres to live as wife with any male comrade to whom she is to be assigned assistant. However, this system sometimes brought trouble too as in the cases of Nagarjote in Naxalbari and Debra and Gopiballavpur in Midnapore district.

(VIII) In case of a principal unit, or when a conference is

being attended by many "Central Unit" figures, specially trained Naxalite agents should carry on the watch and conduct a twenty-four hour round the clock patrol with extreme vigilance and loaded revolvers in their pockets to meet with possible emergencies.

(IX) Neither the organisations nor any individuals in the party should be allowed to cultivate much relationships between themselves. When it becomes necessary to contact another unit or individual, they must refer the matter to their superior, even though a low-level consultation might be much more convenient and simple.

(X) No contact should ever be permitted between the CPI(ML) individual and outside world except those necessitated by his official duties. In other words, he should not be allowed to have friends either inside or outside his party. Furthermore, he should not write letters to, or receive letters from his own family.

(XI) Every Naxalite worker dispatched to do underground work in the government controlled areas or departments should try his best to penetrate into every echelon on society, making friends with lot of people and hiding himself under a safe disguise of a seemingly indisputable identity and an assumed name.

(XII) Mutual Help Association should be created, in fact semipublic in nature, which aims to help and seek to release party comrades who are arrested, as his idea has been working successfully in many other South-East countries and Indian States of Andhra, Kerala, Bihar, Assam, West Bengal, UP, Punjab. The constituents of this organisation should be mostly Naxalite sympathizers who will have acquired considerable political, financial or social background and prestige. This Mutual Help Association should raise a relief fund which may be used at pay the expenses of arrested comrades and their dependents, which may include, of course, the lawyers' fees and some forms of bribes.

The CPI(ML) considers attacks on educational institutions as a first step towards a cultural revolution and a revolt against the bourgeois-controlled education system. Burning of portraits of so-called national leaders, kings and military rulers and books written by them and on them should be intensified in all the districts, such as those of and on Gandhi, Nehru, Tagore, Vivekananda, Rammohan Roy, Netaji Kings of Nepal, Sikkim, Bhutan and rulers of Burma and Pakistan; and this take should particularly be continued by Naxalite students and youths without being deceived by any illusion of careerism and the movement should be carried on with double vigore following the example set by our Chinese and Vietnamese comrades, the Red Guard followers of our Great Chairman Mao Tse-tung.

They should set up small Red Guard Units in Nepal, Bhutan, NEFA, Sikkim and all the districts and villages of Assam, Manipur, Nagaland, Mizo Hills, West Bengal, Bihar, UP, Punjab, Andhra Pradesh, Kerala, Tamil Nadu, Maharashtra, Gujarat, Rajasthan, Delhi, Kashmir, Himachal Pradesh, Mysore, Orissa and Goa as that was the pattern of Red Guard movement being carried on by our counter-parts in China, Laos, Burma, Philippines, Cambodia, Vietnam, Malaysia, Thailand, Japan, Korea and Okinawa. That way our Red Guards would be able to help faster armed peasant and Pakistan where peasantry makes majority of population.

If necessary, the students should discontinue their studies in schools and colleges for the time being as the brave students in our Great Chairman Mao Tse Tung's people's China in order to accomplish the Cultural Revolution. The CPI(ML) Polit Bureau congratulates and greets the daring students with Laal Salaam for their brave deeds in many parts of Indian and particularly in Kerala, Andhra Pradesh, Bihar, Assam and West Bengal in recent months; and it call as them to carry on the same with double vigour as the whole party is with them in all eventuality, of course, leased by Chairman Mao Tse-tung.

The CPI(ML) expresses its firm belief that a people's Liberation Army to be formed by the combination of numerous Red Guard units and Naxalite guerrillas at an appropriate time, will march through the hills and villages of Nepal, Sikkim, Bhutan, Nefa and the plains of Assam, Bengal and Bihar and Orissa within a year or two and the same is going to be an historic march with certainty.

As is being practiced by them in many parts of India the militant students and youths should depend on the determination of the people and on bombs, spears, swards, bows and arrows, guns and evolvers and other lethal weapons for carrying forward the party programme.

The CPI(ML) would like to warn them against manoevring tactics of revisionist elements who believe in bourgeois parliamentary politics and who might have erupt into the revolutionary party as also other so-called revolutionary groups. This should copy the tactics of the 1930 Chittagong Armoury raid revolutionaries for the capture of arms.

Every comrade should take the CPI(ML) Party oath not be divulger of our party secrets even in a most difficult circumstance. Such potential cadres should be given intense training in hit- and run tactics, bombs-making, sword-fighting and use of guns, pistols, revolvers, stenguns and such other weapons on guerrilla pattern taking the leaf from the book of valiant Red Guard of China.

Chairman Mao's thoughts should be hand written or typed and cyclostyled in simple Bengali, Hindi, Nepali, Bhutanese or in local dialect in different regions for their distribution in all the Indian States, besides, Nepal, Sikkim and Bhutan and Nagaland.

Nothing of this secret guideline should be divulged to any one else than our CPI(ML) cadres.

LAAL SALAAM
To our Daring Naxalite/Youths
Long Live Chairman Mao Tse Tung
Sd/- Ch. Mazumdar
Chairman, CPI(ML)
Dated: 1st July 1970
MDR-25.9.70

ANNEXURE II

Only for CCMs

CC First Meeting Resolutions

[January 28-31, 2007]

1. Resolutions on the Central Bodies: [Can be orally reported to all SCs]

CCMs should report orally to all SCs only regarding the election of CC, formation of PB, CMC, RBs and five Central Departments, but should not report to any one at any level including SCs regarding the number of members and alternate members and their names in CC; and also the number of members and their names in PB, CMC, RBs and five Central Departments; CCMs can be introduced only to the concerned SCs and Central Fractions of MOs, but cannot be introduced below as CCMs or as a member of any particular Central Body or Central Dept".

2. Congress Related Resolutions: [Can be orally reported to SCs]

i. The Congress debates will not be released as it is, but on the important questions there will be detailed articles on the stands passed with a summing up of the debate.

ii. The documents will be printed before the end of March in Hindi and English. It will be translated into the local languages as early as possible,

iii. Souvenir will be published in English and Hindi by end February/March,

iv. The Press Communique and Call to the People will be

released on Feb. 19th night for coverage in the media on the 20th.

v. A Congress Special PW issue will be brought out.
vi. The Congress documents should be taken down as an education programme by all SCs and Depts and plan according to the tasks and one year program decided by the CC.
vii. Interview on the Congress has to be given to the media.

3. Resolutions of SUCOMO on Coordination: (for concerned Committees and MO Fractions)

The following are the suggested methods for coordination for all-India activities of the Mass Organisations:

i. Sucomo comrades should have direct links with State Sucomos and/or the SCM in charge of State Mass Organisations,
ii. Central Mass Organisation leaders should have direct links with the MO leaders at the state level and immediately convey decisions taken by A1M0 ECs through the MO channels,
iii. The two levels of communication must go on simultaneously, i.e. at the party level and the MO level,
iv. Mostly any call for all-India mobilisation should be given by the Party well in advance. It should also be conveyed to State MOs through the Central MOs as their programs,
v. For prompt political intervention, particularly for A3, the Central MO leaders should directly convey directives to the state units and the local units should act on the call given centrally. The local units should take up the issue according to their ability,
vi. The State Sucomo and/or the SCM in-charge of MOs should always be given detailed account of the MO activities and the problems, so that there can be correct and effective intervention,
vii. At all levels the MO leaders should not be given

multifarious activities by the party committees and should allow concentrating on the MOs work,

viii. A3 should have a perspective of building it structures UG. A3 should itself not form cover organisations; the latter should be formed by the party directly,

ix. The State SuCoMO/MO in-charge from the SC must pay full attention to build the MOs at their state level and must take initiative in this direction.

4. Resolutions of USCO: [For CC; some points of these resolutions are meant for discussion in the next PB meeting to finalize]

The Urban Sub-Committee (USCO) met for two hours on 30th January, 2007 and discussed the tentative plan for urban work. The following decisions were taken:

i. The Urban Perspective Paper draft should be finalised in the next meeting and placed before the PB. The two papers on urban work—the paper newly prepared for the unified Party and the paper of erstwhile PW will be distributed to all CCMs and their opinions on the papers to be obtained by March 31, 2007. The USCO will finalise the draft taking into consideration the opinions received from the CCMs. The draft will be placed before the PB up to——.

ii. Concrete guidelines will be prepared for work in the working class front in particular. This is mainly meant for the party committees and organizers working in working class front,

iii. Short Notes will be prepared elaborating the methods of work and giving examples of our experiences in various sectors such as PSUs, MNCs and other organized sectors, contract and casual labour in the unorganized sector, etc. These Notes will be of help to the party committees and organizers working in these sectors,

iv. USCO will strive to synthesise from time to time the experiences obtained in various parts of the country in the urban front. Suggestions and recommendations will be placed before the CC/PB before sending below,

v. The main areas of work in the working class are identified as: 1) the coal-mineral belt in and around the areas of our struggle in Eastern and Central India; 2) Golden Corridor; 3) other industrial areas; 4) Railways; 5) MCD workers,

vi. USCO will also guide the work in the areas coming under it. Cadres and leadership should be allotted for this purpose by the CC to strengthen the work in the industrial front. The main focus should be on allotting cadres for work in the core sector in Central India and railways.

To all CCMs:

Dear comrades,

We are enclosing the urban documents of erstwhile PW and the new draft prepared by some comrades to all CCMs. Please send your opinions on these documents before 31st March so as the urban committee can finalise the draft and place it before the PB. The new urban draft is in Hindi. We shall try to send it in English also within a fortnight.

We also request you to send your experiences in the urban work and work in the working class front in particular within the same date. This will be of help to the urban committee in its discussions while finalising the urban policy paper.

With revolutionary greetings,

Urban Committee

1st February, 2007

5. Draft Resolutions of SCOPE: [For CC to finalize in the next PB meeting]

A. The SCOPE will bring out the following booklets as a basic course within the next six months:

i. Communist Party History — com. Rahul

ii. Agrarian Revolution — com. Sujoy

iii. Indian Ruling Classes — Get done by Sujoy

iv. What is Maoism/MLM — com. Pradeep
v. What is Imperialism, Globalisation, etc — com. Raja

B. The following study material is suggested to be prepared in one year and classes taken for leadership by the RBs:
   i. History of Chinese Communist Party — corns. Birendra, Prakash and Rahul
   ii. Nepal Revolution — corns. Bimal, Chetan and Ambar
   iii. Philippines Revolution — corns. Kishore, Sonu and Yogesh
   iv. Peru Revolution — corns. Vijay and Balraj
   v. Indian revolution — corns. GS and Kishan

6. Resolutions of CMSC: [For CMSC and concerned SCs]

i. One member from BJSAC area to be included in CMSC. The name to be decided in consultation with BJSAC.
ii. The women's workshop will be held by the CMSC and NRB will help,
iii. Funds for CMSC will be provided by SWRB till next CC meeting.

7. Resolution on the XX Organisation and Problems between DKSZC and CGSC: [For DKSZC & CGSC]

CC opined that formation of Zonal Organizing Committee with XX comrades by the CGSC and Concerned CCMs was premature. The work in the urban areas will continue as it is between the DKSZC and CGSC for the present. The Zonal Organizing Committee should be continued with fewer members and slowly developed in to ZC by testing in practice. The representative comrades from the two sides of XX background will be brought to a common meeting to resolve the problems. This meeting will be attended and guided by concerned SCMs from DK and CG. Com. Gan and CGSC must take full precautions while working secretly with ZOC comrades and XX background comrades. There must be good coordination between **DK** SZC and CG SC.

9. Resolutions of CMC : Sending CMC resolutions along with these CC Resolutions.

10. Budget Planning.

11. Finalisation of Policy Papers: [Can be reported for all SCs]

The next PB will finalise the following papers after taking the views of all CCMs:

i. Financial Policy
ii. Urban Policy;
iii. Women's Perspective

12. Tasks and One-year Programme: [Tasks Up to PMs and One-year Program for all SCs & SMCs]

A one-year programme will be taken up based on the following tasks drawn up in the POR adopted in the Congress:

The Principal & Central Task before the Party

While strengthening the three weapons of our revolution the principal and central task must be to advance the guerrilla war to a qualitatively higher stage of mobile war and transform the PLGA into PLA in order to establish base areas in the strategic areas of DK and BJ. Also intensify the guerrilla war in other guerrilla zones, and develop red resistance areas in the perspective areas and complete the preparations for building guerrilla zones in these and other areas also. To orient the entire party PLGA and masses towards this principle and central task. To achieve this we must formulate the following politcal, military and UF tasks:

Political Tasks

1) Smash the countrywide multi-pronged fascist armed offensive of the central and state governments led by the Joint Task Force and JOC,: fight back the counter-revolutionary attack by central and state forces and state-sponsored salwa judum, sendra, cobras, and other private mercenary armed gangs by firmly relying on

class line and mass line and effectively mobilising the PLGA forces and the masses.! Carry out tactical counter offensive campaigns to annihilate the enemy forces bit by bit throughout the guerrilla zones and other zones of armed struggle!

2) Intensify the guerrilla war in AOB and mobilise all forces to defeat the enemy's cruel offensive and to regain the initiative in war! Consolidate our Party, strengthen the PLGA, Expand our organs of political power; build broad-based mass fronts and increase our overall subjective strength and expand our area of armed struggle to help transform the guerrilla zone into base area.
3) Concentrate on surviving and reviving the movement in AP and NT. Pay attention to preserve our forces in the ongoing all-round brutal enemy offensive while resisting the enemy in a planned way to the extent possible. Establish the relations with the masses and concentrate on political mobilisation and consolidation and increase our subjective forces. Adopt strictly secret methods of organisation throughout the zones.
4) Accumulate the subjective forces in BJO while carrying out attacks on the class enemies and reactionary classes and developing the guerrilla war to the possible extent.
5) Develop the agrarian revolutionary war in 3U, North Chattisgarh and Orissa. Concentrate on building a strong mass base, consolidate the organisation while continuing the attacks on the class enemies and the state. Complete preparations for developing guerrilla zones.
6) Concentrate our forces in the other states and perspective areas, arm them, and intensify the armed agrarian revolutionary struggles and complete the preparations with the aim of building guerrilla zones. Build up strong anti-imperialist, anti-feudal, anti-comprador bureaucratic bourgeoisie struggles.
7) Link up the strategic areas between the main zones of

guerrilla war as a special strategic task with a time-bond programme.

8) Have a direction to expand the guerrilla war to newer states and areas with proper balance between consolidation and expansion.
9) Develop, deepen and widen the mass base.

Military Tasks

1) Study Maoist principles of ppw along with the experiences of other revolutionary and nationality struggles and apply it creatively in the concrete conditions.
2) To develop guerrilla war into mobile warfare and PLGA into PLA in every GZ establish and consolidate commissions and commands.
3) To defeat the enemy offensive develop our forces on a war footing and develop our striking capacity.
4) In order to transform the PLGA into the PLA, we have to establish auxiliary departments like intelligence, supply, communication, training, production, etc.
5) With the aim of forming battallions in DK and BJ, develop companies on a wide scale as the primary unit of the PLA
6) Build up militias on a wide scale and arm and train them.

UF Tasks

1) Strengthen the strategic and tactical UFs.
2) While advancing the peoples war in the main zones develop the UF in the form of the four class alliance and establish and strengthen RPCs from the local to the zone level.
3) Develop the widest possible UF against displacement and the associated imperialist model of development.
4) Unite with all forces who oppose the imperialist-dictated policies of globalisation, liberalisation and privatisation pursued by the traitorous ruling class parties in the centre and the state governments.

5) Coordinate the ppw with the ongoing armed struggles of the various nationalities in Kashmir, Assam, Nagaland, Manipur and other parts of the North East.
6) Build a broad front of minorities, particularly Muslims against Hindu fascism.
7) Organise dalits against all forms of caste oppression.
8) Mobiliase women on a big scale against all forms of patriarchy and feudal/imperialist oppression.
9) Mobilise the masses into militant struggles against the fascist repression unleashed by the Indian ruling classes in all fields and wage resolute struggles against all draconian laws.

Organisational Tasks

1) Impart ideological, political education throughout the entire party.
2) To ideologically, politically organisationally Bolshevise the Party, build up the unity of thought and action, and with iron discipline act as a.
3) Make the Party committees self-reliant, with initiative and capable to lead successfully the movement in their areas.
4) Build a strong underground party with a stable nucleus of PRs and an extensive network of part time units. Build a secret appartus which is impregnable to enemy attacks. Bolshevise the party by purging itof all alien trends. Concentrate on a recruitment drive to increase the party membership and the PRs to enhance the Party's strength. Give special emphasis on recruiting party cadres from the basic classes and promoting them from the working class, poor and landless peasants and from the special social groups like adivasis, women, Muslims and dalits.
5) Within the framework of democratic centralism all committees must initiate political and military tactics in a creative and lively way not merely depending on instructions of the higher committees but using their own initiative.

Urban Tasks

1) To get specialisation in urban work depute, our forces and leadership in a planned way with a time-bound programme.
2) Build up a strong Develop the class struggles in the urban area by concentrating mainly on the working class. Develop the secret network in the urban areas and build a powerful movement of the workers; specifically in the core sector.
3) Build a vast student and youth movement which will act as a big recruiting ground for the party.
4) Build up a strong urban revolutionary movement oriented towards peoples war

Keeping in mind the above tasks the following programme has to be chalked out:

(i) In the next two months the Congress documents should be taken down as an education programme.
(ii) The TCOC should be taken up from 7th to 9th month in all guerrilla zones. And in the other zones it will take related programs of exposure, etc.
(iii) Mass political campaigns should be taken up on issues such as Displacement, Agrarian crisis and suicides, etc.
(iv) July Martyrs Week should be organised in a big way.

ANNEXURE III

Financial Policy of CPI (Maoist)

I. Policy

The collection and allocation of funds is one of the important factors for the implementation of the general political and military line of the party. The Central Committee has to formulate a financial policy. It has to thereby ensure proper collection and allotment of the funds to not only the party and the army but also to the united front. The Communist party should have a clear cut proletarian outlook both in the collection of funds and in their expenditure. Funds should be allocated keeping always in mind the needs of the war, political propaganda and the people. There is always an ample scope for the entry of non-proletarian trends due to the influence of the feudal and imperialist culture. This results in economic wastage and corruption, etc. The conscientious party members must always have to struggle against these wrong trends. All the party members should live very simple lives and should always keep in mind that every paisa expended by them is the product of sweat and blood of the toiling masses and that it should therefore be not wasted.

1. There are three resources in the main for fulfilling our economic needs. One is the party membership fee, levy and the contributions of the people and the second one is by confiscating the wealth and the income sources of the enemy and the third is the taxes we collect in the guerilla zones and base areas by following

progressive tax system. At present income through independent production is not an important source of income for us. This is possible only after the establishment of the base areas.

Our sources of income are limited but our areas of operation are expanding. The intensity of the war is increasing and area of movement is expanding. So our needs and expenditure are increasing also. It is natural for the incomes of the different regions to be unequal as there is unequal development of the movement. It is also fact that our income is not increasing par with the growing expenditure. Therefore it is quite necessary for us to strive to achieve balance between income and expenditure.

So, to achieve the above said balance, to fulfill ever increasing needs of the war, political propaganda and to uplift the life standards of the people, it is necessary to improve the economic resources and regulate the expenditure. For this a centralized financial policy and planning is quite essential for our party. That means, all the income and expenditure should be planned centrally. This centralized policy and plan should be implemented throughout the party form the higher committee to lower committee according to the committee system.

2. Though we work in the light of the above centralized general policy, it is difficult for the CC to fulfill all the needs of conducting revolutionary war in a vast country like India. Moreover even when seen from the angle of protracted people's war, making the areas self-sufficient is also of prime importance. While implementing the centralized financial policy we have to keep in mind the above said important factor also. Therefore by making our areas of struggle self-sufficient on the one hand and proper implementation of the centralized policy on the other we can fulfill the need of war efficiently. For this the State and Zonal

committees should have to play a crucial role in planning, procurement of funds and regulation of expenditures.

3. According to the plan given by the SCs, the ZCs should be the basic units for the collection of funds, expenditure and accounting. The SCs/SACs/SZCs will leave one year reserve funds with them and take the rest. CC also will leave one year reserve funds with the states and take the rest. This should be implemented except under special circumstances. Self-sufficiency should be achieved at all levels. To fulfill all the needs of central committee to conduct revolutionary war is the responsibility of the ZCs and SCs that should be carried out by them.
4. The lower committees will submit their budget and their accounts to the ZCs/DVCs/DCs and these committees to look after their needs. ZCs/DVCs/DCs, RCs and the SCs/SACs/SZCs will submit their budgets and accounts with their respective higher committees. It is well and good if the expenditures of the committees are met with their own incomes. Otherwise, the higher committees may make necessary allotments for time being and also formulate a time-bound plan to make them self-sufficient and see to it that they are implemented. In this way, it will also be possible for the central committee to make suitable allotments for various regions and departments where it is needed.
5. The Central Committee will formulate guidelines regarding financial matters of our Party, allocate funds according to the budget plan and co-ordinate with various states and the departments. It also maintains the central reserves, prepares the financial statements and budget planning yearly and definitely checks up the financial matters of the lower level committees. The CC looks after the financial matters such as checking the wrong trends arising in the Party in respective of

financial matters by identifying them in time, helping in the extension of the movement to new areas and rendering financial assistance to the Party units where the movement is weak. For this, audit bureaus should be formed at the state and central levels. The funds collected by states and other wings of the Party shall be considered as the central reserves of the Party. It submits the final financial report for the period between two Congresses for the approval of the Congress.

6. SAC/SZC/SCs will allocate funds according to the budget plan and co-ordinate with various Regions and Zones and departments. It also maintains the state reserves, prepares the financial statements and budget planning and accounts yearly and submits them to the CC and checks up the financial matters of the lower level committees. The SCs looks after the financial matters such as checking the wrong trends arising in the Party in financial matters by identifying them in time, helping in the extension of the movement to new areas and rendering financial assistance to the Party units where the movement is weak. It submits the final financial report for the period between two state Conferences for the approval of the Conference.
7. The ZCs will allocate funds according to the budget plan and co-ordinate with various lower level committees up to AC and the departments. It also maintains the Zonal reserves, prepares the financial statements and budget planning and accounts yearly and submits them to the SCs. It will check up the financial matters of the lower level committees. The ZC looks after the financial matters such as checking the wrong trends arising in the Zone in financial matters by identifying them in time, helping in the extension of the movement to new areas and rendering financial assistance to the Party units where the movement is weak. It submits the final financial report for the period between two Zonal Conferences for the approval of the Conference.

8. All the party members should submit their accounts in every meeting of their resoective committees and all the committees should finalize their accounts in their every meeting.
9. Our centralized financial policy comes into effect through the implementation of the decisions taken by CC on financial matters in the States, and their direct guiding of regional and zonal committees in accordance with the central financial policy. ZCs and the RCs must obtain the approval of the SCs for their plans for the collection and allocation of funds.
10. The SCs examines and ratifies the annual budgets of the lower level committees ranging from the Area Committee to the regional committee. The State Committee guides the lower committees so that they prepare guidelines about funds needed and to draw up and implement budget plan. When new annual budget allocations have not been approved in time, the RCs and ZCs can add additional allocation of 20% over their last budget. The whole new budget may be allocated as expenditure from the reserves with them, and subsequently the approval of the higher committee must be obtained. If new additional expenses come to the fore after the allocation of the new budget, the respective committees by themselves can allocate additional allocations up to 10% out of their annual budget. If additional expenses are needed over this, they should not be made with out the approval of the State Committee. Similarly the State Committees can spend up to 10% over their budget, and if any thing more is needed, they must obtain permission from the CC. When the holding of CC, SC meetings gets delayed or when new problem arises due to repression, the State/ Central Committee members can allocate budget amounts for their own needs and for the needs of the departments they are leading, equivalent to their last annual expenditure.

11. The budget year for our Party will be from January to December. All committees and departments under the state committees should annually prepare and send their budget proposals for the forthcoming year once in a year to concerned higher committees for its approval.
12. Necessary funds should be allocated for the RPCs of various layers that are coming into existence in the guerilla zones marching towards the liberated areas, so that production can be enhanced and various welfare measures implemented. But from the beginning, they have to strive to become self-sufficient by improving the production, developing co-operatives among the people, bring about changes in land relations and collect taxes.
13. Whenever a part of the movement area (generally a few districts) in one state is merged with another movement area in the adjacent state to accord with the needs of the movement - for extension and development of the movement - or where an important struggle area from a single state is separated and formed into special zone, all the reserves of such regions will temporarily remain with the erstwhile State Committee. However, keeping in mind the financial needs of the new regions and the possibilities for fund collection open to them, the allocation of reserves should be decided by the CC.

II. Collection and Allocation of Funds

1. Collection of Funds

(a) **From Party Members:** Membership fee should be collected regularly from Part-time Party Members without fail. Levy should be collected compulsorily from them taking into account their incomes. Professional Revolutionaries should accept the money and other goods sent by their friends and relatives. However the consciousness among them should be raised that this is the party's property.

(b) **From the People: It** will be our bounden duty to foster among the people the political consciousness that "we (people) must meet the financial needs of the Party". We should collect contributions from people of all walks of life except from counter revolutionaries. This can be in the form of cash or grain or in other kinds. We should collect grain extensively during harvesting season in the rural areas.

We should collect funds, through the form of 'work days', which are marked with shramdan (voluntary contribution of labour) and in the form of contributions from workers and employees. On the occasions of mass meetings contributions from the people should be collected by all possible means, by visiting each household in villages and towns. These funds constitute the lifeblood of our movement.

(c) **Through the confiscation of properties of people's enemies:** As a part of the class struggle raids should be conducted on the properties of big landlords and notorious money lenders both in rural and urban areas either en masse with the cooperation of the people or by the PLGA units itself, and all kinds of valuable properties should be confiscated and handed over as party funds. On occasions when raids are conducted solely for meeting the needs of the people as per Party directive, all that is confiscated should go to the people. When the Party feels it is necessary, it can take some part of the money obtained through such raids with the permission of the people.

(d) **Through Taxes:** Various contract jobs, businesses, and collection of raw materials is going on in the movement areas. Even while waging struggle against their exploitation, taxes should be imposed on the total amount of their businesses.

As the national bourgeoisie, Petty-businessmen and traders are part in the New Democratic Revolution we shall collect contributions from all of them category-wise according to their capacity. We will collect taxes from them in our guerrilla zones and perspective areas. We shall not collect taxes from the public construction works such as schools, hospitals, and from ration shops and projects, etc., but strive to enhance the people's control/checking on them.

(e) **Confiscations:** As the needs of the movement grow, raids should be conducted on public-private banks and cash and gold should be confiscated. The income obtained from these raids will also constitute one of the important resources for the Party.

(f) All the collections should be done only by issuing proper receipts.

2. Allocations

Party funds have to be allocated mainly for the following heads. Depending on the needs of the movement, the allotments should be done carefully under different heads while preparing the budget itself. The higher committees also should carefully examine the proposals for the budget and make necessary cuts. CC, central audit bureaus and state audit bureaus will make necessary cuts even when the funds are scarce.

(a) Maintenance of Committees and tech mechanism
(b) Extension to New Areas
(c) Military needs
(d) Party Magazines and Propaganda
(e) Political Training
(f) Mass organisations
(g) RPCs
(h) Medical
(i) Other needs

(a) **Maintenance of Committees and Tech-mechanism:** The meeting expenses of the committees, traveling expenses of its members, expenses for maintaining tech mechanism and along with these, the expenses for the purchase of necessary equipment and other related expenses, all come under the head - maintenance expenses of committees. Necessary funds should be allocated for them.

(b) **Extension to new Areas:** At the time of extending to new areas we cannot immediately depend on the people for all needs. In such times, assistance has to be given until the party committee of that area becomes financially self-sufficient.

(c) **Military Needs:** In the main, three types of expenditure come under military needs. One - for the maintenance and management, fatigue needs and the training of the PLGA forces; two - purchase of arms, ammunition and explosives; three - various departments like production and R&D of arms, ammunition and explosives, and Communications, Intelligence, Logistics, Supply, Medical and such other important departments.

(d) **Maintenance of Professional Revolutionaries:** The Professional Revolutionaries have to depend mainly on the people to meet their needs. Where the needs are not met, respective party committees have to allocate necessary funds.

(e) **Political and Ideological Training:** The need for imparting political ideological training to party members, party committees at all levels and in all fronts grows day by day. Classes, workshops, seminars, study camps have to be conducted and libraries have to be set up as a part of this. Hence, funds should be allocated specially for conducting these.

(f) **Party Literature and Propaganda:** Several types of journals along with the writings of Marxist teachers will be required in all regional languages where Party branches function for the propagation of revolutionary politics and movement and for imparting political education to party members and the for raising the consciousness of the people. The need for other literature, which will be of use in understanding deeply, the experiences and political and ideological debates of various countries, will grow along with the growth of the movement. Several types of other literature too will be required for countering the enemy propaganda, the feudal-imperialist culture and repression and for direct exposition of Party's line to the people. Adequate funds should be allocated to this field due to the importance of revolutionary literature and propaganda.

(g) **Mass Organisations:** The Party should guide mass organisations at all levels, in a way that they become financially self-sufficient by procuring the amounts thy need through membership of the mass organisation and through the collection of contributions directly from the people. During the time when repression goes on intensively and when the mass organisations are functioning secretly and when the need for funds for their programmes arises, those amounts too should be procured from the people. Cover organisations too should depend on the people alone for the funds required for their programmes. When it becomes absolutely necessary, there should be allotments from the party committees, even while giving them guidance to overcome the situation.

(h) **Medical Needs:** The medical needs are growing along with the growth of the party and the movement. The Party committees at various levels should provide funds for meeting the expenses of those wounded in battle; the medical needs of the party committees and guerrilla forces; the medical facilities provided through medical camps, people's clinics and other facilities provided by the mass organisation to the people and so on. The concerned committees should show the medical expenses separately in their expenditure sheet.

(i) **RPCs:** Along with the establishment of the liberated areas and the consolidation of the people's organs of power, they will have relatively independent financial policy and funds and their allocations. Until then, however, the party committees have to make the necessary allocations, to fulfill their needs. RPCs should allot funds for the militia units.

(j) **Other needs:** We have to basically depend on the people for expenses towards the legal aid, jail expenses etc. for the incarcerated revolutionaries and sympathizers, and for the help of their families and of the families of the martyrs in case they have no other go. Whenever those expenses are not met, the respective committees have to make the necessary allotments according to these needs.

ACs and Sub-zonal committees have to be allotted funds needed for four months, ZCs, RCs and commands at Zonal and above have to be allotted funds for six months and SCs for one year. Funds for the specified time periods should be given in advance to those committees which are not self-sufficient. Depending on the war situation in the guerilla zones, budget allocations can be done and reserves kept aside sufficient for one year. State committees should make the necessary resolutions and implement them.

Funds for different departments and for the maintenance of the dens should be given for a period of four months to one year keeping in mind their special needs, covers etc. When huge allotments have to be made for long term purposes, it should be done only with the permission of the respective committees.

Those committees, which have more income than their needs, should not expend more funds than those allocated to them, without the permission of the higher committee.

III. The Financial Policy of the Guerilla Zones and Liberated Areas

All the strategic areas selected by our party for the establishment of liberated areas are backward areas with forests, hills and they basically comprise of tribal people. So it is imperative for us to increase production and productivity along with the transformation of the production relations.

We have to take up activities with the aim of establishing

new production relations in place of the economic policies that serve the interests of the landlords and imperialists. For this, land reforms should be implemented, lands of the landlords occupied and distributed among the agricultural labourers and poor peasantry. Indiscriminate felling of the forest should be controlled and fallow lands and un-cultivated forest lands should be extensively brought into cultivation.

Modern agricultural methods should be employed using the local resources for improving the agricultural productivity. We should train up the people to adopt better methods in the growing of vegetables, and rearing pigs, poultry etc.

Efforts should be made to develop business, handicrafts and cottage industries like soaps, shoes, oil mills etc. and those industries which depend on the forest products. These should be encouraged both collectively and individually. Constructions like tanks, ponds, watersheds, drainage channels, irrigation canals, bridges, schools, hospitals, veterinary hospitals, that fulfill the collective needs, should be taken up. Primary Health Centers and schools for primary education should be established and run regularly and effectively. We should rely on the voluntary contribution of free labour by the people for the implementation of the above policies, and the RPCs should collect the additional funds needed through various sources.

i. RPCs will collect taxes and contributions from people, businessmen, contractors etc. and fines from anti-people elements. This could be in cash or in kind.
ii. They will collect royalties from the big businessmen and contractors.
iii. They will issue bonds, when necessary, to collect capital for the people's government.

When the RPCs are not self-sufficient with the funds collected through the above means, respective party committees should allocate up to 15% of their funds.

IV. Legal Assistance and Assistance To the Families of Victims of Repression

(a) Legal Assistance

There is a need for funds for providing legal assistance to thousands of sympathizers and activists who are facing court cases. Funds are needed for the engagement of lawyers, for offering sureties in court affairs, for court fees, for the controlling of false witnesses etc. Money will also be needed for various needs of the comrades in jails.

Funds for this should be collected through various methods and forms -from the families of the jailed, from the people's enemies who are responsible for the cases, from the common funds of the villages and through donation campaigns etc. When sufficient funds are not raised through these methods, party committees should allocate necessary funds. However, we should not let the attitude of depending entirely on the party prevail.

(b) For the Families and Villages of Victims of Repression

For those who become homeless, having lost houses, harvests, production implements due to repression, help should be extended by mobilising people. Financial support is needed apart from moral support. We should also try to see that help is extended to the utterly poverty stricken families of martyr comrades. Contributions collection campaign should be taken up for this. Efforts should be made to see that the collection and distribution of these funds takes place under the supervision of special committees. The distribution of funds should be allotted to fulfill the needs. When enough funds can not be collected by RPCs through these methods, minimum party funds should be allotted.

(c) Assistance for Families of Party Members and PLGA Members

Generally, we are not giving assistance for the needs of families of party and forces. We have been educating our comrades and their families that it is not possible for us to extend financial assistance to them and they should solve their financial problems on their own and that one should be prepared even if one's family undergoes suffering to some extent and that sacrifice is the only solution to this problem. However, where these families absolutely have no other alternative, the concerned committees should draw up plans to extend assistance through the following methods:

(i) Assistance through village mass organisations
(ii) Assistance through friends and relatives arranged through our encouragement
(iii) Direct assistance from the Party

One should have the understanding that even through all this assistance we will be still able to raise funds and distribute only small amounts. Funds should be raised through these three methods to the extent possible and allotted to the families. Along with this, political consciousness too should be instilled. Necessary funds should be allotted for the direct assistance that party provides.

V. Wrong Trends in Financial Matters

The wrong tendencies which are emerging in financial matters

(a) Regarding party funds and expenditure:

i) Additional expenses being incurred due to dependence on the market for articles that can be procured by depending on people.

ii) Not caring about money due to the increase in financial resources,

iii) Making huge expenditures with individual decisions and without any committee decisions; not submitting accounts to the committees and lack of checking of the accounts of the committees as well as of the various units under the committees and taking a liberal approach towards the wastage by the committee members and the lack of thorough criticism and self-criticism.

iv) The wastage that occurs in collective life due to lack of fixed responsibility,

v) Wastage due to liberalism on the part of leadership who appease the petty-bourgeois wishes of comrades who lacks sufficient political consciousness,

vi) Though a time limit is fixed and quota system exists as to what extent various goods are to be used, violation of that system, and those allocations, reluctance to use articles which can be used for some more time and obtaining new articles,

vii) Giving loans for the personal needs of the sympathizers,

viii) Corruption of party funds

(b) For comrades living in dens the ground for the emergence of alien class tendencies always exists. The main tendencies in financial matters that arise are as follows:

i) Not sticking to limits regarding food, medicine, clothes, household and other articles: making purchases of various types without permission in the name of necessity

ii) Using rickshaws, autos and taxies irrespective of the need for them in local travels, where one can walk or use cycle or bus.

iii) Wasting time and money in the name of passing time or entertainment.

To rectify these defects comrades should be made to realize their shortcomings through discussions and concrete methods and suggestions should be indicated. And limits should be imposed.

(c) Money dumps of huge amounts should not be kept with comrades in whom political and organisational vacillation has began irrespective of the level they may belong, nor should the dumps be kept even under their supervision. While setting up dumps in struggle areas large amount should not be kept at one place. In plains and urban areas party funds should not be kept with those who are exposed to the enemy; with those who do not have sufficient revolutionary political consciousness and with those who are addicted to vices. Any one should not take and utilize the un-allotted funds from the dumps.

(d) In-spite of collecting funds properly by the committees and members even when there are such opportunities, depending on the higher committees. Not implementing collective decisions during collection and taking individual and liberal decisions and not giving proper accounts.

(e) The wrong trend of not depending on the people and lack of thriftiness.

Such trends are growing at all levels from top to bottom. For correcting these, we should enhance the political consciousness among comrades at all levels and strict discipline should be observed.

Comrades,

Today our party is leading a merciless class war. In this situation, systematizing our economic activities and our economic condition is the immediate need of the hour. Keeping this in view we have to implement this financial policy in such a way that a very disciplined and efficient economy can be brought about from top to bottom in the party, PLGA, mass organisations, UF organisations and all the departments; proper balance can be achieved between the income and expenditure of the party and our needs and resources so that the revolutionary war can be advanced; every paise is saved to fulfill the increasing war needs; no work shall stop owing to the paucity of funds and not even a single paise be expended anywhere unnecessarily. In this way, we have to strive hard to systematize the economic life of our party like the disciplined life of the proletariat.

All the leaders and cadres of our party, army and mass organisations at all levels should adopt the simple life style and hard work of the proletariat. We must get rid off the petti-bourgeoisie values, standards and habits and adopt the proletariat values, standards and habits.

Comrades, we have to lay the foundation of new democratic economy. So we have to nourish and develop the new democratic aspects in the economy of our party. We know that the very meaning of Socialism is well disciplined, well systematized and well planned system. Come, let us implement this centralized financial policy with resolve and on priority basis to build the whole economy of the party on this foundation.

12 December, 2007

With Revolutionary Greetings,
Central Committee,
CPI (Maoist)

ANNEXURE IV

Company Drills of People's Liberation Guerilla Army (PLGA)

We formed PLGA in 2000 as per our political and military line, with the aim of making the Indian New Democratic Revolution successful. The Peoples' Army strives to destroy the political power of the exploiting classes and establish the people's political power. The Ninth Congress directed us to immediately start work to build guerilla bases in the guerilla zones with the great aim of liberating Dandakaranya. We are building the company as the main force in the PLGA to facilitate achieving the tasks the Ninth Congress directed. The Company will develop guerilla war quantitatively and qualitatively and develops the mobile war. We must orgnise the Company with the aim of building more Companies and Battalions in the coming days. In addition to conducting war actions with this aim, we have to improve military discipline and military training with this aim. The Company Party Committee must understand the importance of it as the main force in People's War and glide the Company. We arc providing information about a few Company drills to help you run the Company. Let us develop these drills in a more detailed and extensive manner depending on the experiences in daily life. In China and Vietnam, there were 120 members in a company. In the bourgeois armies there are 130. In some red armies, there are three rifle platoons, artillery squad, heavy-machine gun squad recoilless rifle squad, recce squad and other such sections. With the present leadership forces and the weapons in view, we have decided the following formation.

On special occasions, when the number is between 46-49, there must be two platoons. When the number is between 70-120, we must divide them into three platoons. The Company headquarter must not be part of anyone platoon but must be separate.

The number of members in the various political and military classes, Conferences, Plenums, Camps and meetings is ranging from 46-65. At times it is even reaching 120 and more. Apart from the defense team we can form three platoons with the given number. If we bring so many members under one command, we can have the form of company. In view of the necessity of the level of our struggle, we are concentrating in more numbers in ambush, raids and short surprise attacks.

Since there are more members, it is very important to maintain secrecy. If we lose secrecy it will be a danger to the existence of the Company. The Company must have the nature of developing great fighting capacity.

Formation of Company

- Company headquarter (HQ) section
- Three Platoons
- Company headquarter section
- Company Party Committee Secretary- Political commissar
- Company Commander
- Company Deputy Commander
- Company Party Committee Secretary guard
- Company Commander guard
- Runner
- Runner
- Runner
- LMG person
- LMG assistant
- Communications person
- Communications person
- Platoon headquarter section
- Platoon Commander

- Platoon Deputy Commander
- Platoon Commander guard - runner
- Communication person
- Another three members
- Sections in the Platoon
- Section Commander
- Section Deputy
- Section Commander guard
- Another five members
- Artillery section
- LMG person
- LMG assistant
- Two members to carry grenade launchers
- Two assistants for those carrying grenade launchers
- Three mortar rocket personnel
- Artillery section Commander

Note:

Medical department, communications department, recce team and a supply department are established in the Company to enhance the fighting capacity. Comrades from these departments are placed in the respective sections.

The scout team must go in front of the Company during journey. It will go 1-3 kms front of the first platoon. In the camps it will be part of a section in a platoon.

Since there are ten members in the artillery section in the second platoon one each from the three sections in the first, second and the third platoons will be lesser.

The leadership committees must strive to establish the Company with all the departments and all the necessary aspects when the number of members, leadership and weapons improve.

Formation

Company will normally move in the above said formation. The first group is in the beginning. The Headquarters and the recce group will be at its back. The second platoon is at its back.

The third platoon comes next. Members from the second or the third platoon will be taken and send to flanks. This is called flank guards. Out of these, 2-5 members will work as the left flank of the Company HQ. 2-5 persons will be kept as right flank. In view of the necessities of war the Deputy Commander of the Company will be with any platoon.

Recce groups are the *eyes* of the Company. On some occasions, the recce groups are formed from members from Militia and Secondary forces. At present we are forming-recce group from the various sections of various platoons. As the Company strengthens, we will have to form a permanent recce group. They inform the HQ of the movements of the enemy forces. They fight only for protecting themselves. They must have communication equipment to pass over information.

- Company recce group (during journey)
- Company Commander
- Company communications person
- Commanders of support weapons groups. They will always be together.
- Company recce group (during retaliation in journey or in raid)

Before making reccy the Commander will issue temporary directions. After the reccy the commander will give orders again. They are called official orders. After the official orders the commander will say 'over'.

Note: We can utilize the Secondary and the Base classes as reserves.

Reserves can be put in the level of platoon also. It is very essential to have reserves in the level of Company. They will be in the control of the Company Commander and will be helpful on various occasions. Normally when our forces are advancing or in the upper hand and if the other platoons are able to withhold the enemy effectively, the reserve forces can go and help in defeating the enemy.

It is not correct to use reserves in conditions where we cannot defeat the enemy. This will create more critical conditions to us. The company commander must not send reserves as soon as the platoon commanders say they are facing critical condition. They must think and send. We have to follow this method when we are making an attack on the enemy positions. We have to send the reserves in places where the enemy might directly enter.

Control in Journey

We have to send scout patrol teams for clearance during journeys.

There must be ten members in the first section in the first platoon to face the enemy if they come across.

There will be 2-5 members in the flanks. They too fight only for their protection.

If necessary and if we have the communication equipment, the scouts might travel 5-10 kms front. Or else they will walk 1-3 kms distant.

The platoons will disperse (decentralize) and assemble (centralize) in order to maintain secrecy and due to the enemy repression. During other conditions, the company might move as separate platoons or all the platoons can go together. When the company is going in formation it is possible to appoint flank security Company will move according to the necessities of war.

The Company Commander must observe whether the platoons and the front guards are coming with stipulated distance or not. They have to see whether they are maintaining proper distance or not and guide them. They must also have good relations with the Platoon Commanders.

The Company Commander will maintain relations with the flanks, take reports from the roads, rivers and streams and coordinate all the platoons. ......

If the first platoon suspects enemy it will send the first section and check. If it encounters the enemy it will withhold them. Thus it will facilitate the journey of the Company.

If it comes across the enemy the first platoon will follow the 'Y' formation and suppresses the enemy through firing. It will give information to the Company Commander.

We have to maintain proper distance between the various sections and the various platoons. Thus the Company will not be caught in the enemy ambush.

It will take up an action on the basis of platoon. It will not move as a company. It will move in Company formation on special occasions.

We must assign the Secondary and Base forces in all the approach routes and identify the enemy. If the enemy is moving around, we have to create losses. Thus we must protect the main force. The Company must work so that the enemy does not understand.

When the enemy encircles the Company camp, during combing or when to retreat by giving a blow to the enemy, the Company will fight as a unit.

There is an artillery section in the Companies. One section of each platoon will have an MG. These sections will have rocket launchers too.

If the front guard is 600 metres before the Company and does firing it will be possible for us to take proper positions and fight.

Order group: Platoon Commanders, Company Commander, Company Deputy Commander, Company Party Committee Secretary (Political Commissar) will attend the order group meeting. If there are units to help the commanders of those units, mainly the commanders of artillery will be part of the order group. Commanders and Commissars will be the leaders of the military units. There is a clear division of work between them. The Military Commanders will be responsible to implement the orders relating to military affairs. Political Commissars will be responsible to implement the tasks relating to political affairs. The Platoon Deputies will not be part of the order group. When the Platoon Commanders participate in the order group meetings, the Platoon deputies will take the responsibility of respective platoons. Note: When Battalion is formed, the first Company will work as the front guard. The second and the third Companies will move at the back.

Company Battle Drills

The Battle Drills explain how the platoons and sections must move according to the conditions they come across and how to interpret fire and movement. All Military actions are not alike. The actions vary according to the conditions. Their nature differs according to the situation of the enemy, our situation, the geographical situation and the support of the masses. So it is essential to understand the changing conditions creatively. **If** we **review the right and wrong of the past actions and understand the ordinary rules and** maneuverings **(fire and movement) properly, it will reduce the** speed **of** assessing **the actual condition and the** process of taking decision. The Company drills help to emphasise on creating offensive response immediately. A drill starts from planning an action to getting organized after defeating the enemy. It might be necessary to take a counter action when we see the enemy or go away from them. The drills depend on the conditions. We are giving the details of specific drills here.

When we come across the enemy

Company moves in 'V' formation when it needs to counter the enemy.

Scouts pass information to the HQ when they come across the enemy. As soon as they receive information - the front guard section must take a parallel position on one side. All the platoons take positions in perimeter, means in a round. The forces will be deployed according to the orders of the commander.

After everyone change into 'V' formation, the first and the second platoon will go together on the starting line (they will go to SLA and then to the grouping line GL) and change to parallel line. They fight with the enemy in parallel line formation. The section working as front guard until then will come and join the third platoon. The groups in the flanks will stay there. Logistics will be at the back (round position).

If the enemy is chasing us from the back, the headquarter will go in between the second and the third platoons. After the firing is over all the members will gather again. They will then move in single line formation and then another attack or travel will be decided.

When we come across the enemy from the front

When we come across the enemy from the front or if the enemy sights the front guard, the front guard will immediately fire on the enemy. The enemies fires in response and this will make all the members in the formation know the positions of the enemy Immediately after this, the Company Commander will take up race alongwith the platoon commanders to assess the number of enemy personnel, positions of the weapons and terrain.

The Deputy Commander will continue the necessary preparations for the attack.

After the Company Commander meets the Deputy Commander they will discuss with the platoon commanders, plan and give the necessary directions. This plan is important. All the members will set their watches corresponding to that of the Commander. Later they decide upon the signals and passwords.

The Platoon Commanders will go to their respective platoons and implement the orders. They will explain the plan to the members.

The Company Commander directs the deployment of mortar, anti-tank guns, rocket launchers and other such things in consultation with the group commander.

How to counter if the enemy forces attack from the backside of the enemy?

When we understand that the enemy would attack from the backside, we must make slight changes in the formation, come into V formation and move.

If the attack is from the sides

The platoon that is attacked must turn into assault formation. The second platoon must go to the sides and give cover fire. The third platoon must go into flank.

Method of mutual support in camp

If the enemy attacks the Company, they will try to isolate a part of the Company and to stop concentrating fighting power in that area. In this situation, we must have one more position to fire on the enemy from the rear and flanks. As soon as they are warned of enemy attack, the squad must go into self-defense positions and be ready to face the enemy.

Method of retreat when the enemy attacks while the formation is moving

First, the A and the C, section must come on to a parallel line. B section must also be parallel. After the platoon HQ receives retreat signal from the Company commander, the platoon commander must give retreat signal to the A and C, section commanders.

A and C must leave the IMG groups and retreat until 200 metres away from the gathering points.

B section must stay there and fire. Later it must leave the IMG group and come to the gathering point.

A and C sections reach the platoon gathering point before the B section comes. The platoon commander arrives with the A and C sections and reports to the Company Commander. Later the commander will retreat the B section.

Another method

Initially the first and the second platoons will fight with the enemy for some time. Later the first and the second platoons will retreat. Later the third platoon will retreat.

Method (four steps) to retreat when the enemy attacks the journey or camp

Platoons must follow four steps to move away from the enemy attack. They have to lessen the number of their platoons or move out as firing teams, squads or platoons.

When the enemy firing is rapid and it is very essential to withdraw, the squad team leaders will order their team members to go from the back as a method of moving away from the enemy.

While going back one team will provide cover firing to another. They will follow the fire and movement method.

If the enemy firing is less or more, the firing groups must follow the fire and movement method and retreat.

As squads, if the enemy firing is less or if it is not necessary to lessen the squads as they have moved away to a certain distance, or if there is no necessity of military action from the firing teams or firing groups, they will go back as platoon squads.

If the platoons are not under enemy attack or if they know that the enemy is coming and decide to withdraw, they will do so as platoons.

Withdrawing when there is no pressure or when there is less pressure

If a platoon changes its positions in order to fight, the rest of the Company will withdraw. This will take place with speed, secrecy and by deception. Such a withdrawal must be done during nighttime. Vacating camps is one such example.

When the enemy is not attacking the camp, Company will disperse (decentralize) and retreat. It will leave a part to cover the withdrawal through deception, firing or military action. It might leave a platoon or one squad of each platoon. Mixed platoon is the best method.

When the enemy attacks during the retreat of the Company from the camp, it must be covered with firing. The Company must withdraw after it goes to a certain distance. If it is still in contact with the enemy, they must fire until the contact is broken. Then the Company must reach a common point to go to a safe place.

Withdrawal under pressure

Intensity of enemy attack decides the method of withdrawal. Platoon withdraws as it fights. It maneuvers from the rear and moves away from the enemy. Soldiers, fire teams and squads will withdraw first. Thus they will be able to make suppressive firing when the soldiers, teams and squads in contact, are withdrawing.

Flank maneuvering when the enemy attacks in journey or camp

As soon as the enemy attacks, we have to send a race team to observe their movements. Another race team must be sent towards the retreat direction.

Then important equipment and members must be sent back. Then we must take up maneuverings.

When we know that the enemy forces are less in number, the first platoon must be in its position and fire on the enemy. The second and the third platoons will attack the enemy flanks. They will retreat after attacking the enemy flanks for sometime.

Hasty attack

As soon as the Commander receives information about the number of the enemy soldiers, about the ambush, about the temporary self-defense arrangements of the enemy and other such things, the commander will analyse the situation and takes decisions. When we make an attack without giving any chance to the enemy to retreat, it is called hasty attack.

As soon as the Commander receives information about the enemy he/she will give a signal. Then he/she will discuss with the Deputy Commander. Later the commander will go) for race and the deputy commander will check the positions of the platoons.

When the company is caught in ambush

Normally the whole company will not be caught in ambush. It maintains certain distance to avoid the same.

When the enemy arranges ambush in our way of journey, we can attack the enemy on their flanks or the rear because we have the sufficient number. We must keep the ordinary rules, maneuvers in view and move our forces depending on our condition.

When the A section of the first platoon is caught in ambush

When the A section of the first platoon is caught in an ambush the Commander of the respective platoon must take initiative and send the B section to the right flank and C section to the left flank. He/She must send information to the Company Commander.

The Company Commander might send the right and left flanks and make an attack on the enemy from the rear. Then there must be coordination between the first and the second platoons.

If the enemy arranges ambush in 'L' formation on one side and arranges stop group on the other.

When the enemy arranges ambush in 'L' formation on one side and stop group on the other, the second section must go to the right and third section to the left flanks of the enemy.

The section caught in ambush will face certain losses. The rest of them must take favorable positions and resist the enemy.

If there is no stop group, the third section of the first platoon will go to the sides, advance and attack from the rear. The first section of the second platoon will go to the right and the second section to the left and clear the place. Or it will attack the rear.

When the enemy arranges ambush on the rear of the company and attacks

When the enemy arranges ambush on the rear of the company the first and the second platoons will attack the enemy flanks. This rule applies in the front or the back.

To cross open places

If the company needs to cross an open area, the first platoon must totally across and clear. The second and the third platoons must cross only later.

When crossing bridges and dangerous spots

While crossing bridges and other such dangerous places the first platoon first crosses and observes the surroundings. It arranges a protective ring later the second and the third platoons cross the area. The platoon that arranged the protective ring until then will become the third platoon. This rule applies to the platoon too.

Delay tactics

We have to face the enemy by arranging delaying tactics to attack the enemy, for self-defense or when we know that the enemy is going to attack the camp as a self-defense of the camp, for the protection of the leadership. If we plan to attack and force the enemy into unfavorable conditions as part of defense, the units will take up actions for delaying. They force the enemy to deploy to make another attack. Thus they will slow the enemy movements. The delaying force withdraws into another position before the enemy attacks. The delaying force must follow these primary rules.

It must be as mobile as the enemy Or it must lower the mobility of the enemy to the level of its fighting capacity.

It must maintain contact with the enemy to escape from the enemy maneuver.

It must protect the freedom of maneuvering through withdrawing alone, the squads and platoons can move away from the enemy (the distance must be between 300-500 kms). The distance might be less in a terrain with hills and valley,

Once a distance is over, the platoon must go into the next position and make self-defense. Then it will be able to force the enemy to deploy again.

With such tactics we can lessen the advance of the enemy and create losses to their forces and equipment. We can use ambushes, snipers, hurdles, minefields and clamors.

Methods of the Company camp

Before the Company decides the place for camping the order group must take the responsibility to check the enemy in the surroundings, to do race, to arrange the initial self-defense and to arrange the sentry posts. This group will decide the initial positions of everyone. It will protect security to the area. It will occupy the places that have cover and are secret. It directs so that everyone will come out of their covers and go to the respective places, when the main unit arrives. Firing arcs are allotted to everyone for mutual support and to cover the vacancies in observation and firing Observation posts are arranged and members assigned.

Observation posts, sentryposts, bunkers and mine fields are arranged. Everyone is allotted self-defense positions and firing arcs. The order group also arranges the necessary trenches and concealments for the race teams and defense teams. It will camouflage the whole camp.

Map 1: Naxalites' Map of Golapalli-Batiguda Ambush

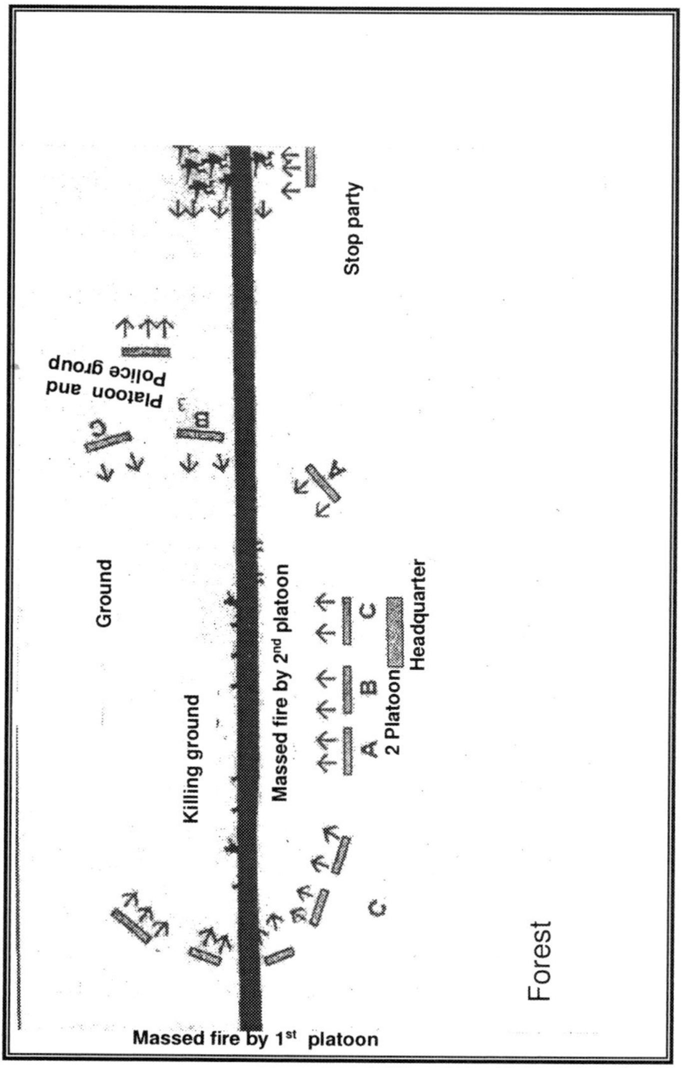

Map 2: Naxalites' Drawing Ambush of Motorcycle Party, 2008

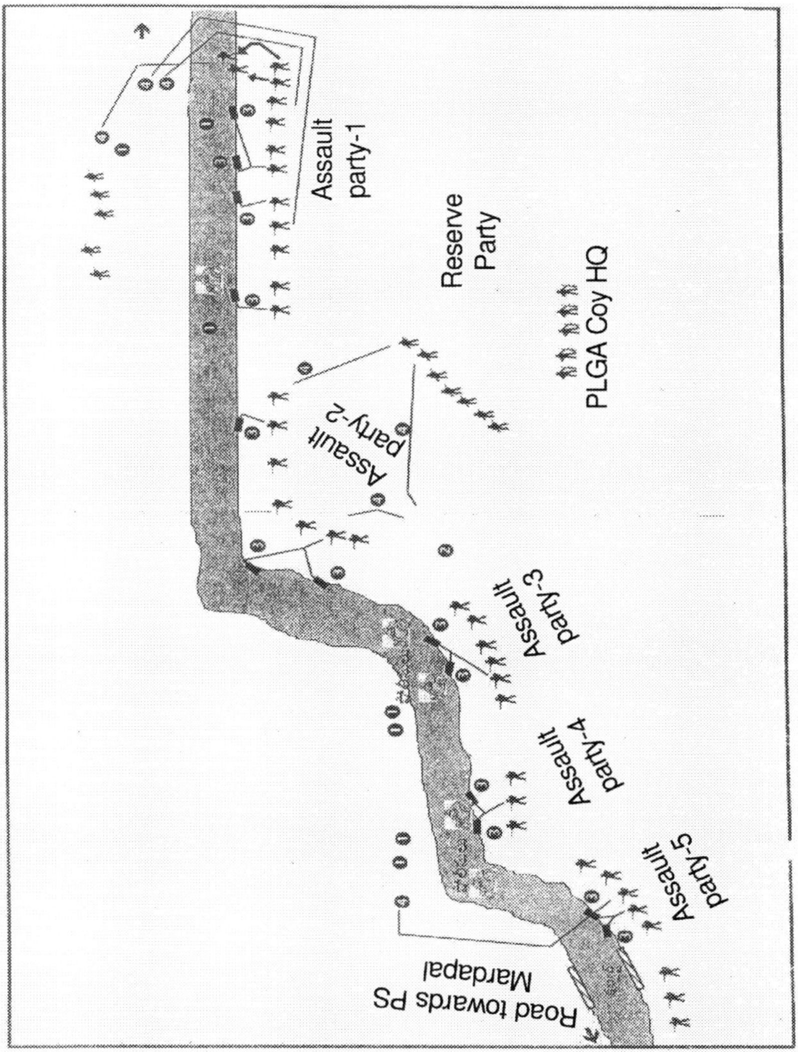

Map 3: Naxal Position when their HQ is Attacked

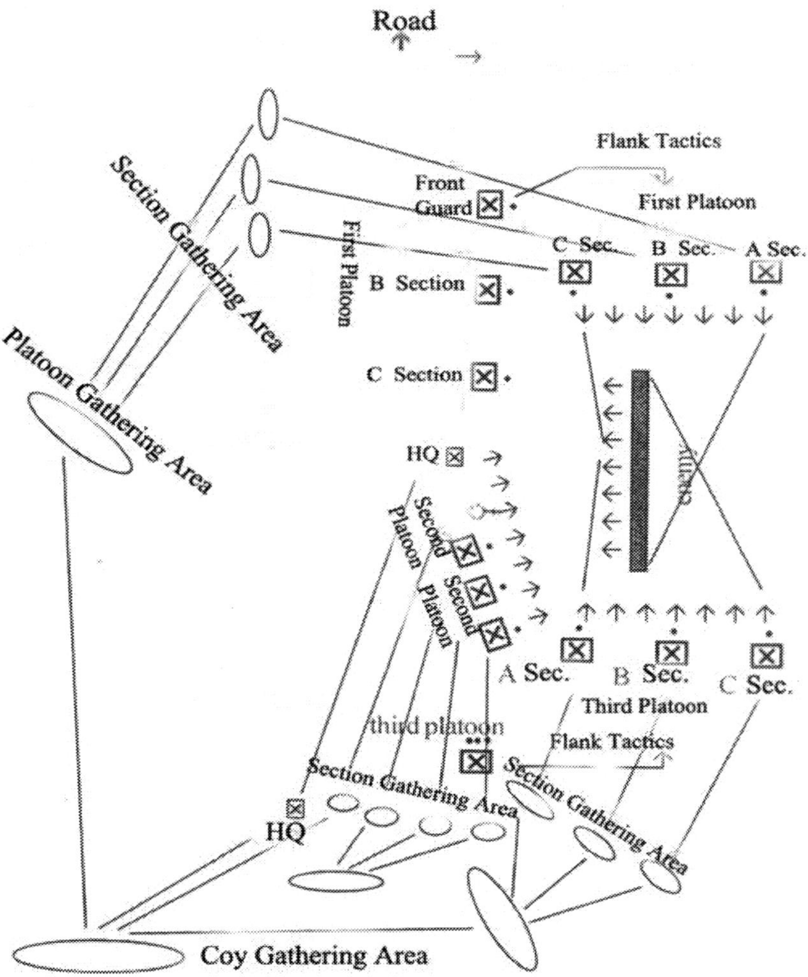

Map 4: Combat Drill Steps

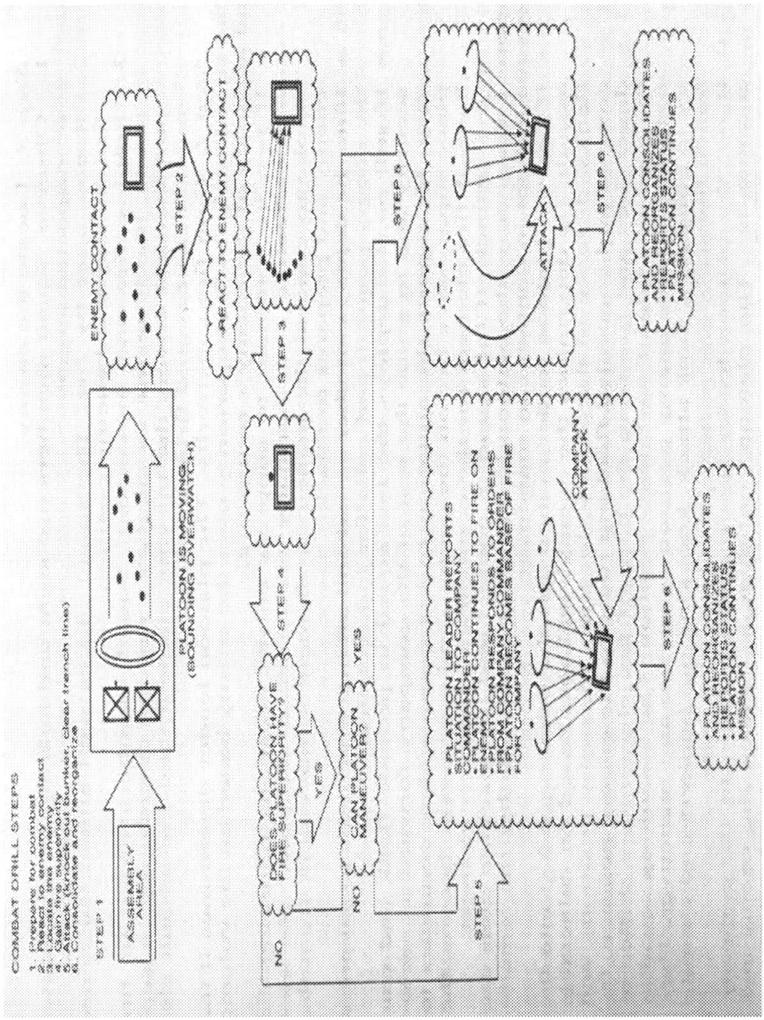

Map 5: Force Position when Coy is Attacked during Retreat

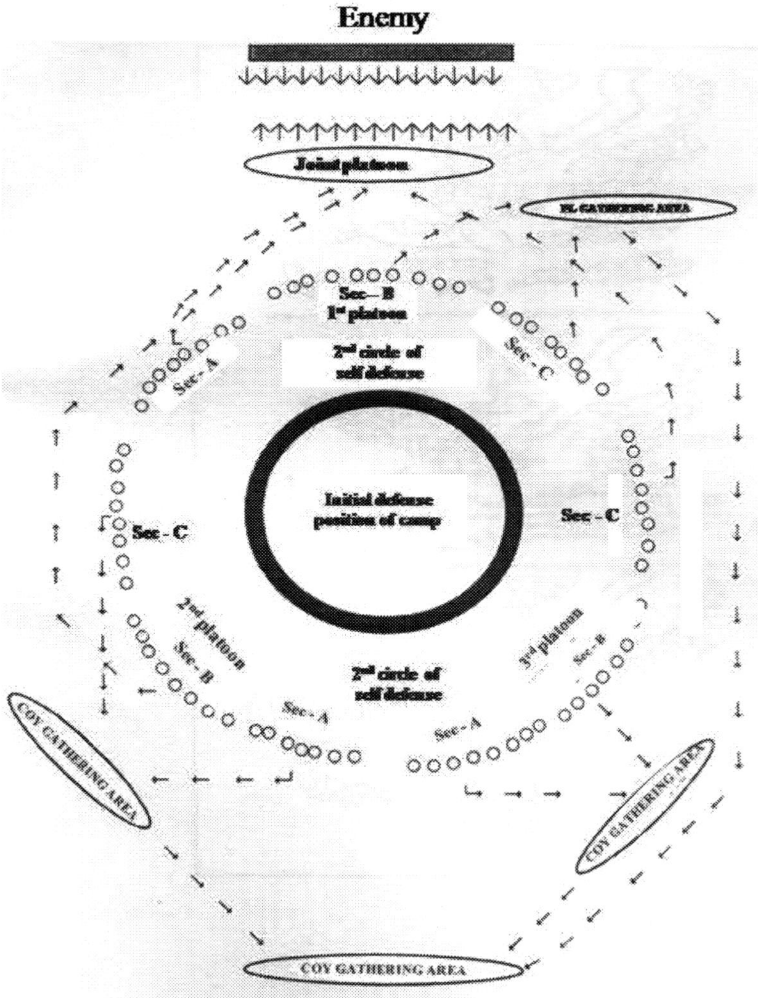

Map 6: L Formation Ambush

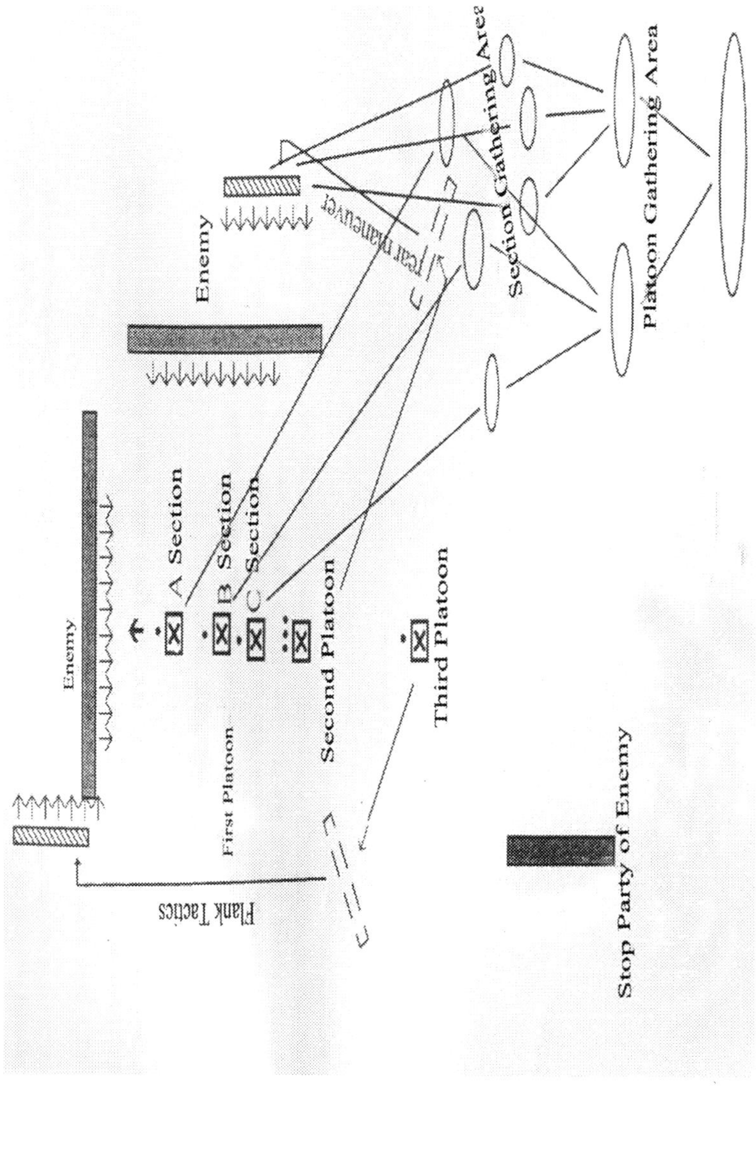

Map 7: When First Section of First Platoon is Ambushed

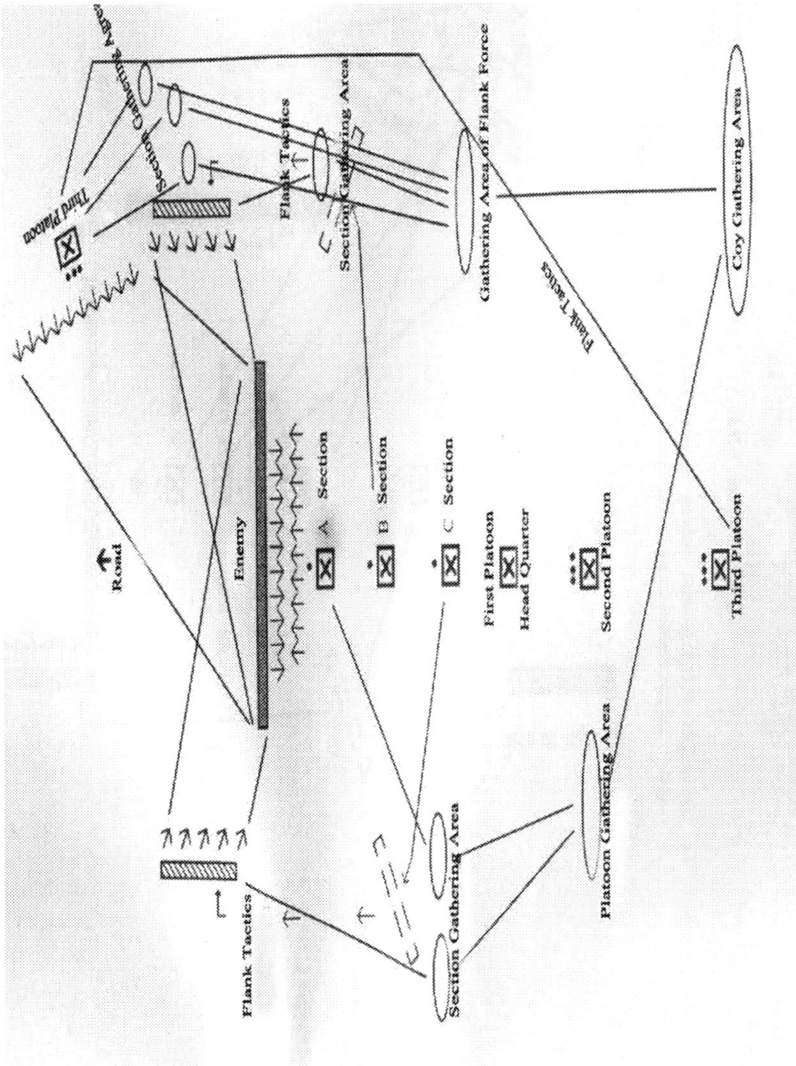

Map 8: Enemy Contact on Far side and on Road or Trail

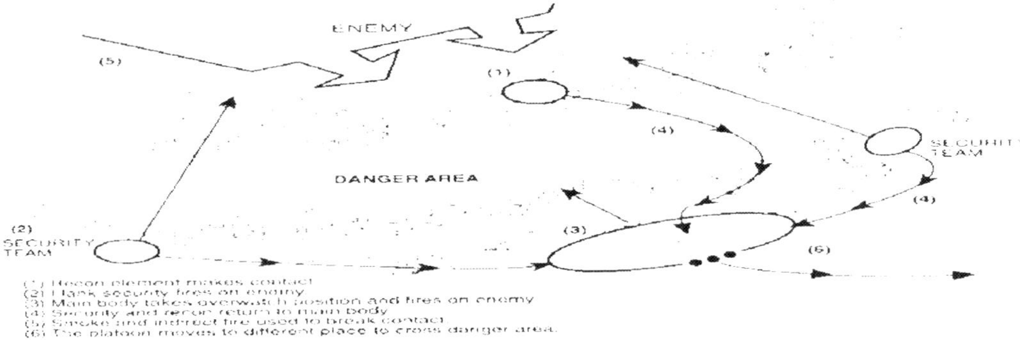

Enemy contact on far side.

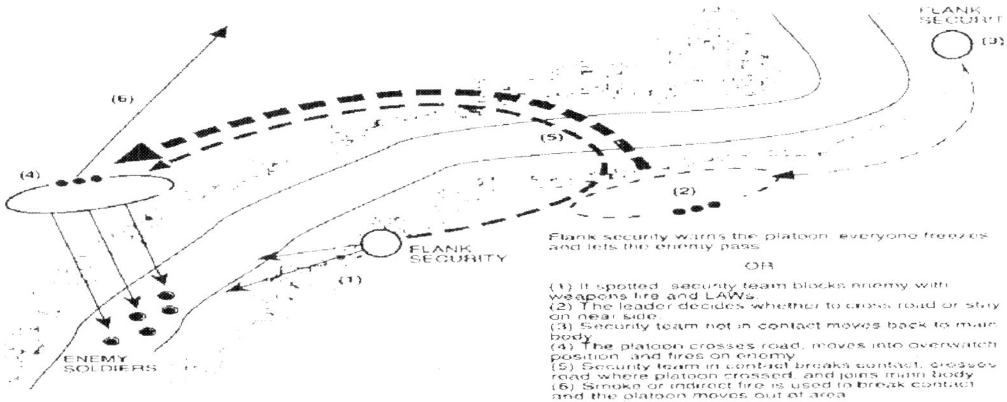

Map 9: Force Maneuvers during Attack on Platoon from Flank

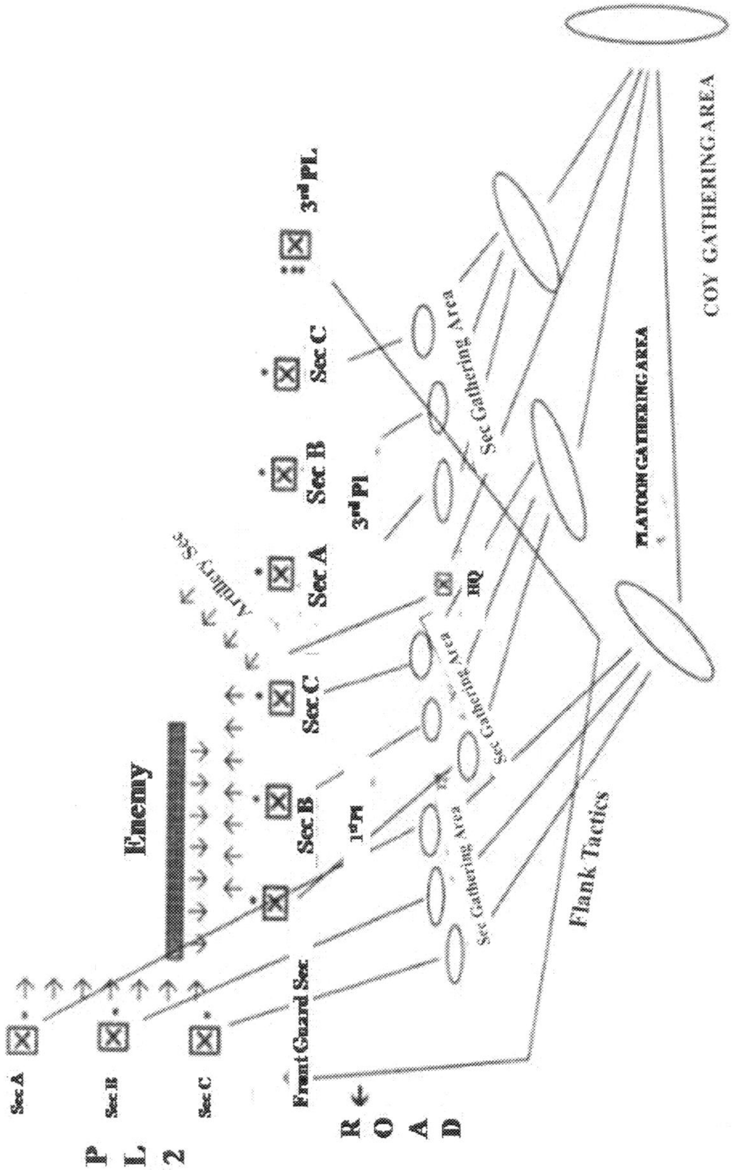

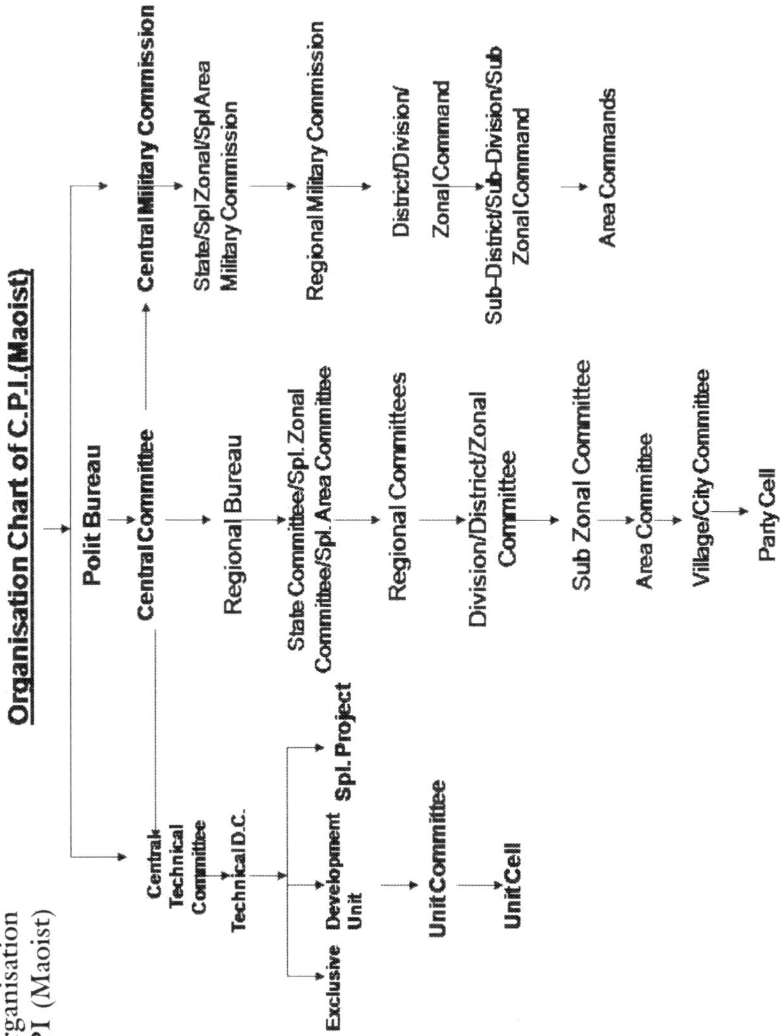

Chart 1: Organisation Chart of CPI (Maoist)

Chart 2: AICCCR–1968

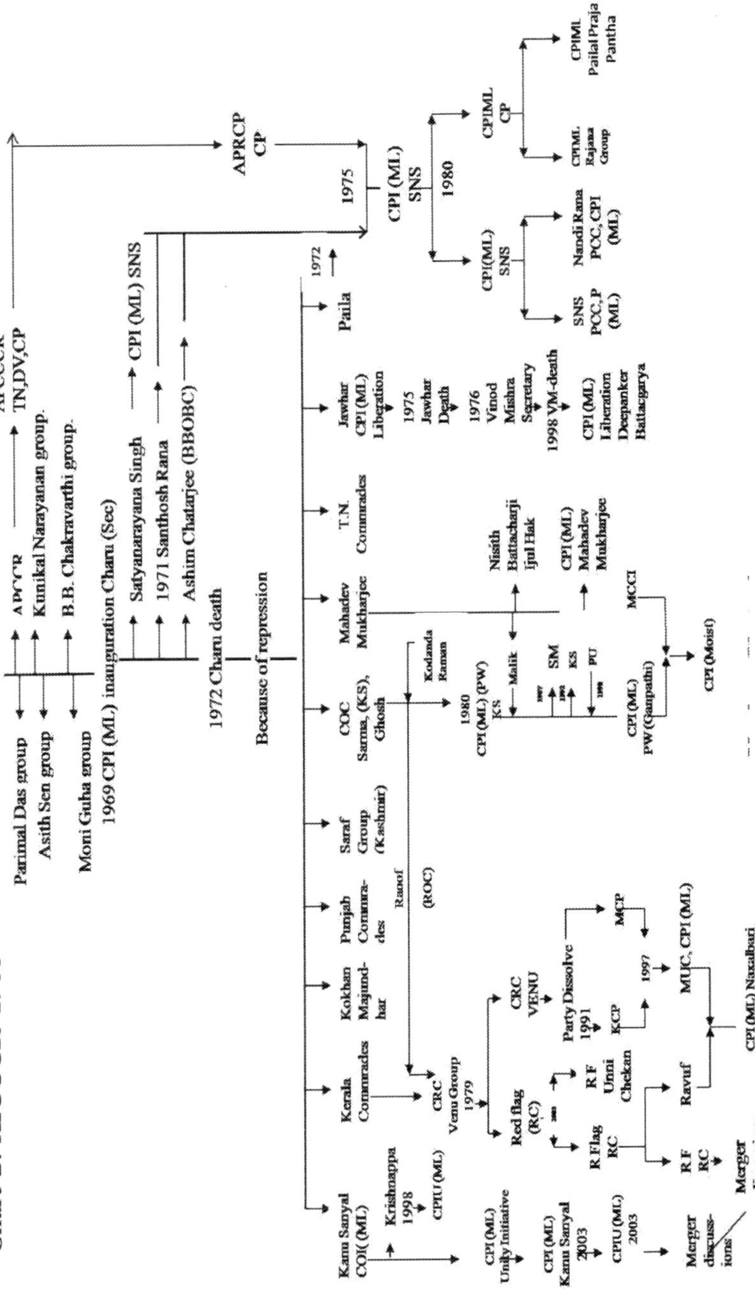

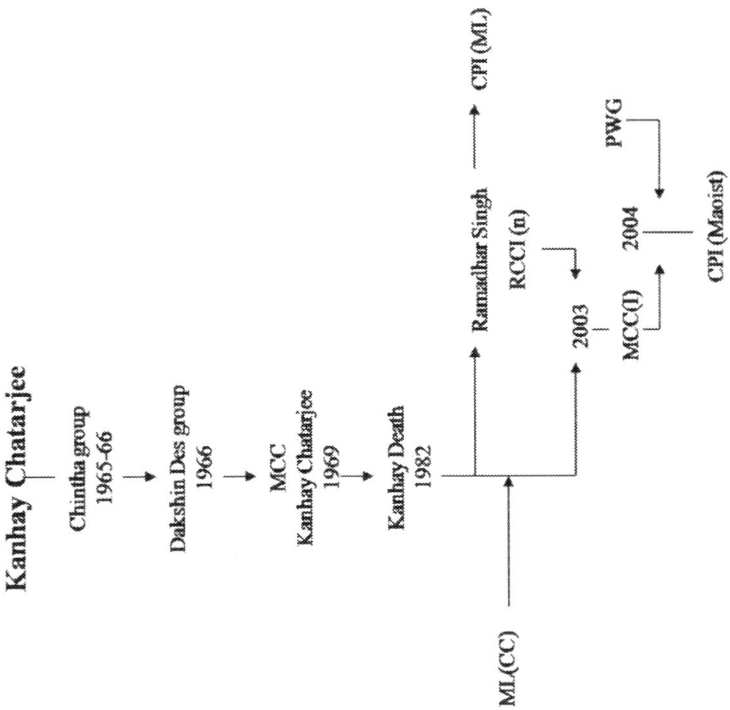
Kanhay Chatarjee
Chintha group
1965-66
Dakshin Des group
1966
MCC
Kanhay Chatarjee
1969
Kanhay Death
1982
ML(CC)
Ramadhar Singh
CPI (ML)
RCCI (m)
2003
MCC(I)
PWG
2004
CPI (Maoist)

Bibliography

Adam B Lowther (2008) *Americans and Asymmetric Conflict* (Lebanon, Somalia and Afghanistan) Pentagon Press, New Delhi.

Albert Camus, *The Rebel*, London: Penguin, 2000,

Alastair Finlan (2008) *Special Forces, Strategy and War on Terror* (Warfare by other means), Routledge New York.

Art of War by Sun Tzu translated by James Callvel.

Azad, *Maoists in India Writings and Interviews*, Friends of Azad, 2010

B.H. Liddlehart; *Strategy the Indirect Approach*, Natraj publishers, Dehra Dun 2003.

Colin S. Gray (2008) *Fighting Talk* (Forty Maxims on War, Peace, And Strategy)

Capt. B.H. Liddell Hart (1964) *Mao-Tse-Tung & Che Guevara, Guerrilla Warfare*. Cassell & Company LTD London.

Clausewitz Carl von, 1997, *On War*, Wordsworth Editions Limited.

CSM James J. Gallagher USA (Ret.) (1994) *Low-Intensity Conflict, A Guide for Tactics, Techniques, and Procedures*. Lancer Publishers & Distributors New Delhi.

Daniel Marston, Carter Malkasian (2008), *Counterinsurgency in Modern Warfare*, Osprey Publishing, Oxford.

David Galula, *Counterinsurgency Warfare Theory and Practice*, New Delhi: Pentagon Press, 2008.

David G.J. Jr. and McKeldn III T.R. Ed., 2009, *Ideas as Weapons Influence and Perception in Modern Warfare*, Pentagon Press New Delhi.

Donatella della Porta, (2006) *Social Movement, Political Violence, and State*, Cambridge University Press New Work.

Edgar O' Balance (1995) *The Wars In Vietnam* 1954-1973, Natraj Publishers, Dehra Dun.

Edward N. Luttwak, *Strategy (The Logic of War and Peace)* Published by The Belknap Press of Harvard University Press (2001)

Frank Kitson (1992) *Low Intensity Operations, Subversion Insurgency & Peacekeeping*, Natraj Publishers, Dehra Dun.

Ghosh, Suniti Kumar, *Naxalbari Before and After Reminiscences and Appraisal*, New Age Publishers (P) Ltd. Kolkata (2009).

Gorriti Gustav and translated by Robin Kirk, 1999, *'The Shining Path'—A History of the Millenarian War in Peru*, University of North Carolina Press,

Guevara, C. (1969) *Guerilla Warfare*, London: Penguin Books.

Henry Mintzberg, A. Bruce Ahlstrand, B. Josheph Lampel, C. *Strategy Safari the Complete Guide Through the Wilds of Strategic Management*, Pearson Education (Singapore) (2005).

John A. Nagal (2005) *Learning to Eat Soup with a Knife*, The University of Chicago Press, Chicago and London.

John Keegan (1978) *The Face of Battle*. Penguin Books, London.

J.P. Cross (1992) *Jungle Warfare (Experiences and Encounters)* The English Book Depot, Dehra Dun.

Mao Tse-Tung *On War*, Natraj Publication, Dehradun (2008).

James C. Scott (1998) *Seeing Like A State (How Certain Schemes to Improve the Human Condition Have Failed)*, Yale University Press New Haven and London.

K. Aravinda Rao (1996) *Naxalite Terrorism (Social and Legal Issues)*, East West Books (Madras) Pvt. Ltd.

Laqueur Walter, 2009 *Guerrilla Warfare*, New Brunswick, New Jersey.

Liddell Hart (1934) '*T.E. Lawrence in Arabia and After*, Natraj Publishers Dehra Dun.

Louise Willmot *On War Carl von Clausewitz* (1997), Publications Wordsworth, London.

Lt. Col. Joshua Potter, USA, Commander Gary Stubblefield, USN (Ret.), and Mark Monday, Ambush (A

Professional's Guide to Preparing & Preventing Ambushes. Lancer Publishers & Distributors, Paladin Press, New Delhi, 2011.

Lt. Col. Raymond A. Millen, USA (2006) *Command Legacy (A Tactical Primer for Junior Leaders of Infantry Units)*, Bookmart Publishers New Delhi.

Mao-tse-Tung *On War (Strategy, Guerrilla Warfare, and Doctrine)* (2008), Natraj Publishers Dehra Dun.

Napolean D. Valeriano Charles T.R. Bohannan (2008) *Classis of the Counterinsurgency Era, Counter-Guerrilla Operations* (The Philippine Experience), Pentagon Press, New Delhi.

Prakash Singh (2006) *The Naxalite Movement in India*. Rupa & Co. New Delhi.

Regis Debray, *The Revolution on Trial*, New York: Penguin Books, 1974.

Robert Taber (2008), *War of the Flea* (The Classic Study of Guerrilla Warfare) Bookmart Publishers, New Delhi.

Robert F. Thompson, *Defeating Communist Insurgency: Experiences from Malaya and Vietnam* (London: Chatto and Windus, 1972)

Sen, Samer, Debabrata Panda, Ashish Lahiri; *Naxalbari: A Frontier Anthology*, Vol. 1, Calcutta: Kathashilpa, June 1978.

S.L.A. Marshall (1997) *Men against Fire (The Problem of Battle Command in Future War)* Natraj Publishers Dehra Dun.

Thomas A. Marks (1996) *Maoist Insurgency Since Vietnam*, Frank Cass & Co. Ltd. London.

Thomas A. Marks, *Maoist People's War in Post-Vietnam Asia*, Studies in Insurgency and Terrorism No. 1, White Lotus Press, Thailand (2007).

Thomas E. Ricks, *Fiasco: The American Military Adventure in Iraq*, (2006), Penguin books, London.

Vo Nguyen Giap, *People's War People's Army: The Viet-Cong Instruction Manual For Under Developed Countries*, (Dehradun: Natraj Publications, 2002).

Newspapers

Amrit Sandesh.

Dainik Bhaskar.

Deshbandhu.

Haribhumi.

Highway Channel.

Hindustan Times.

Hitvada.

Pioneer.

The Hindu.

Times of India (New Delhi).

UNI

Magazines and Pamphlets

David Kilcullen, 'Counter-insurgency Redux.' Survival winter 2006-2007.

Ganpati's Interview to Peoples March 2005 July.

Hoffman B. and McCormick G.H., July-Aug 2004, Terrorism signaling and suicide attack Conflict Terrorism, Vol. 27, No. 4.

Jane's Insurgency 1998, and 99.

Maoists Tactical United Front & Urban Movement, Dr. P.V.

Ramanna, Presented during weekly fellow' Seminar IDSA New Delhi, 2007.

Maritna Ottaway, Rebuilding State Institutions in Collapsed States, Development & Change 33, No.5.

Nayak Nihar Geo-politics, Vol. 2 (2010).

Nayak, Giridhari, *Strategy Analysis*, Vol. 34, No. 4 July 2010.

Nayak, Giridhari, *U.K. Police Journal*, Vol. 78, 2005

Naxalites document Polit Bureau report of 2006.

Naxalites document, DKSZC Report.

Naxals' 9th Congress Document.

New Strachan, The Lost Meaning of Strategy, Survival, 47 autumn 2005.

Pascale Combelles Siegel, Perception Management: IO's Stepchild?

Peoples March-July 2000.

Ramana, P.V., Maoists Tactical United Front and Urban Movement,

Sandipani Dash, Research Associate, Institute for Conflict Management, South Asia Intelligence Review (SAIR), Weekly Assessments and Briefings, August 2010.

Small Wars & Insurgencies Conceptualization of Guerrilla Warfare 2004.

Status Paper on The Naxal Problem, Ministry of Home Affairs, Internal Security Division 31-10-2006.

Status Paper on Naxalism as on November 30, 2007, Ministry of Home Affairs, Govt. of India.

Steven R. Ratner Saving Failed States Foreign Policy 89 winter 1993.

'The Strategy & Tactics of Indian Revolution" Published by Central Committee (P) CPI(Maoist) (2004)

Thomas, Marks, The Maoists in Nepal, Strategies of Subversion and Subterfuge, Fault lines Vol. 19, April 2008.

Index